AF540229

DOMESTIC ANIMAL DIVERSITY

DOMESTIC ANIMAL DIVERSITY

By

Dr. Amita Sarkar

Deptt. of Zoology

Agra College, Agra

(Uttar Pradesh)

(India)

DISCOVERY PUBLISHING HOUSE PVT. LTD.

NEW DELHI-110 002

Published by:
Tilak Wasan

DISCOVERY PUBLISHING HOUSE PVT. LTD.
4383/4B, Ansari Road, Darya Ganj
New Delhi-110 002 (India)
Phone : +91-11-23279245, 43596064-65
Fax : +91-11-23253475
E-mail : discoverypublishinghouse@gmail.com
sales@discoverypublishinggroup.com
parul.wasan@gmail.com
web : www.discoverypublishinggroup.com

First Edition: **2013**

ISBN: 978-93-5056-253-6

Domestic Animal Diversity

Printed at:
Aditi Fine Art Press
Delhi

PREFACE

Domestic Animal Diversity covers the spectrum of genetic differences within each breed, and across all breeds within each domestic animal species, together with the species differences. This variety is available for the sustainable intensification of food and agriculture production.

Industrial livestock production and also increasingly livestock production in mixed crop-livestock systems use a very limited range of animal breeds. This has already led to the extinction of some local livestock breeds and to the genetic erosion of others.

Specific genetically determined capacities in local breeds to cope with the climatic, nutritional and disease challenge may already have been lost.

Despite agricultural advances, an estimated 826 million people, or about 13 per cent of the world's population, still go hungry. The development of high-performing livestock and poultry breeds has greatly contributed to the increase of food production, especially in temperate climates. These advances in technology are increasingly being adopted in tropical regions, but their indiscriminate export into tropical countries has at times ended in failure. The animals cannot stand the heat, they need optimal inputs and more easily develop diseases. To overcome these weaknesses, the ongoing approach is the widespread promotion of crossbreeding high-yielding breeds with hardy and well adapted local animals. The price of this and other developments is high: local breeds are disappearing at a rate of two breeds a week. This has far-reaching consequences, not only for our generation but also for the generations to come. Genetic resources are among the most valuable assets that a country holds. Human societies have, for at least 12000 years, recognized the importance of these assets and have been engaged in the domestication of wild plants and animals to meet a variety of needs. Domestic animals make a major contribution to human requirements for food in the form of meat, milk, milk products, eggs, fibre, fertilizer for crops as well as drought power. The number of domestic animal species contributing to agriculture is low, with less than 30 species being used extensively, and with less than 14 species accounting for over 90 per cent of global livestock production. However, whilst the number of species being used in the livestock sector is low, the genetic diversity of these species has been used extremely effectively. Farmers and breeders have successfully selected animals for a variety of traits and production environments, resulting in the development of over 6000 breeds of livestock. From just nine of the 14 most important species (cattle, horse, ass, pig, sheep, buffalo, goat, chicken and duck) as many as 4000 breeds have been developed and used worldwide. The FAO's Domestic Animal Diversity Information System had, in March 2005, records of over 6900 breeds in 35 species from 180 countries, including information on origin, population, risk status, performance and morphology. Of these, over 700 are already extinct and it is estimated that 30 per cent of the world's breeds are at risk of extinction.

—Author

CONTENTS

1 Introduction

Domestic Animal Diversity covers the spectrum of genetic differences within each breed, and across all breeds within each domestic animal species, together with the species differences. This variety is available for the sustainable intensification of food and agriculture production.

Industrial livestock production and also increasingly livestock production in mixed crop-livestock systems use a very limited range of animal breeds. This has already led to the extinction of some local livestock breeds and to the genetic erosion of others.

Specific genetically determined capacities in local breeds to cope with the climatic, nutritional and disease challenge may already have been lost.

Despite agricultural advances, an estimated 826 million people, or about 13 per cent of the world's population, still go hungry. The development of high-performing livestock and poultry breeds has greatly contributed to the increase of food production, especially in temperate climates. These advances in technology are increasingly being adopted in tropical regions, but their indiscriminate export into tropical countries has at times ended in failure. The animals cannot stand the heat, they need optimal inputs and more easily develop diseases. To overcome these weaknesses, the ongoing approach is the widespread promotion of crossbreeding high-yielding breeds with hardy and well adapted local animals. The price of this and other developments is high: local breeds are disappearing at a rate of two breeds a week. This has far-reaching consequences, not only for our generation but also for the generations to come. Genetic resources are among the most valuable assets that a country holds. Human societies have, for at least

12000 years, recognized the importance of these assets and have been engaged in the domestication of wild plants and animals to meet a variety of needs. Domestic animals make a major contribution to human requirements for food in the form of meat, milk, milk products, eggs, fibre, fertilizer for crops as well as drought power. The number of domestic animal species contributing to agriculture is low, with less than 30 species being used extensively, and with less than 14 species accounting for over 90 per cent of global livestock production. However, whilst the number of species being used in the livestock sector is low, the genetic diversity of these species has been used extremely effectively. Farmers and breeders have successfully selected animals for a variety of traits and production environments, resulting in the development of over 6000 breeds of livestock. From just nine of the 14 most important species (cattle, horse, ass, pig, sheep, buffalo, goat, chicken and duck) as many as 4000 breeds have been developed and used worldwide. The FAO's Domestic Animal Diversity Information System had, in March 2005, records of over 6900 breeds in 35 species from 180 countries, including information on origin, population, risk status, performance and morphology. Of these, over 700 are already extinct and it is estimated that 30 per cent of the world's breeds are at risk of extinction.

Contribution from Diversity

These breeds commonly possess valuable traits such as adaptation to harsh conditions, including tolerance of parasitic and infectious diseases, drought and poor quality feed. They are being replaced in both developed and developing countries by a few high production breeds which, to be successful, require high inputs, skilled management and comparatively benign environments.

Within the agricultural context, animal biodiversity is the genetic variability (or diversity) between breeds and within breeds of the same species. Within agricultural systems biological diversity is often referred to as 'Agrobiodiversity'.

There is still a large diversity in the genotypes of livestock species. This results from natural selection, reproduction in isolation, and from breeding for specific purposes. However, agrobiodiversity is declining due to an increase in communication, changed demand for livestock products and services, and innovations in the livestock sector resulting in more uniform conditions for livestock.

Gradual Change

This results from changes in the environment and therefore of genotype - environment interactions and natural selection. Investments are made to protect livestock from harsh conditions, feeding is improved and diseases are controlled with curative and preventative measures. Locally this results in a gradual change in genetic composition. Globally, the result is a reduction in agrobiodiversity. This process takes place in all livestock production systems.

Global Decline

Global decline in genetic diversity is also the result of the use of increased numbers of livestock from a small number of selected breeds. Changes in the productive environment create opportunities for use of exotic breeds where many years of selection has concentrated on production characteristics. Through replacement and cross-breeding the local variation in genetic composition initially increases but decreases as the characteristic of the local breeds are lost over time. The number of highly productive breeds is relatively small. Technical innovations in transport, communication and reproduction (hatcheries, AI, embryo transfer) facilitate the use of these few breeds on a world-wide basis and their representation in the livestock population is increasing.

The import of exotic breeds can result in activities within the livestock sector that are uneconomic and/or have a negative impact on the environment. In many cases these activities are subsidized or otherwise provided for by development programmes. Measurements to support livestock production include for example:

- tsetse control to create an environment for Trypanosomiasis sensitive cattle breeds;
- tick and tick borne disease control to reduce losses and enhance productivity of exotic breeds and cross breeds.

More recently alternative approaches have been promoted, but usually at a small scale, *e.g.*:

- re-introduction of trypano-tolerant breeds and selection on trypano-tolerance in Western and Central Africa;
- cross-breeding and selection for tick and tick borne disease tolerance in Australia and Eastern Africa.

The focus in the earlier approaches is on changing the environment to create opportunities for exotic breeds to be productive. In the more recent approach the focus is on accepting certain constraints of the environment and using breeds that can cope with these constraints. A parallel can been seen in the crop sector: chemical pest control versus selection on disease resistance.

Maintenance of the genetic diversity of livestock is therefore important.

The demand for milk, meat and eggs is developing faster than that for other livestock products and services as such as hair, wool, animal traction and transport (where demand is usually decreasing). In the competition for scarce resources, species and breeds renowned for these more traditional products and services (camels, donkeys, horses, buffalo, elephants, llama's, yak, wool sheep, etc) are at the loosing end, also in the resource driven farming systems. Gradually nomads and farmers replace traditional species and breeds by species and breeds that have a greater productivity and therefore higher economic value in the short term. As a result, population sizes of these traditional breeds is decreasing, their management gets poorer and performances decline. Some of these breeds have been included in breeding programmes aiming at safeguarding them for the purpose of genetic diversity. However, these programmes are costly and can only survive when external parties show an interest in keeping them.

The impact of the environment on the genetic composition of breeds and the use of certain species is highest in the extensive grazing and the mixed farming grazing systems. Because of the large diversity in ecological settings there is a large diversity in genetic composition amongst the breeds in these systems. Many of these systems make use of environments that are marginal for other uses but rely for certain periods of the year on environments that have a higher potential (*i.e.* flood plains and mountain valleys). Increased competition for the use of these areas is a thread for these extensive livestock systems and so for the global genetic diversity of livestock species.

Advantages of Agrobiodiversity

The present high-input high-output industrial agricultural systems are characterized by the use of high levels of fertilizers and good quality feed concentrates. Within these systems veterinary treatment with drugs for preventive and clinical use is sometimes practiced at a high level. Environmental problems and resistance against drugs can create conditions for animal production in which higher levels of feed conversion efficiency and disease resistance are required. The conservation of biodiversity is required as sources of genes, which are necessary as an insurance against changes in production circumstances, or the threat of a new disease. Animal production geneticists world-wide are searching for genes which influence the production, quality of products, and the health or reproduction traits of animals. In this search, crosses between breeds with extreme characteristics play an important role. This type of crossbreeding requires a high level of biodiversity within the species. The existence of many local breeds contribute to such a biodiversity.

Results of experience and research show that greater levels of agrobiodiversity can:

- Contribute to improved disease resistance;
- Diversify products and income opportunities, and reduce risks to individuals and nations;
- Increase productivity, food security, and economic returns;
- Reduce dependency on external inputs;
- Improve human nutrition;
- Help maximize effective use of resources and the environment;
- Conserve ecosystem structure, reduce the pressure of agriculture on the environment, and help maximize effective use of resources and the environment;
- Make farming systems more stable, robust, and sustainable, and contribute to sustainable intensification.

Breed not at risk: A breed where the total number of breeding females and males is greater than 1000 and 20 respectively; or the population size approaches 1000 and the percentage of purebred females is close to 100 per cent, and the overall population size is increasing.

Endangered breed: A breed where the total number of breeding females is between 100 and 1000 or the total number of breeding males is less than or equal to 20 and greater than five; or the overall population size is close to, but slightly above 100 and increasing and the percentage of pure-bred females is above 80 per cent; or the overall population size is close to, but slightly above 1000 and decreasing and the percentage of pure-bred females is below 80 per cent.

Critical breed: A breed where the total number of breeding females is less than 100 or the total number of breeding males is less than or equal to five; or the overall population size is close to, but slightly above 100 and decreasing, and the percentage of pure-bred females is below 80 per cent.

Extinct breed: A breed where it is no longer possible to recreate the breed population. Extinction is absolute when there are no breeding males (semen), breeding females (oocytes), nor embryos remaining.

Maintained breed: (Critical-maintained breed and endangered-maintained breed) categories where critical or endangered breeds are being maintained by an active public conservation programme or within a commercial or research facility.

Genetic diversity of livestock is being lost. The number of breeds has markedly declined over the past half century. Up to 30 per cent of global mammalian and avian livestock breeds (*i.e.*, 1,200 to 1,500 breeds) are currently at risk of being lost and cannot be replaced. Breeds become rare, either because their characteristics do not suit contemporary demand or because their qualities have not been recognized. When a breed population falls to about 1,000 animals, it is considered rare and endangered. Examples given by Thrupp (1998) serve to emphasize the nature and extent of the more on PSR.

"FAO estimates that somewhere in the world at least one breed of traditional livestock dies out every week. Many traditional breeds have disappeared as farmers focus on new breeds of cattle, pigs, sheep, and chickens. Of the 3,831 breeds of cattle, water buffalo, goats, pigs, sheep, horses, and donkeys believed to have existed in this century, 16 per cent have become extinct, and a further 15 per cent are rare. Some 474 of extant livestock breeds can be regarded as rare. A further 617 have become extinct since 1892. Over 80 breeds of cattle are found in Africa, and some are being replaced by exotic breeds. These losses weaken the potential of breeding programmes that could improve hardiness of livestock."

A number of factors are considered as being mainly responsible for the declining genetic diversity of livestock:

- Destruction of the native habitats of some livestock breeds;
- The development of genetically uniform livestock breeds;
- Farmer and/or consumer preferences for certain varieties and breeds (and changes in these consumer preferences over time);
- Market forces from competing commercial groups (e.g. supermarkets) where low prices are viewed as being more important than quality and taste.

Of these, commercial interests are considered as creating the most important pressures on livestock diversity. Factors in determining the direction and nature of change include:

- Growth performance (productivity). This is by far the most important factor.
- Pest and disease resistance. This is less important to large scale commercial producers where the widespread use of antibiotics, pesticides and other chemicals compensates for loss of disease resistance. In general, the loss of diversity reduces the resistance to disease.
- Ease of handling.
- Adaptation to current levels of technology, and to a relatively minor extent, consumer choice. Policies and international markets that support and favour high performance varieties, a uniformity of product, and use of chemical controls (e.g. subsidies, credit, market standards).

- The focus of producers on short-term returns at the expense of longer-term social and ecological/environmental factors.
- Disparities in resource distribution and disrespect for local knowledge and indigenous livestock management practices.

The overall result is the loss of local breeds and a decrease in levels of agricultural species diversity. Important consequences of this reduced diversity are a loss of disease resistance and loss of tolerance to different environmental conditions. In addition, local knowledge about diversity is lost as uniform industrial type agricultural technologies predominate.

Ironically, the loss of indigenous breeds that are able to exploit vegetation in the more extreme environments may also seriously affect the capacity of some societies to live in significant areas of the world in a sustainable manner.

Lack of appreciation of the value of indigenous breeds and their importance in niche adaptation. Incentives to introduce exotic and more uniform breeds from industrialized countries on the basis of greater productivity without consideration of other factors such as disease resistance. Product-focussed selection Undue emphasis placed on a specific product or trait, leading to the rapid dissemination of one breed of animal at the expense of others. Changes in land use Conversion of rangelands and mixed farming systems for agriculture, game parks, and industrial use. Changes in knowledge The idea that 'modern/imported is best' has led to the loss of knowledge about traditional livestock husbandry practices and to the erosion of domestic animal diversity.

Change in Technology Replacement of animal draught and transport by mechanization, leading to permanent change of farming systems. Artificial insemination and embryo transfer leading to rapid replacement of indigenous breeds. Change in Economy Decline in economic the viability of traditional livestock production systems. Intensification Livestock populations that rely on veterinary services and on improved feeding conditions. Heavy investment in preventative and curative veterinary measures, and in feeding, housing and management. Multipurpose local species and breeds replaced by those with higher milk, meat, egg production (including cross-breeds and pure-bred exotics).

Cross-breeding Predominance of sires from a few selected breeds in widespread cross-breeding programmes can lead to loss of features expressed by specialized breeds. Storage Failure of cryopreservation equipment (used to freeze semen, ova and embryos) or lack of refrigerant, inadequate maintenance of frozen semen from breeds that are not in demand.

Conflict Wars and other forms of socio-political instability can lead to livestock owners moving their stock out of their usual area, thus increasing the possibility of mixing with other breeds thereby potentially losing a location-specific breed. Disaster Natural disasters such as floods, drought or famine, and spread of new diseases (*e.g.* as a result of increased international communication and trade) can result in whole breeds dying out.

Declining livestock diversity has serious consequences for current livestock production and future capacity to meet unforeseen challenges and opportunities. Livestock diversity is being lost partly because of commercial production.

For instance, commercial production of egg chickens, meat chickens, and turkeys is dominated by fewer than 10 multinational breeding companies. Breed-level diversity within egg and meat-producing types is low because common breed origins and intense selection for similar production goals have promoted genetic uniformity. Similarly, records in the Domestic Animal Diversity database indicates that China possessed 128 pig breeds, of which 10 are now extinct and a further 10 are either critical or endangered as they are replaced with western breeds.

Traditional pastoralists have often tended to foster biodiversity, in both plants and animals. Many pastoral societies have developed elaborate systems that result in the preservation of genetic resources. Pastoralists have deliberately developed livestock to meet different needs and conditions.

For example, a least 12 breeds of camel are known from southern Sudan alone. However, wealthier sectors of society are now accumulating large livestock holdings through purchase of animals from different areas and tribal groups — with the resulting cross-breeding making camels of one generic type.

It is clear that livestock breeds are not biological taxa but rather represent the outcome of social processes. They are therefore unlikely to survive outside the social contexts and production systems that formed them. However, these losses weaken the potential of breeding programmes that could improve hardiness of livestock.

Commercial breeds of livestock possess greater genetic variability than most crop varieties do. This diversity allows intensification of selection within breeds to be a fruitful approach for improving livestock productivity. However, if continued emphasis on breed replacement and increasing selection intensity (*e.g.* for greater productivity) take place at the expense of maintenance of genetic diversity, including the advantages of disease resistance and environmental adaptation, there may be significant long-term costs. As an example, Holstein cattle have become the pre-eminent dairy breed world-wide and have enjoyed sustained improvements in milk production potential, but only at the cost of declining genetic diversity within the breed.

Despite significant advances in the preservation of genetic diversity of crop varieties, for example through *ex-situ* preservation of germplasm and seed banks, little attention has been paid to conserving the genetic diversity of livestock species. The current dependence on *in situ* conservation by hobbyists is inadequate. Moreover, this form of breed preservation is currently largely limited to Europe and America. The significant livestock diversity in Africa, Asia and South America is largely unprotected.

State is therefore characterized by:

- Change in the number of individual livestock breeds that are routinely used by grazing, mixed and industrial livestock production systems;
- Increased uniformity of livestock products Increased genetic uniformity within individual livestock breeds;
- Increasing sedentarization of livestock production;
- Declining economic viability of traditional livestock production systems Impact.

High Performance Breeds May Not Be High Performers

For decades, local or indigenous livestock breeds were regarded as inferior to the high-performance breeds developed in the North. Cross-breeding with exotic animals has led to the dilution of indigenous breeds, and this is one of several factors responsible for a very severe narrowing of the genetic base of our domesticated animals. But now more and more reports are indicating that the performance of indigenous breeds is equal to or even better than that of improved or cross-bred animals. In India, for instance, the enormous rise in the country's milk output is due to indigenous buffaloes, rather than cross-bred cattle. In Ethiopia, a detailed study comparing the outputs of improved goats (Anglo-Nubian x Somali) with those of local breeds revealed that improved goats, while they grew faster, were much more susceptible to weight loss during the dry season, thus offsetting the previous gains. Although they gave more milk per animal, this was not the case when the yield was calculated in relationship to body weight.

Disease Resistance of Indigenous Breeds

One of the important traits of indigenous breeds concerns their ability to cope with local diseases. For instance, the Red Masai sheep has proven to be genetically resistant, or less prone, to infestation with intestinal worms .

The Uda sheep of Northern Nigeria is much less susceptible to foot rot, while the Kuri cattle kept along the shores of Lake Tchad are very resistant to insect bites. N'dama and some other breeds of indigenous African cattle are resistant to infection with trypanosomes. Such disease resistance is compromised when animals are selected only for high productivity. For example, the Orma Boran cattle kept by the Orma people in the Tana River District of Kenya are much more resistant to trypanosomes than their relative, the Improved Kenya Boran, which has been selected for meat gains over several generations. Thus in areas where tsetse pressure is high, the Orma Boran gains weight faster than the Improved Kenyan Boran. Similarly, local 'backyard' chickens are likely to be more resistant to diseases and to certain parasites than are the 'improved' breeds.

It is important that the genetic diversity of rare and endangered livestock breeds and their wild relatives and ancestral lines be preserved as insurance against future needs.

Formal government-sponsored international programmes for *in-situ* and *ex-situ* preservation of livestock genetic diversity need to be established. This is gradually becoming established through the efforts of the FAO Domestic Animal Diversity programme. However, there needs to be a far greater awareness of the problem. In addition, the native habitats of the wild relatives of livestock species must be preserved. Investments in preserving this natural capital could yield net pay-offs in both agricultural productivity and profitability. Such investments should be considered in any economic cost-benefit analyses of alternative production regimes.

A move towards sustainable agriculture requires changes in production methods, concepts, and policies, as well as the participation of local people. Scientific advancements in genetics and "improved" varieties can have important roles. However, these need to be reoriented towards conserving and using diversity in farming systems — rather than replacing diversity with uniformity. The following principles are important:

- It is possible, with appropriate agricultural practices, for significant genetic diversity to be maintained within agricultural production systems, both within individual farms and among farms across a region;
- Participation and empowerment of farmers and indigenous peoples, and protection of their rights, are important means of conserving agro-biodiversity in research and development;
- Creating a supportive policy environment, including the elimination of incentives for uniform varieties, and implementing policies for local rights to genetic resources are important for agricultural biodiversity enhancement and food security;

- Application of agro-ecological principles helps conserve and enhance diversity on farms and can increase sustainable productivity;
- Adaptation of methods to local agro-ecological and socio-economic conditions, building upon existing successful methods and local knowledge, is essential to link biodiversity and agriculture and to meet livelihood needs;
- Conservation of plant and animal genetic resources, including in-situ methods, protects biodiversity to enhance current livelihood security as well as future needs;
- Reforming genetic research and breeding programmes for enhancement of agricultural diversity is essential and can also have production benefits.

Response must therefore be characterized by:

- Development and transfer of technologies relevant to the sustainable use of biological diversity, including agricultural diversity;
- Development of policies and programmes targeted at the maintenance of local breeds of livestock;
- Creation of an enabling environment for economically viable production systems utilizing local breeds. Provision of incentives for the maintenance of local breeds;
- Monitoring numbers and population sizes of local breeds;
- Research targeted towards the identification and utilization of important characteristics inherent in local breeds of livestock;
- A reassessment of the value of products and services from local breeds in comparison with alternatives by fully taking into account the environmental costs and the real costs of veterinary services, disease control and other services.

Conservation of Livestock Diversity

Conservation of animal genetic resources is essential to enable farmers to adapt to changing environmental conditions and consumer demands. Variation in environmental conditions such as disease outbreaks, drought, floods and climatic anomalies, as well as changes in consumer preferences, is inevitable. It is therefore in the best interest of societies to ensure that farmers and breeders have access to the widest possible range of animal genetic resources so that they can effectively respond to change. It is impossible to predict the nature of the change, but change is certain, and the livestock sector must not be left without its animal genetic diversity insurance policy.

Conservation of animal genetic resources is also essential to fully realize the investment that has been made over many human generations in developing these resources. Also, ensuring the conservation of wild species will provide opportunities to further develop and expand the livestock sector. Identification of wild species with potential to contribute to agriculture, and integration of agricultural biodiversity conservation strategies and plans with general biodiversity conservation initiatives is essential.

Conservation of animal genetic diversity is a global issue, as all countries benefit from the use and development of domestic animals and their many products. Conservation of animal genetic diversity over the long-term, will enable countries and their farmers to better respond to changing environmental conditions and consumer preferences, to pursue new economic opportunities and to reduce their vulnerability to food shortages.

Conservation and sustainable use of animal genetic resources are essential to support and inform the biotechnology industry and other industries that are dependent on genetic resources. Technological developments are increasingly improving our capacity to use and develop genetic resources, and thus, it is imperative that the current rapid erosion of animal genetic resources is addressed.

2 Animal-rearing

Animal-rearing has its origins in the transition of cultures to settled farming communities rather than hunter-gatherer lifestyles. Animals are 'domesticated' when their breeding and living conditions are controlled by humans. Over time, the collective behaviour, life cycle, and physiology of livestock have changed radically. Many modern farm animals are unsuited to life in the wild. Dogs were domesticated in East Asia about 15,000 years ago. Goats and sheep were domesticated around 8000 BCE in Asia. Swine or pigs were domesticated by 7000 BCE in the Middle East and China. The earliest evidence of horse domestication dates to around 4000 BCE.

Older English sources, such as the King James Version of the Bible, refer to livestock in general as 'cattle', as opposed to the word 'deer', which then was used for wild animals which were not owned. The word *cattle* is derived from Middle English *chatel*, which meant all kinds of movable personal property, including of course livestock, which was differentiated from non-movable real-estate ('real property'). In later English, sometimes smaller livestock was called 'small cattle' in that sense of movable property on land, which was not automatically bought or sold with the land. Today, the modern meaning of 'cattle', without a qualifier, usually refers to domesticated bovines. Other species of the genus *Bos* sometimes are called wild cattle.Livestock (also cattle) refers to one or more domesticated animals raised in an agricultural setting to produce commodities such as food, fibre and labour. The term 'livestock' as used in this article does not include poultry or farmed fish; however the inclusion of these, especially poultry, within the meaning of 'livestock' is common.

Livestock generally are raised for subsistence or for profit. Raising animals (animal husbandry) is an important component of modern agriculture. It has been practised in many cultures since the transition to farming from hunter-gather lifestyles.

The term 'livestock' is nebulous and may be defined narrowly or broadly. On a broader view, livestock refers to any breed or population of animal kept by humans for a useful, commercial purpose. This can mean domestic animals, semi-domestic animals, or captive wild animals. Semi-domesticated refers to animals which are only lightly domesticated or of disputed status. These populations may also be in the process of domestication. Some people may use the term livestock to refer just to domestic animals or even just to red meat animals.

'Livestock' are defined, in part, by their end purpose as the production of food, fibre and/or labour.

The economic value of livestock includes:

Meat

The production of a useful form of dietary protein and energy.

Dairy Products

Mammalian livestock can be used as a source of milk, which can in turn easily be processed into other dairy products, such as yogurt, cheese, butter, ice cream, kefir, and kumis. Using livestock for this purpose can often yield several times the food energy of slaughtering the animal outright.

Fibre

Livestock produce a range of fibre/textiles. For example, sheep and goats produce wool and mohair; cows, deer, and sheep skins can be made into leather; and bones, hooves and horns of livestock can be used.

Fertilizer

Manure can be spread on fields to increase crop yields. This is an important reason why historically, plant and animal domestication have been intimately linked. Manure is also used to make plaster for walls and floors, and can be used as a fuel for fires. The blood and bone of animals are also used as fertilizer.

Labour

Animals such as horses, donkey, and yaks can be used for mechanical energy. Prior to steam power, livestock were the only available source of non-human labour. They are still used for this purpose in many places of the world, including ploughing fields, transporting goods, and military functions.

Land Management

The grazing of livestock is sometimes used as a way to control weeds and undergrowth. For example, in areas prone to wild fires, goats and sheep are set to graze on dry scrub which removes combustible material and reduces the risk of fires.

During the history of animal husbandry, many secondary products have arisen in an attempt to increase carcass utilization and reduce waste. For example, animal offal and non-edible parts may be transformed into products such as pet food and fertilizer. In the past, such waste products were sometimes also fed to livestock as well. However, intra-species recycling poses a disease risk, threatening animal and even human health. Due primarily to BSE (mad cow disease), feeding animal scraps to animals has been banned in many countries, at least in regards to ruminants and pigs.

Farming practices vary dramatically worldwide and between types of animals. Livestock are generally kept in an enclosure, are fed by human-provided food and are intentionally bred, but some livestock are not enclosed, or are fed by access to natural foods, or are allowed to breed freely, or any combination thereof. Livestock raising historically was part of a nomadic or pastoral form of material culture. The herding of camels and reindeer in some parts of the world remains unassociated with sedentary agriculture. The transhumance form of herding in the Sierra Nevada Mountains of California still continues, as cattle, sheep or goats are moved from winter pasture in lower elevation valleys to spring and summer pasture in the foothills and alpine regions, as the seasons progress. Cattle were raised on the open range in the Western United States and Canada, on the Pampas of Argentina, and other prairie and steppe regions of the world.

The enclosure of livestock in pastures and barns is a relatively new development in the history of agriculture. When cattle are enclosed, the type of 'enclosure' may vary from a small crate, a large fenced pasture or a paddock. The type of feed may vary from natural growing grass, to highly sophisticated processed feed. Animals are usually intentionally bred through artificial insemination or through supervised mating. Indoor production systems are generally used only for pigs and poultry, as well as for veal cattle. Indoor animals are generally farmed intensively, as large space requirements would make indoor farming unprofitable and impossible. However, indoor farming systems are controversial due to the waste they produce, odour problems, the potential for groundwater contamination and animal welfare concerns. (For further discussion on intensively farmed livestock, see factory farming, and intensive pig farming).

Other livestock are farmed outside, although the size of enclosure and level of supervision may vary. In large open ranges animals may be only occasionally inspected or yarded in 'round-ups' or a muster (livestock). Herding dogs may be used for mustering livestock as are cowboys, stockmen and jackaroos on horses, or with vehicles and also by helicopters. Since the advent of barbed wire (in the 1870s) and electric fence technology, fencing pastures has become much more feasible and pasture management simplified. Rotation of pasturage is a modern technique for improving nutrition and health while avoiding environmental damage to the land. In some cases very large numbers of animals may be kept in indoor or outdoor feeding operations (on feedlots), where the animals' feed is processed, offsite or onsite, and stored on site then fed to the animals.

Livestock — especially cattle — may be branded to indicate ownership and age, but in modern farming identification is more likely to be indicated by means of ear tags than branding. Sheep are also frequently marked by means of ear marks and/or ear tags. As fears of mad cow disease and other epidemic illnesses mount, the use of implants to monitor and trace animals in the food production system is increasingly common, and sometimes required by government regulations.

Modern farming techniques seek to minimize human involvement, increase yield, and improve animal health. Economics, quality and consumer safety all play a role in how animals are raised. Drug use and feed supplements (or even feed type) may be regulated, or prohibited, to ensure yield is not increased at the expense of consumer health, safety or animal welfare. Practices vary around the world, for example growth hormone use is permitted in the United States, but not in stock to be sold to the European Union. The improvement of health, using modern farming techniques, on the part of animals has come into question. Feeding corn to cattle, which have historically eaten grasses, is an example; where the cattle are less adapted, the rumen pH changes to more acidic, leading to liver damage and other difficulties. The US F.D.A. still allows feedlots to feed non-ruminant animal proteins to cattle. For example, feeding chicken manure and poultry meal is acceptable for cattle, and beef or pork meat and bone meal is being fed to chickens.

Predation

Livestock farmers had suffered from wild animal predation and theft by rustlers. In North America, gray wolf, grizzly bear, cougar, black bear, and coyote are sometimes considered a threat to livestock. In Eurasia and Africa, wolf, brown bear, leopard, tiger, lion, dhole, black bear, spotted hyena, and others caused livestock deaths. In Australia, the dingo, foxes, wedge-tailed eagles, hunting and domestic dogs (especially) cause problems for graziers because they often kill for fun. In Latin America, feral dogs cause livestock deaths in nightfall.

Disease

Livestock diseases compromise animal welfare, reduce productivity, and can infect humans. Animal diseases may be tolerated, reduced through animal husbandry, or reduced through antibiotics and vaccines. In developing countries, animal diseases are tolerated in animal husbandry, resulting in considerably reduced productivity, especially given the low health-status of many developing country herds. Disease management for gains in productivity is often the first step taken in implementing an agriculture policy.

Disease management can be achieved through changes in animal husbandry. These measures may aim to control spread using biosecurity measures, such as controlling animal mixing, controlling entry to farm lots and the use of protective clothing, and quarantining sick animals. Diseases also may be controlled by the use of vaccines and antibiotics. Antibiotics in sub-therapeutic doses may also be used as a growth-promoter, increasing growth by 10-15 per cent. The issue of antibiotic resistance has limited the practices of preventative dosing such as antibiotic-laced feed. Countries will often require the use of veterinary certificates before transporting, selling or showing animals. Disease-free areas often rigorously enforce rules for entry of potentially diseased animals, including quarantine.

Since many livestock are herd animals, they were historically driven to market "on the hoof" to a town or other central location. During the period after the American Civil War, the abundance of Longhorn cattle in Texas, and the demand for beef in Northern markets, led to the implementation of the Old West cattle drive. The method is still used in some parts of the world. Truck transport is now common in developed countries. Local and regional livestock auctions and commodity markets facilitate trade in livestock. In other areas, livestock may be bought and sold in a bazaar, such as may be found in many parts of Central Asia, or a flea market type setting.

Stock shows and fairs are events where people bring their best livestock to compete with one another. Organizations like 4-H, Block and Bridle, and FFA encourage young people to raise livestock for show purposes. Special feeds are purchased and hours may be spent prior to the show grooming the animal to look its best. In cattle, sheep, and swine shows, the winning animals are frequently auctioned off to the highest bidder, and the funds are placed into a scholarship fund for its owner. The movie *Grand Champion*, released in 2004, is the story of a young Texas boy's experience raising a prize steer.

The issue of raising livestock for human benefit raises the issue of the relationship between humans and animals, in terms of the status of animals and obligations of people. Animal welfare is the viewpoint that animals under human care should be treated in such a way that they do not suffer unnecessarily. What is 'unnecessary' suffering may vary. Generally, though, the animal welfare perspective is based on an interpretation of scientific research on farming practices. By contrast, animal rights is the viewpoint that using animals for human benefit is, by its nature, generally exploitation, regardless of the farming practices used. Animal rights activists would generally be vegan or vegetarian, whereas it is consistent with the animal welfare perspective to eat meat, depending on production processes.

Animal welfare groups generally seek to generate public discussion on livestock raising practices and secure greater regulation and scrutiny of livestock industry practices. Animal rights groups usually seek the abolition of livestock farming, although some groups may recognise the necessity of achieving more stringent regulation first. Animal welfare groups, such as the RSPCA, are often, in first world countries, given a voice at governmental level in the development of policy. Animal rights groups find it harder to find methods of input, and may go further and advocate civil disobedience or violence.

A number of animal husbandry practices have been the subject of campaigns in the 1990s and 2000s and have led to legislation in some countries. Confinement of livestock in small and unnatural spaces is often done for economic or health reasons. Animals may be kept in the minimum size of cage or pen with little or no space to exercise. Where livestock are used as a source of power, they may be pushed beyond their limits to the point of exhaustion. The public visibility of this abuse meant it was one of the first areas to receive legislation in the nineteenth century in European countries, but it still goes on in parts of Asia. Broiler hens may be de-beaked, pigs may have deciduous teeth pulled, cattle may be de-horned and branded, dairy cows and sheep may have tails cropped, merino sheep may be mulesed, and many types of male animals are castrated. Animals may be transported long distances to market and slaughter. Overcrowded conditions, heat from tropical-area shipping and lack of food, water and rest breaks have been subject to legislation and protest. Slaughter of livestock was an early target for legislation. Campaigns continue to target Halal and Kosher religious ritual slaughter.

Environmental Impact

At first reports like the United Nations report 'Livestock's Long Shadow' cast a pall over the livestock sector (primarily cattle, chickens, and pigs) for 'emerging as one of the top two or three most significant contributors to our most serious environmental problems.' The United Nations controversially included emissions from deforestation as part of its methodology. Rather than the 18 per cent figure that placed on the sector as major contributor to emissions, the real figure, less deforestation is actually 12 per cent . In April 2008, the [United States Environmental Protection Agency] released a major stocktake of emissions in the United States entitled *Inventory of U.S. Greenhouse Gas Emissions and Sinks: 1990-2006* . On 6.1 it found "In 2006, the agricultural sector was responsible for emissions of 454.1 teragrams of CO_2 equivalent (Tg CO_2 Eq.), or 6 per cent of total U.S. greenhouse gas emissions." By way of comparison, transportation in the US produces more than 25 per cent of all emissions.

The issue of livestock as a major policy focus remains, especially when dealing with problems of deforestation in neotropical areas, land degradation, climate change and air pollution, water shortage and water pollution, and loss of biodiversity. A research team at Obihiro University of Agriculture and Veterinary Medicine in Hokkaido found that supplementing the animals' diet with cysteine, a type of amino acid, and nitrate can reduce the methane gas produced, without jeopardising the cattle's productivity or the quality of their meat and milk.

Researchers in Australia are looking into the possibility of reducing methane from cattle and sheep by introducing digestive bacteria from kangaroo intestines into livestock.

Research from the University of Botswana in 2008 has found that farmers' common practice of overstocking cattle to cope with drought losses made ecosystems more vulnerable and risked long term damage to cattle herds, in turn, by actually depleting scarce biomass. The study of the Kgatleng district of Botswana predicted that by 2050, the cycle of mild drought is likely to become shorter for the region (18 months instead of two years) due to climate change.

Legal Definitions

United States federal legislation sometimes more narrowly defines the term to make specified agricultural commodities either eligible, or ineligible, for a programme or activity. For example, the Livestock Mandatory Reporting Act of 1999 (P.L. 106-78, Title IX) defines livestock only as cattle, swine, and lambs. However, 1988 disaster assistance legislation defined the term as "cattle, sheep, goats, swine, poultry (including egg-producing poultry), equine animals used for food or in the production of food, fish used for food, and other animals designated by the Secretary".

3 Species of Cattle

Cattle were originally identified as three separate species. These were *Bos taurus*, the European or 'taurine' cattle (including similar types from Africa and Asia); *Bos indicus*, the zebu; and the extinct *Bos primigenius*, the aurochs. The aurochs is ancestral to both zebu and taurine cattle. Recently these three have increasingly been grouped as one species, with *Bos primigenius taurus*, *Bos primigenius indicus* and *Bos primigenius primigenius* as the subspecies.

Complicating the matter is the ability of cattle to interbreed with other closely related species. Hybrid individuals and even breeds exist, not only between taurine cattle and zebu (including the sanga cattle breeds, *Bos taurus africanus*) but also between one or both of these and some other members of the genus *Bos*: yak (called a dzo or 'yattle'), banteng and gaur. Hybrids (such as the beefalo breed) can also occur between taurine cattle and either species of bison, which some authors consider to be in the genus *Bos* as well. The hybrid origin of some types may not be obvious — for example, genetic testing of the Dwarf Lulu breed, the only taurine-type cattle in Nepal, found them to be a mix of taurine cattle, zebu and yak. Cattle cannot successfully be hybridized with more distantly related bovines such as water buffalo or African buffalo.

The aurochs originally ranged throughout Europe, North Africa, and much of Asia. In historical times its range became restricted to Europe, and the last known individual died in Masovia, Poland, in about 1627. Breeders have attempted to recreate cattle of similar appearance to aurochs by crossing traditional types of domesticated cattle, creating the Heck cattle breed.

Cattle (colloquially cows) are the most common type of large domesticated ungulates. They are a prominent modern member of the subfamily Bovinae, are the most widespread species of the genus *Bos*, and are most commonly classified collectively as *Bos primigenius*. Cattle are raised as livestock for meat (beef and veal), as dairy animals for milk and other dairy products, and as draft animals (pulling carts, plows and the like). Other products include leather and dung for manure or fuel. In some countries, such as India, cattle are sacred. It is estimated that there are 1.3 billion cattle in the world today. In 2009, cattle became the first livestock animal to have its genome mapped.

Cattle did not originate as the term for bovine animals. It was borrowed from Old French *catel*, itself from Latin *caput*, head, and originally meant movable personal property, especially livestock of any kind, as opposed to real property (the land, to also include wild or small free-roaming animals such as chickens, which would be sold as part of the land). The word is closely related to "chattel" (a unit of personal property) and 'capital' in the economic sense. The term replaced earlier Old English *feoh* 'cattle, property' (cf. German: *Vieh*, Gothic: faihu).

The word *cow* came via Anglo-Saxon *cu* (plural), from Common Indo-European (genitive *gowes*) = 'a bovine animal', compare Persian *Gâv*, Sanskrit *go*, Welsh *buwch*.

In older English sources such as the King James Version of the Bible, 'cattle' refers to livestock, as opposed to 'deer' which refers to wildlife. 'Wild cattle' may refer to feral cattle or to undomesticated species of the genus *Bos*. Today, when used without any other qualifier, the modern meaning of 'cattle' is usually restricted to domesticated bovines.

In general, the same words are used in different parts of the world but with minor differences in the definitions. The terminology described here contrasts the differences in definition between the United Kingdom and other British influenced parts of world such as Canada, Australia, New Zealand, Ireland, and the United States.

An *intact* (*i.e.*, not castrated) adult male is called a *bull*. A wild, young, unmarked bull is known as a *micky* in Australia. An un branded bovine of either sex is called a 'maverick' in the USA and Canada.

An adult female that has had a calf (or two, depending on regional usage) is a *cow*. A young female before she has had a calf of her own and is under three years of age is called a *heifer* (pronounced , 'heffer'). A young female that has had only one calf is occasionally called a *first-calf heifer*.

Young cattle of both sexes are called *calves* until they are weaned, then *weaners* until they are a year old in some areas; in other areas, particularly with male beef cattle, they may be known as *feeder-calves* or simply *feeders*. After that, they are referred to as *yearlings* or *stirks* if between one and two years of age.

A castrated male is called a *steer* in the United States; older steers are often called *bullocks* in other parts of the world but in North America this term refers to a young bull. *Piker bullocks* are micky bulls that were caught, castrated and then later lost. In Australia, the term 'Japanese ox' is used for grain fed steers in the weight range of 500 to 650 kg that are destined for the Japanese meat trade. In North America, draft cattle under four years old are called *working steers*. Improper or late castration on a bull results in it becoming a coarse steer known as a *stag* in Australia, Canada and New Zealand. In some countries an incompletely castrated male is known also as a *rig*.

A castrated male (occasionally a female or in some areas a bull) kept for draft purposes is called an *ox* (plural *oxen*); 'ox' may also be used to refer to some carcase products from any adult cattle, such as *ox-hide*, *ox-blood* or *ox-liver*.

A *springer* is a cow or heifer close to calving.

In all cattle species, a female that is the twin of a bull usually becomes an infertile partial intersex, and is a *freemartin*.

Neat (horned oxen, from which neatsfoot oil is derived), *beef* (young ox) and *beefing* (young animal fit for slaughtering) are obsolete terms, although *poll*, *pollard* or *polled cattle* are still terms in use for naturally hornless animals, or in some areas also for those that have been disbudded.

Cattle raised for human consumption are called *beef cattle*. Within the beef cattle industry in parts of the United States, the older term *beef* (plural *beeves*) is still used to refer to an animal of either gender. Some Australian, Canadian, New Zealand and British people use the term *beast*, especially for single animals when the gender is unknown.

Cattle of certain breeds bred specifically for milk production are called *milking* or *dairy cattle*.; a cow kept to provide milk for one family may be called a *house cow* or *milker*.

The adjective applying to cattle in general is usually *bovine*. The terms 'bull', 'cow' and 'calf' are also used by extension to denote the gender or age of other large animals, including whales, hippopotamuses, camels, elk and elephants.

Cattle can only be used in the plural and not in the singular: it is a plurale tantum. Thus one may refer to 'three cattle' or 'some cattle', but not 'one cattle'. There is no universally used singular form in modern English of 'cattle', other than the sex- and age-specific terms such as cow, bull, steer and heifer. Historically, 'ox' was a non-gender-specific term for adult cattle, but generally this is now used only for draft cattle, especially adult castrated males. The term is also incorporated into the names of other species such as the musk ox and 'grunting ox' (yak), and is used in some areas to describe certain cattle products such as ox-hide and ox-tail.

'Cow' is in general use as a singular for the collective 'cattle', despite the objections by those who insist it to be a female-specific term. Although the phrase 'that cow is a bull' is absurd from a lexicographic standpoint, the word 'cow' is easy to use when a singular is needed and the sex is unknown or irrelevant - when 'there is a cow in the road', for example. Further, any herd of fully mature cattle in or near a pasture is statistically likely to consist mostly of cows, so the term is probably accurate even in the restrictive sense. Other than the few bulls needed for breeding, the vast majority of male cattle are castrated as calves and slaughtered for meat before the age of three years. Thus, in a pastured herd, any calves or herd bulls usually are clearly distinguishable from the cows due to distinctively different sizes and clear anatomical differences. Merriam-Webster, a U.S. dictionary, recognizes the non-sex-specific use of 'cow' as an alternate definition, whereas Collins, a UK dictionary, does not.

Colloquially, more general non-specific terms may denote cattle when a singular form is needed. Australian, New Zealand and British farmers use the term 'beast' or 'cattle beast'. 'Bovine' is also used in Britain. The term 'critter' is common in the western United States and Canada, particularly when referring to young cattle. In some areas of the American South (particularly the Appalachian region), where both dairy and beef cattle are present, an individual animal was once called a 'beef critter', though that term is becoming archaic.

Cattle raised for human consumption are called 'beef cattle'. Within the beef cattle industry in parts of the United States, the term 'beef' (plural 'beeves') is still used in its archaic sense to refer to an animal of either gender. Cows of certain breeds that are kept for the milk they give are called 'dairy cows' or 'milking cows' (formerly 'milch cows' — 'milch' was pronounced as 'milk'). Most young male offspring of dairy cows are sold for veal, and may be referred to as *veal calves.*

The term 'dogies' is used to describe orphaned calves in the context of ranch work in the American west, as in 'Keep them dogies moving'. In some places, a cow kept to provide milk for one family is called a 'house cow'. Other obsolete terms for cattle include 'neat' (this use survives in 'neatsfoot oil', extracted from the feet and legs of cattle), and 'beefing' (young animal fit for slaughter).

An onomatopoeic term for one of the commonest sounds made by cattle is 'moo', and this sound is also called *lowing*. There are a number of other sounds made by cattle, including calves *bawling*, and bulls *bellowing*. The bullroarer makes a sound similar to a territorial call made by bulls.

Cattle have one stomach with four compartments. They are the rumen, reticulum, omasum, and abomasum, with the rumen being the largest compartment. The reticulum, the smallest compartment, is known as the 'honeycomb'. Cattle sometimes consume metal objects which are deposited in the reticulum and irritation from the metal objects causes hardware disease. The omasum's main function is to absorb water and nutrients from the digestible feed. The omasum is known as the 'many plies'. The abomasum is like the human stomach; this is why it is known as the 'true stomach'.

Cattle are ruminants, meaning that they have a digestive system that allows use of otherwise indigestible foods by regurgitating and rechewing them as 'cud'. The cud is then reswallowed and further digested by specialised microorganisms in the rumen. These microbes are primarily responsible for decomposing cellulose and other carbohydrates into volatile fatty acids that cattle use as their primary metabolic fuel. The microbes inside the rumen are also able to synthesize amino acids from non-protein nitrogenous sources, such as urea and ammonia. As these microbes reproduce in the rumen, older generations die and their carcasses continue on through the digestive tract. These carcasses are then partially digested by the cattle, allowing them to gain a high quality protein source. These features allow cattle to thrive on grasses and other vegetation.

The gestation period for a cow is nine months. A newborn calf weighs 25 to 45 kilograms (55 to 99 lb). The world record for the heaviest bull was 1,740 kilograms (3,840 lb), a Chianina named Donetto, when he was exhibited at the Arezzo show in 1955. The heaviest steer was eight year old 'Old Ben', a Shorthorn/Hereford cross weighing in at 2,140 kilograms (4,720 lb) in 1910. Steers are generally killed before reaching 750 kilograms (1,650 lb). Breeding stock usually live to about 15 years (occasionally as much as 25 years). The oldest recorded cow, Big Bertha, died at the age of 48 in 1993.

A common misconception about cattle (particularly bulls) is that they are enraged by the colour red (something provocative is often said to be 'like a red flag to a bull'). This is incorrect, as cattle are red-green colour-blind. The myth arose from the use of red capes in the sport of bullfighting; in fact, two different capes are used. The capote is a large, flowing cape that is magenta and yellow. The more famous muleta is the smaller, red cape, used exclusively for the final, fatal segment of the fight. It is not the colour of the cape that angers the bull, but rather the movement of the fabric that irritates the bull and incites it to charge.

Although cattle cannot distinguish red from green, they do have two kinds of colour receptors in the cone cells in their retinas. Thus they are dichromatic, the same as most other mammals (including dogs, cats, horses and up to ten per cent of male humans; see also colour vision). They are able to distinguish some colours, particularly blue from yellow, in the same way as most other non-primate land mammals.

Cattle occupy a unique role in human history, domesticated since at least the early Neolithic. They are raised for meat (beef cattle), dairy products and hides. They are also used as draft animals and in certain sports. Some consider cattle the oldest form of wealth, and cattle raiding consequently one of the earliest forms of theft.

Cattle are often raised by allowing herds to graze on the grasses of large tracts of rangeland. Raising cattle in this manner allows the use of land that might be unsuitable for growing crops. The most common interactions with cattle involve daily feeding, cleaning and milking. Many routine husbandry practices involve ear tagging, dehorning, loading, medical operations, vaccinations and hoof care, as well as training for agricultural shows and preparations. There are also some cultural differences in working with cattle- the cattle husbandry of Fulani men rests on behavioural techniques, whereas in Europe cattle are controlled primarily by physical means like fences. Breeders use cattle husbandry to reduce M. bovis infection susceptibility by selective breeding and maintaining herd health to avoid concurrent disease.

Cattle are farmed for beef, veal, dairy, leather and they are less commonly used for conservation grazing, simply to maintain grassland for wildlife — for example, in Epping Forest, England. They are often used in some of the most wild places for livestock. Depending on the breed, cattle can survive on hill grazing, heaths, marshes, moors and semi desert. Modern cows are more commercial than older breeds and, having become more specialized, are less versatile. For this reason many smaller farmers still favour old breeds, like the dairy breed of cattle Jersey.

In Portugal, Spain, Southern France and some Latin American countries, bulls are used in the activity of bullfighting; a similar activity, Jallikattu, is seen in South India; in many other countries this is illegal. Other activities such as bull riding are seen as part of a rodeo, especially in North America. Bull-leaping, a central ritual in Bronze Age Minoan culture, still exists in southwestern France. In modern times, cattle are also entered into agricultural competitions. These competitions can involve live cattle or cattle carcases in hoof and hook events.

In terms of food intake by humans, consumption of cattle is less efficient than of grain or vegetables with regard to land use, and hence cattle grazing consumes more area than such other agricultural production when raised on grains. Nonetheless, cattle and other forms of domesticated animals can sometimes help to use plant resources in areas not easily amenable to other forms of agriculture.

Cattle today are the basis of a multi-billion dollar industry worldwide. The international trade in beef for 2000 was over $30 billion and represented only 23 per cent of world beef production. (Clay 2004). The production of milk, which is also made into cheese, butter, yogurt, and other dairy products, is comparable in economic size to beef production and provides an important part of the food supply for many of the world's people. Cattle hides, used for leather to make shoes, couches and clothing, are another widespread product. Cattle remain broadly used as draft animals in many developing countries, such as India.

A 400-page United Nations report from the Food and Agriculture Organization (FAO) states that cattle farming is "responsible for 18 per cent of greenhouse gases". The production of cattle to feed and clothe humans stresses ecosystems around the world, and is assessed to be one of the top three environmental problems in the world on a local to global scale.

The report, entitled *Livestock's Long Shadow*, also surveys the environmental damage from sheep, chickens, pigs and goats. But in almost every case, the world's 1.5 billion cattle are cited as the greatest adverse impact with respect to climate change as well as species extinction. The report concludes that, unless changes are made, the massive damage reckoned to be due to livestock may more than double by 2050, as demand for meat increases. One of the cited changes suggests that intensification of the livestock industry may be suggested, since intensification leads to less land for a given level of production.

Some microbes respire in the cattle gut by an anaerobic process known as methanogenesis (producing the gas methane). Cattle emit a large volume of methane, 95 per cent of it through eructation or burping, not flatulence. As the carbon in the methane comes from the digestion of vegetation produced by photosynthesis, its release into the air by this process would normally be considered harmless, because there is no net increase in carbon in the atmosphere—it's removed as carbon dioxide from the air by photosynthesis and returned to it as methane. Methane is a more potent greenhouse gas than carbon dioxide, having a warming effect 23 to 50 times greater, and according to Takahashi and Young "even a small increase in methane concentration in the atmosphere exerts a potentially significant contribution to global warming". Further analysis of the methane gas produced by livestock as a contributor to the increase in greenhouse gases is provided by Weart. Research is underway on methods of reducing this source of methane, by the use of dietary supplements, or treatments to reduce the proportion of methanogenetic microbes, perhaps by vaccination.

Cattle are fed a concentrated high-corn diet which produces rapid weight gain, but this has side effects which include increased acidity in the digestive system. When improperly handled, manure and other byproducts of concentrated agriculture also have environmental consequences.

Grazing by cattle at low intensities can create a favourable environment for native herbs and forbs; however, in most world regions cattle are reducing biodiversity due to overgrazing driven by food demands by an expanding human population.

Health

Cow urine is commonly used in India for medical purposes. It is distilled and then consumed by patients seeking treatment for a wide variety of illness. At present, there is no conclusive medical evidence that this has any effect.

Oxen (singular ox) are large and heavyset breeds of *Bos taurus* cattle trained as draft animals. Often they are adult, castrated males. Usually an ox is over four years old due to the need for training and to allow it to grow to full size. Oxen are used for plowing, transport, hauling cargo, grain-grinding by trampling or by powering machines, irrigation by powering pumps, and wagon drawing. Oxen were commonly used to skid logs in forests, and sometimes still are, in low-impact select-cut logging. Oxen are most often used in teams of two, paired, for light work such as carting. In the past, teams might have been larger, with some teams exceeding twenty animals when used for logging.

An ox is a mature bovine who has learned to respond appropriately to a teamster's signals. These signals are given by verbal commands or by noise (whip cracks). In North America, the commands are:

1. *get up*;
2. *whoa*;
3. *back up*;
4. *gee* (turn right); and
5. *haw* (turn left).

U.S. ox trainers favoured larger males for their ability to work.

Oxen can pull harder and longer than horses. Though not as fast as horses, they are less prone to injury because they are more sure-footed.

Many oxen are used worldwide, especially in developing countries.

Oxen are also used as food products, including their blood, livers, kidneys, hearts, hides, and tails.

Cattle are venerated within the Hindu religion of India. According to Vedic scriptures they are to be treated with the same respect 'as one's mother' because of the milk they provide; "The cow is my mother" (Mahabharata) They appear in numerous stories from the Puranas and Vedas. The deity Krishna was brought up in a family of cowherders, and given the name Govinda (protector of the cows). Also Shiva is traditionally said to ride on the back of a bull named Nandi. In ancient rural India every household had a few cows which provided a constant supply of milk and a few bulls that helped as draft animals.

Observant Hindus, even though they might eat meat of other animals, almost always abstain from beef, and the slaughter of cows is considered a heinous sin in mainstream Orthodox Hinduism. Slaughter of cows (including oxen, bulls and calves) is forbidden by law in almost all the states of the Indian Union. Illegal slaughter of cows in India is sometimes the reason for religious riots between Hindus and Muslims. McDonalds outlets in India serve only vegetarian, chicken or fishburgers. At one time the death sentence was imposed for killing a cow in India, and as late as 1960, an individual could serve three months in jail for killing a pedestrian, but one year for injuring a cow, and life imprisonment for killing a cow.

The Evangelist St. Luke is depicted as an ox in Christian art.

In Judaism, as described in Numbers 19:2, the ashes of a sacrificed unblemished red heifer that has never been yoked can be used for ritual purification of people who came into contact with a corpse.

The ox is one of the 12-year cycle of animals which appear in the Chinese zodiac related to the Chinese calendar.

The constellation.Taurus represents a bull.

An apocryphal story has it that a cow started the Great Chicago Fire by kicking over a kerosene lamp. Michael Ahern, the reporter who created the cow story, admitted in 1893 that he had fabricated it for more colourful copy.

On February 18, 1930, Elm Farm Ollie became the first cow to fly in an airplane and also the first cow to be milked in an airplane.

The first known law requiring branding in North America was enacted on February 5, 1644, by Connecticut. It said that all cattle and pigs had to have a registered brand or earmark by May 1, 1644.

The akabeko (*red cow*) is a traditional toy from the Aizu region of Japan that is thought to ward off illness.

The case of *Sherwood vs. Walker* — involving a supposedly barren heifer that was actually pregnant—first enunciated the concept of mutual mistake as a means of destroying the meeting of the minds in contract law.

The Maasai tribe of East Africa traditionally believe that all cows on earth are the God-given property of the Maasai.

4 The Domestic Goat

The domestic goat (*Capra aegagrus hircus*) is a subspecies of goat domesticated from the wild goat of southwest Asia and Eastern Europe. The goat is a member of the Bovidae family and is closely related to the sheep as both are in the goat-antelope subfamily Caprinae. There are over three hundred distinct breeds of goat.

Goats are one of the oldest domesticated species. Goats have been used for their milk, meat, hair, and skins over much of the world. In the twentieth century they also gained in popularity as pets.

Female goats are referred to as *does* or *nannies*, intact males as *bucks* or *billies*; their offspring are *kids.* Note that many goat breeders prefer the terms 'buck' and 'doe' to 'billy' and 'nanny'. Castrated males are *wethers.* Goat meat from younger animals is called *kid* or *cabrito,* and from older animals is sometimes called *chevon,* or in some areas 'mutton'.

The Modern English word *goat* comes from the Old English *gat* which meant 'she-goat', and this in turn derived from Proto-Germanic **gaitaz* (cf. Old Norse and Dutch *geit* 'goat', German *Geiß* 'she-goat', and Gothic *gaits* 'goat'), ultimately from Proto-Indo-European **ghaidos* meaning 'young goat' but also 'jump' (cf. Latin *haedus* 'kid', Old Church Slavonic *zajeci* 'hare', Sanskrit *jihite* 'he jumps'). To refer to the male of the species, Old English used *bucca* (which survives as 'buck') until a shift to *he-goat* (and *she-goat*) occurred in the late 12th century. 'Nanny goat' originated in the 18th century and 'billy goat' in the 19th.

Goats are among the earliest animals domesticated by humans. The most recent genetic analysis confirms the archaeological evidence that the

Anatolian Zagros are the likely origin of almost all domestic goats today. Another major genetic source of modern goats is the Bezoar goat; distributed from the mountainous regions of Asia Minor across the Middle East to Sind.

Neolithic farmers began to keep them for easy access to milk and meat, primarily, also for their dung, which was used as fuel and their bones, hair, and sinew for clothing, building, and tools. The earliest remnants of domesticated goats dating 10,000 years before present are found in Ganj Dareh in Iranian Kurdistan. Goat remains have been found at archaeological sites in Jericho, Choga, Mami, Djeitun and Cayonu; dating the domestication of goats in western Asia at between 8000 and 9000 years ago. Domestic goats were generally kept in herds that wandered on hills or other grazing areas, often tended by goatherds who were frequently children or adolescents, similar to the more widely known shepherd. These methods of herding are still used today.

Historically, goat hide has been used for water and wine bottles in both travelling and transporting wine for sale. It has also been used to produce parchment.

Most goats naturally have two horns, of various shapes and sizes depending on the breed. All goats have horns unless they are 'polled' meaning they have one parent with a dominant polled gene. There have been incidents of polycerate goats (having as many as eight horns), although this is a genetic rarity thought to be inherited. Their horns are made of living bone surrounded by keratin and other proteins, and are used for defense, dominance, and territoriality.

Goats are ruminants. They have a four-chambered stomach consisting of the rumen, the reticulum, the omasum, and the abomasum.

Goats have horizontal slit-shaped pupils, an adaptation which increases peripheral depth perception. Because goats' irises are usually pale, the pupils are much more visible than in animals with horizontal pupils, but very dark irises, such as cattle, deer, most horses and many sheep.

Both male and female goats have beards, and many types of goat (most commonly dairy goats, dairy-cross boers, and pygmy goats) may have wattles, one dangling from each side of the neck.

Some breeds of sheep and goats look similar, but they can usually be told apart because goat tails are short and point up, whereas sheep tails hang down and are usually longer and bigger — though some (like those of Northern European short-tailed sheep) are short, and longer ones are often docked. In some climates, goats are able to breed at any time of the year. In temperate climates and among the Swiss breeds, the breeding season commences as the day length shortens, and ends in early spring. Does of any breed come into heat every 21 days for 2 to 48 hours. A doe in heat typically flags her tail often, stays near the buck if one is present, becomes more vocal, and may also show a decrease in appetite and milk production for the duration of the heat.

Bucks (intact males) of Swiss and northern breeds come into rut in the fall as with the doe's heat cycles. Rut is characterized by a decrease in appetite and obsessive interest in the does.

In addition to natural mating, artificial insemination has gained popularity among goat breeders, as it allows easy access to a wide variety of bloodlines.

Gestation length is approximately 150 days. Twins are the usual result, with single and triplet births also common. Less frequent are litters of quadruplet, quintuplet, and even sextuplet kids. Birthing, known as *kidding*, generally occurs uneventfully. Right before kidding the doe will have a sunken area around the tail and hip. Also she will have heavy breathing, a worried look, become restless and show great display of affection for her keeper. The mother often eats the placenta, which gives her much needed nutrients, helps stanch her bleeding, and parallels the behaviour of wild herbivores such as deer to reduce the lure of the birth scent for predators.

Freshening (coming into milk production) occurs at kidding. Milk production varies with the breed, age, quality, and diet of the doe; dairy goats generally produce between 660 to 1,800 L (1,500 and 4,000 lb) of milk per 305 day lactation. On average, a good quality dairy doe will give at least 6 lb (2.7 l) of milk per day while she is in milk. A first time milker may produce less, or as much as 16 lb (7.3 l), or more of milk in exceptional cases. After the 305 day lactation, the doe will 'dry off', typically after she has been bred. Occasionally, goats that have not been bred and are continuously milked will continue lactation beyond the typical 305 days. Meat, fibre, and pet breeds are not usually milked and simply produce enough for the kids until weaning.

Male lactation is also known to occur in goats.

Goats are reputed to be willing to eat almost anything, except tin cans and cardboard boxes. While goats will not actually eat inedible material, they are browsing animals, not grazers like cattle and sheep, and (coupled with their natural curiosity) will chew on and taste just about anything resembling plant matter in order to decide whether it is good to eat, including cardboard and paper labels from tin cans. Another possibility is that the goats are curious about the unusual smells of leftover food in discarded cans or boxes.

Aside from sampling many things, goats are quite particular in what they actually consume, preferring to browse on the tips of woody shrubs and trees, as well as the occasional broad-leaved plant. However, it can fairly be said that their plant diet is extremely varied, and includes some species which are otherwise toxic. They will seldom consume soiled food or contaminated water unless facing starvation. This is one reason goat rearing is most often free ranging, since stall-fed goat rearing involves extensive upkeep and is seldom commercially viable.

Goats prefer to browse on shrubbery and weeds, more like deer than sheep, preferring them to grasses. Nightshade is poisonous; wilted fruit tree leaves can also kill goats. Silage (corn stalks) is not good for goats, but haylage can be used if consumed immediately after opening. Alfalfa is their favourite hay; fescue is the least palatable and least nutritious. Mold in a goat's feed can make it sick and possibly kill it. Goats should not be fed grass showing any signs of mold.

The digestive physiology of a very young kid (like the young of other ruminants) is essentially the same as that of a monogastric animal. Milk digestion begins in the abomasum, the milk having bypassed the rumen via closure of the reticular/esophageal groove during suckling. At birth, the rumen is undeveloped, but as the kid begins to consume solid feed, the rumen soon increases in size and in its capacity to absorb nutrients.

Goats are extremely curious and intelligent. They are easily trained to pull carts and walk on leads. Ches McCartney, nicknamed 'the goat man', toured the United States for over three decades in a wagon pulled by a herd of pet goats. They are also known for escaping their pens. Goats will test fences, either intentionally or simply because they are handy to climb on. If any of the fencing can be spread, pushed over or down, or otherwise be overcome, the goats will escape. Being very intelligent, once a weakness in the fence has been discovered, it will be exploited repeatedly. Goats are very coordinated and can climb and hold their balance in the most precarious places. Goats are also widely known for their ability to climb trees, although the tree generally has to be on somewhat of an angle. The vocalization goats make is called bleating.

Goats have an intensely inquisitive and intelligent nature: they will explore anything new or unfamiliar in their surroundings. They do so primarily with their prehensile upper lip and tongue. This is why they investigate items such as buttons, camera cases or clothing (and many other things besides) by nibbling at them, occasionally even eating them.

A goat is useful to humans either living or dead, first as a renewable provider of milk and fiber, and then as meat and hide. Some charities provide goats to impoverished people in poor countries, because goats are easier and cheaper to manage than cattle, and have multiple uses. In addition, goats are used for driving and packing purposes.

For instance, the intestine is used to make 'catgut', which is still in use as a material for internal human surgical sutures and strings for musical instruments. The horn of the goat, which signifies wellbeing (Cornucopia), is also used to make spoons.

The taste of goat kid meat is similar to that of spring lamb meat; in fact, in the English-speaking islands of the Caribbean, and in some parts of Asia, particularly Pakistan and India, the word 'mutton' is used to describe both goat and lamb meat. However, some compare the taste of goat meat to veal or venison, depending on the age and condition of the goat. Its flavor is said to be primarily linked to the presence of 4-methyloctanoic and 4-methylnonanoic acid. It can be prepared in a variety of ways including stewed, baked, grilled, barbecued, minced, canned, fried, curried, or made into sausage. Due to its low fat content, the meat can toughen at high temperatures without additional moisture. One of the most popular goats grown for meat is the South African Boer, introduced into the United States in the early 1990s. The New Zealand Kiko is also considered a meat breed, as is the myotonic or 'fainting goat', a breed originating in Tennessee.

Goats produce approximately two per cent of the world's total annual milk supply. Some goats are bred specifically for milk. If the strong-smelling buck is not separated from the does, his scent will affect the milk.

Doe milk naturally has small, well-emulsified fat globules, which means the cream remains suspended in the milk, instead of rising to the top, as in raw cow milk; therefore, it does not need to be homogenized. Indeed, if the milk is going to be used to make cheese it is recommended that it is not homogenized as this changes the structure of the milk impacting the culture's ability to coagulate the milk and the final quality and yield of cheese.

Dairy goats in their prime, which is generally around the third or fourth lactation cycle, average 6 to 8 pounds (2.7 to 3.6 kg) of milk production daily (roughly 3 to 4 US quarts (2.7 to 3.6 litres)) during a ten-month lactation, producing more just after freshening and gradually dropping in production toward the end of their lactation. The milk generally averages 3.5 per cent butterfat. A doe may be expected to reach her heaviest production during her third or fourth lactation.

Doe milk is commonly processed into cheese, butter, ice cream, yoghurt, cajeta and other products. Goat cheese is known as *chèvre* in France, after the French word for 'goat'. Some varieties include Rocamadour and Montrachet. Goat butter is white because goats produce milk with the yellow beta-carotene converted to a colourless form of vitamin A.

The American Academy of Paediatrics discourages feeding infants milk derived from goats. An April 2010 case report summarizes their recommendation and presents "a comprehensive review of the consequences associated with this dangerous practice," also stating, "Many infants are exclusively fed unmodified goat's milk as a result of cultural beliefs as well as exposure to false online information. Anecdotal reports have described a host of morbidities associated with that practice, including severe electrolyte abnormalities, metabolic acidosis, megaloblastic anemia, allergic reactions including life-threatening anaphylactic shock, hemolytic uremic syndrome, and infections." Untreated caprine brucellosis results in a two per cent case fatality rate. According to the United States Department of Agriculture (USDA), doe milk is not recommended for human infants because it contains "inadequate quantities of iron, folate, vitamins C and D, thiamin, niacin, vitamin B_6, and pantothenic acid to meet an infant's nutritional needs" and may cause harm to an infant's kidneys and could cause metabolic damage.

The Department of Health in the United Kingdom has repeatedly released statements stating on various occasions that "Goats' milk is not suitable for babies, and infant formulas and follow-on formulas based on goats' milk protein have not been approved for use in Europe," and "infant milks based on goats' milk protein are not suitable as a source of nutrition for infants".

On the other hand, some farming groups promote the practice. For example Small Farm Today in 2005 claimed beneficial use in invalid and convalescent diets, proposing that glycerol ethers, possibly important in nutrition for nursing infants, are much higher in doe milk than in cow milk. A 1970 book on animal breeding claimed that doe milk differs from cow or human milk by having higher digestibility, distinct alkalinity, higher buffering capacity, and certain therapeutic values in human medicine and nutrition. George Mateljan suggested that doe milk can replace ewe milk or cow milk in diets of those who are allergic to certain mammals' milk. However, like cow milk, doe milk has lactose (sugar), and may cause gastrointestinal problems for individuals with lactose intolerance. In fact, the level of lactose is similar to that of bovine milk.

The Angora breed of goats produces long, curling, lustrous locks of mohair. The entire body of the goat is covered with mohair and there are no guard hairs. The locks constantly grow and can be four inches or more in length. Angora crossbreeds, such as the pygora and the nigora, have been created to produce mohair and/or cashgora on a smaller, easier-to-manage animal. The wool is shorn (cut from the body) twice a year, with an average yield of about 10 pounds.

Most goats have softer insulating hairs nearer the skin, and longer guard hairs on the surface. The desirable fiber for the textile industry is the former, and it goes by several names (down, cashmere and pashmina). The coarse guard hairs are of little value as they are too coarse, difficult to spin and difficult to dye. The cashmere goat produces a commercial quantity of cashmere wool, which is one of the most expensive natural fibres commercially produced; cashmere is very fine and soft. The cashmere goat fiber is harvested once a year, yielding around 9 ounces (200 grammes) of down.

In South Asia, cashmere is called 'pashmina' (from Persian *pashmina*, 'fine wool'). In the 18th and early 19th century, Kashmir (then called Cashmere by the English), had a thriving industry producing shawls from goat down imported from Tibet and Tartary through Ladakh. The shawls were introduced into Western Europe when the General in Chief of the French campaign in Egypt (1799–1802) sent one to Paris. Since these shawls were produced in the upper Kashmir and Ladakh region, the wool came to be known as 'cashmere'.

Goat breeders' clubs frequently hold shows, where goats are judged on traits relating to conformation, udder quality, evidence of high production, longevity, build and muscling (meat goats and pet goats) and fiber production and the fibre itself (fibre goats). People who show their goats usually keep registered stock and the offspring of award-winning animals command a higher price. Registered goats, in general, are usually higher-priced if for no other reason than that records have been kept proving their ancestry and the production and other data of their sires, dams, and other ancestors. A registered doe is usually less of a gamble than buying a doe at random (as at an auction or sale barn) because of these records and the reputation of the breeder. Children's clubs such as 4-H also allow goats to be shown. Children's shows often include a showmanship class, where the cleanliness and presentation of both the animal and the exhibitor as well as the handler's ability and skill in handling the goat are scored. In a showmanship class, conformation is irrelevant since this is not what is being judged.

Various 'Dairy Goat Scorecards' (milking does) are systems used for judging shows in the US. The American Dairy Goat Association (ADGA) scorecard for an adult doe includes a point system of a hundred total with major categories that include general appearance, the dairy character of a doe (physical traits that aid and increase milk production), body capacity, and specifically for the mammary system. Young stock and bucks are judged by different scorecards which place more emphasis on the other three categories; general appearance, body capacity, and dairy character.

The American Goat Society (AGS) has a similar, but not identical scorecard that is used in their shows. The miniature dairy goats may be judged by either of the two scorecards. The 'Angora Goat scorecard' used by the Coloured Angora Goat Breeder's Association CAGBA (which covers the white and the coloured goats) includes evaluation of an animal's fleece colour, density, uniformity, fineness, and general body confirmation. Disqualifications include: a deformed mouth, broken down pasterns, deformed feet, crooked legs, abnormalities of testicles, missing testicles, more than 3 inch split in scrotum, and close-set or distorted horns.

According to Norse mythology, the god of thunder, Thor, has a chariot that is pulled by the goats Tanngrisnir and Tanngnjóstr. At night when he sets up camp, Thor eats the meat of the goats, but take care that all bones remain whole.

Then he wraps the remains up, and in the morning, the goats always come back to life to pull the chariot. When a farmer's son who is invited to share the meal breaks one of the goats' leg bones to suck the marrow, the animal's leg remains broken in the morning, and the boy is forced to serve Thor as a servant to compensate for the damage.

Possibly related, the Yule Goat is one of the oldest Scandinavian and Northern European Yule and Christmas symbols and traditions. Yule Goat originally denoted the goat that was slaughtered around Yule, but it may also indicate a goat figure made out of straw.

It is also used about the custom of going door-to-door singing carols and getting food and drinks in return, often fruit, cakes and sweets. 'Going Yule Goat' is similar to the British custom was sailing, both with heathen roots. The Gävle Goat is a giant version of the Yule Goat, erected every year in the Swedish city of Gävle.

The Greek god, Pan, is said to have the upper body of a man and the horns and lower body of a goat. Pan was a very lustful god, nearly all of the myths involving him had to do with him chasing nymphs. He is also credited with creating the pan flute.

The goat is one of the twelve-year cycle of animals which appear in the Chinese zodiac related to the Chinese calendar. Each animal is associated with certain personality traits; those born in a year of the goat are predicted to be shy, introverted, creative, and perfectionist.

Several mythological hybrid creatures are believed to consist of parts of the goat, including the Chimera. The Capricorn sign in the Western zodiac is usually depicted as a goat with a fish's tail. Fauns and satyrs are mythological creatures that are part goat and part human. The mineral bromine is named from the Greek word 'br mos', which means 'stench of he-goats'.

Goats are mentioned many times in the Bible. A goat is considered a "clean" animal by Jewish dietary laws and was slaughtered for an honoured guest. It was also acceptable for some kinds of sacrifices. Goat-hair curtains were used in the tent that contained the tabernacle (Exodus 25:4).

Its horns can be used instead of sheep's horn to make a shofar. On Yom Kippur, the festival of the Day of Atonement, two goats were chosen and lots were drawn for them. One was sacrificed and the other allowed to escape into the wilderness, symbolically carrying with it the sins of the community. From this comes the word 'scapegoat'. A leader or king was sometimes compared to a male goat leading the flock. In the New Testament, Jesus told a parable of The Sheep and the Goats.

Popular Christian folk tradition in Europe associated Satan with imagery of goats (see Pan (mythology)). A common superstition in the Middle Ages was that goats whispered lewd sentences in the ears of the saints. The origin of this belief was probably the behavior of the buck in rut, the very epitome of lust. The common medieval depiction of the Devil was that of a goat-like face with horns and small beard (a goatee).

The Black Mass, a probably-mythological 'Satanic mass', was said to involve a black goat , the form in which Satan supposedly manifested himself for worship.

The goat has had a lingering connection with Satanism and pagan religions, even into modern times. The inverted pentagram, a symbol used in Satanism, is said to be shaped like a goat's head. The 'Baphomet of Mendes' refers to a satanic goat-like figure from 19th century occultism.

Goats readily revert to the wild (become feral) if given the opportunity. The only domestic animal known to return to feral life as swiftly is the cat. Feral goats have established themselves in many areas: they occur in Australia, New Zealand, Great Britain, the Galapagos and in many other places. When feral goats reach large populations in habitats which are not adapted to them, they may have serious effects, such as removing native scrub, trees and other vegetation. Feral goats are common in Australia. However, in other circumstances they may become a natural component of the habitat.

5 House Rabbits

Pet rabbits kept indoors are referred to as house rabbits. House rabbits typically have an indoor pen or cage and a rabbit-safe place to run and exercise, such as an exercise pen, living room or family room. Rabbits can be trained to use a litter box and some can learn to come when called. Domestic rabbits that do not live indoors can also often serve as companions for their owners, typically living in an easily accessible hutch outside the home. Some pet rabbits live in outside hutches during the day for the benefit of fresh air and natural daylight and are brought inside at night.

Whether indoor or outdoor, pet rabbits' pens are often equipped with enrichment activities such as shelves, tunnels, balls, and other toys. Pet rabbits are often provided additional space in which to get exercise, simulating the open space a rabbit would traverse in the wild. Exercise pens or lawn pens are often used to provide a safe place for rabbits to run.

A pet rabbit's diet typically consists of unlimited timothy-grass, a small amount of pellets, and a small portion of fresh vegetables and need unrestricted access to fresh clean water. Rabbits are social animals. Rabbits as pets can find their companionship with a variety of creatures, including humans, other rabbits, guinea pigs, and sometimes even cats and dogs. Animal welfare organisations such as the House Rabbit Society advise that rabbits do not make good pets for small children because children generally do not know how to stay quiet, calm, and gentle around rabbits. As prey animals, rabbits are alert, timid creatures that startle easily. They have fragile bones, especially in their backs, that require support on the belly and bottom when picked up. Children 7 years old and older usually have the maturity required to care for a rabbit.

Rabbits are small mammals in the family Leporidae of the order Lagomorpha, found in several parts of the world. There are eight different genera in the family classified as rabbits, including the European rabbit (*Oryctolagus cuniculus*), cottontail rabbits (genus *Sylvilagus*; 13 species), and the Amami rabbit (*Pentalagus furnessi*, an endangered species on Amami Oshima, Japan). There are many other species of rabbit, and these, along with pikas and hares, make up the order Lagomorpha. The male is called a *buck* and the female is a *doe*; a young rabbit is a *kitten* or *kit*.

Rabbit habitats include meadows, woods, forests, grasslands, deserts and wetlands. Rabbits live in groups, and the best known species, the European rabbit, lives in underground burrows, or rabbit holes. A group of burrows is called a warren.

More than half the world's rabbit population resides in North America. They are also native to southwestern Europe, Southeast Asia, Sumatra, some islands of Japan, and in parts of Africa and South America.

They are not naturally found in most of Eurasia, where a number of species of hares are present. Rabbits first entered South America relatively recently, as part of the Great American Interchange. Much of the continent has just one species of rabbit, the tapeti, while most of South America's southern cone is without rabbits.

The European rabbit has been introduced to many places around the world.

Characteristics and Anatomy

The rabbit's long ears, which can be more than 10 cm (4 in) long, are probably an adaptation for detecting predators. They have large, powerful hind legs. The two front paws have 5 toes, the extra called the dewclaw.

The hind feet have 4 toes. They are digitigrade animals; they move around on the tips of their toes. Wild rabbits do not differ much in their body proportions or stance, with full, egg-shaped bodies. Their size can range anywhere from 20 cm (8 in) in length and 0.4 kg in weight to 50 cm (20 in) and more than 2 kg. The fur is most commonly long and soft, with colours such as shades of brown, gray, and buff. The tail is a little plume of brownish fur (white on top for cottontails).

Because the rabbit's epiglottis is engaged over the soft palate except when swallowing, the rabbit is an obligate nasal breather. Rabbits have two sets of incisor teeth, one behind the other. This way they can be distinguished from rodents, with which they are often confused. Carl Linnaeus originally grouped rabbits and rodents under the class Glires; later, they were separated as the predominant opinion was that many of their similarities were a result of convergent evolution. However, recent DNA analysis and the discovery of a common ancestor has supported the view that they share a common lineage, and thus rabbits and rodents are now often referred to together as members of the superclass Glires.

Rabbits are hindgut digesters. This means that most of their digestion takes place in their large intestine and cecum. In rabbits the cecum is about 10 times bigger than the stomach and it along with the large intestine makes up roughly 40 per cent of the rabbit's digestive tract.

The unique musculature of the cecum allows the intestinal tract of the rabbit to separate fibrous material from more digestible material; the fibrous material is passed as feces, while the more nutritious material is encased in a mucous lining as a cecotrope. Cecotropes, sometimes called 'night feces', are high in minerals, vitamins and proteins that are necessary to the rabbit's health. Rabbits eat these to meet their nutritional requirements; the mucous coating allows the nutrients to pass through the acidic stomach for digestion in the intestines. This process allows rabbits to extract the necessary nutrients from their food.

Rabbits are prey animals and are therefore constantly aware of their surroundings. If confronted by a potential threat, a rabbit may freeze and observe then warn others in the warren with powerful thumps on the ground.

Rabbits have a remarkably wide field of vision, and a good deal of it is devoted to overhead scanning. They survive predation by burrowing, hopping away in a zig- zag motion, and, if captured, delivering powerful kicks with their hind legs. Their strong teeth allow them to eat and to bite in order to escape a struggle.

Rabbits have a very rapid reproductive rate. The breeding season for most rabbits lasts 9 months, from February to October. In Australia and New Zealand breeding season is late July to late January. Normal gestation is about 30 days. The average size of the litter varies but is usually between 4 and 12 babies, with larger breeds having larger litters. A kit (baby rabbit) can be weaned at about 4 to 5 weeks of age. This means in one season a single female rabbit can produce as many as 800 children, grandchildren, and great-grandchildren. A doe is ready to breed at about 6 months of age, and a buck at about 7 months. Courtship and mating are very brief, lasting only 30 to 40 seconds. Courtship behaviour involves licking, sniffing, and following the doe. Spraying urine is also a common sexual behaviour. Female rabbits are reflex ovulators. The female rabbit also may or may not lose clumps of hair during the gestation period.

Ovulation begins 10 hours after mating. After mating, the female will make a nest or borough, and line the nest with fur from the dewlap, flanks, and belly. This behavior also exposes the nipples enabling her to better nurse the kits. Kits are altricial, which means they're born blind, naked, and helpless. Passive immunity (immunity acquired by transfer of antibodies or sensitized lymphocytes from another animal) is acquired by kits prior to birth via placental transfer. At 10 to 11 days after birth the baby rabbits' eyes will open and they will start eating on their own at around 14 days old.

Although born naked, they form a soft baby coat of hair within a few days. At the age of 5 to 6 weeks the soft baby coat is replaced with a pre-adult coat. At about 6 to 8 months of age this intermediate coat is replaced by the final adult coat, which is shed twice a year thereafter. Due to the nutritious nature of rabbit milk kits only need to be nursed for a few minutes once or twice a day.

The expected rabbit lifespan is about 9-12 years; the world's longest-lived was 18 years.

Rabbits are herbivores that feed by grazing on grass, forbs, and leafy weeds. In consequence, their diet contains large amounts of cellulose, which is hard to digest. Rabbits solve this problem by passing two distinct types of feces: hard droppings and soft black viscous pellets, the latter of which are immediately eaten. Rabbits reingest their own droppings (rather than chewing the cud as do cows and many other herbivores) to digest their food further and extract sufficient nutrients.

Rabbits graze heavily and rapidly for roughly the first half hour of a grazing period (usually in the late afternoon), followed by about half an hour of more selective feeding. In this time, the rabbit will also excrete many hard fecal pellets, being waste pellets that will not be reingested. If the environment is relatively non-threatening, the rabbit will remain outdoors for many hours, grazing at intervals. While out of the burrow, the rabbit will occasionally reingest its soft, partially digested pellets; this is rarely observed, since the pellets are reingested as they are produced. Reingestion is most common within the burrow between 8 o'clock in the morning and 5 O'clock in the evening, being carried out intermittently within that period.

Hard pellets are made up of hay-like fragments of plant cuticle and stalk, being the final waste product after redigestion of soft pellets. These are only released outside the burrow and are not reingested. Soft pellets are usually produced several hours after grazing, after the hard pellets have all been excreted. They are made up of micro-organisms and undigested plant cell walls.

The chewed plant material collects in the large cecum, a secondary chamber between the large and small intestine containing large quantities of symbiotic bacteria that help with the digestion of cellulose and also produce certain B vitamins. The pellets are about 56 per cent bacteria by dry weight, largely accounting for the pellets being 24.4 per cent protein on average. These pellets remain intact for up to six hours in the stomach; the bacteria within continue to digest the plant carbohydrates. The soft feces form here and contain up to five times the vitamins of hard feces. After being excreted, they are eaten whole by the rabbit and redigested in a special part of the stomach. This double-digestion process enables rabbits to use nutrients that they may have missed during the first passage through the gut, as well as the nutrients formed by the microbial activity and thus ensures that maximum nutrition is derived from the food they eat. This process serves the same purpose within the rabbit as rumination does in cattle and sheep.

Rabbits are incapable of vomiting.

Rabbits are clearly distinguished from hares in that rabbits are altricial, having young that are born blind and hairless. In contrast, hares are generally born with hair and are able to see (precocial). All rabbits except cottontail rabbits live underground in burrows or warrens, while hares live in simple nests above the ground (as do cottontail rabbits), and usually do not live in groups. Hares are generally larger than rabbits, with longer ears, and have black markings on their fur. Hares have not been domesticated, while European rabbits are often kept as house pets. In gardens, they are typically kept in hutches—small, wooden, house-like boxes—that protect the rabbits from the environment and predators.

Leporids such as European rabbits and hares are a food meat in Europe, South America, North America, some parts of the Middle East.

Rabbit is still sold in UK butchers and markets, although not in supermarkets. At farmers markets and the famous Borough Market in London, rabbits will be displayed dead and hanging unbutchered in the traditional style next to braces of pheasant and other small game. Rabbit meat was once commonly sold in Sydney, Australia, the sellers of which giving the name to the rugby league team the South Sydney Rabbitohs, but quickly became unpopular after the disease myxomatosis was introduced in an attempt to wipe out the feral rabbit population (see also Rabbits in Australia).

When used for food, rabbits are both hunted and bred for meat. Snares or guns are usually employed when catching wild rabbits for food. In many regions, rabbits are also bred for meat, a practice called cuniculture. Rabbits can then be killed by hitting the back of their heads, a practice from which the term *rabbit punch* is derived. Rabbit meat is a source of high quality protein. It can be used in most ways chicken meat is used. In fact, well-known chef Mark Bittman says that domesticated rabbit tastes like chicken because both are blank palettes upon which any desired flavors can be layered. Rabbit meat is leaner than beef, pork, and chicken meat. Rabbit products are generally labeled in three ways, the first being Fryer. This is a young rabbit between 4.5 and 5 pounds and up to 9 weeks in age. This type of meat is tender and fine grained. The next product is a Roaster; they are usually over 5 pounds and up to 8 months in age. The flesh is firm and coarse grained and less tender than a fryer. Then there are giblets which include the liver and heart. One of the most common types of rabbit to be bred for meat is New Zealand white rabbit.

There are several health issues associated with the use of rabbits for meat, one of which is tularemia or rabbit fever. Another is so-called rabbit starvation, due most likely to deficiency of essential fatty acids in rabbit meat. Rabbits are a common food item of large pythons, such as Burmese pythons and reticulated pythons, both in the wild and in captivity.

Rabbit pelts are sometimes used for clothing and accessories, such as scarves or hats. Angora rabbits are bred for their long, fine hair, which can be sheared and harvested like sheep wool. Rabbits are very good producers of manure; additionally, their urine, being high in nitrogen, makes lemon trees very productive. Their milk may also be of great medicinal or nutritional benefit due to its high protein content.

Rabbits have been a source of environmental problems when introduced into the wild by humans. As a result of their appetites, and the rate at which they breed, feral rabbit depredation can be problematic for agriculture. Gassing, barriers (fences), shooting, snaring, and ferreting have been used to control rabbit populations, but the most effective measures are diseases such as myxomatosis (myxo or mixi, colloquially) and calicivirus. In Europe, where rabbits are farmed on a large scale, they are protected against myxomatosis and calicivirus with a genetically modified virus. The virus was developed in Spain, and is beneficial to rabbit farmers. If it were to make its way into wild populations in areas such as Australia, it could create a population boom, as those diseases are the most serious threats to rabbit survival. Rabbits in Australia and New Zealand are considered to be such a pest that land owners are legally obliged to control them.

Rabbits are often used as a symbol of fertility or rebirth, and have long been associated with spring and Easter as the Easter Bunny. The species' role as a prey animal also lends itself as a symbol of innocence, another Easter connotation.

Additionally, rabbits are often used as symbols of playful sexuality, which also relates to the human perception of innocence, as well as its reputation as a prolific breeder.

The rabbit often appears in folklore as the trickster archetype, as he uses his cunning to outwit his enemies.

In Aztec mythology, a pantheon of four hundred rabbit gods known as Centzon Totochtin, led by Ometotchtli or Two Rabbit, represented fertility, parties, and drunkenness.

In Central Africa, 'Kalulu' the rabbit is widely known as a tricky character, getting the better of bargains.

In Chinese literature, rabbits accompany Chang'e on the Moon. Also associated with the Chinese New Year (or Lunar New Year), rabbits are also one of the twelve celestial animals in the Chinese Zodiac for the Chinese calendar. It is interesting to note that the Vietnamese lunar new year replaced the rabbit with a cat in their calendar, as rabbits did not inhabit Vietnam.

A rabbit's foot is carried as an amulet believed to bring good luck. This is found in many parts of the world, and with the earliest use being in Europe around 600 B.C.

In Japanese tradition, rabbits live on the Moon where they make mochi, the popular snack of mashed sticky rice. This comes from interpreting the pattern of dark patches on the moon as a rabbit standing on tiptoes on the left pounding on an usu, a Japanese mortar.

In Jewish folklore, rabbits (shfanim) are associated with cowardice, a usage still current in contemporary Israeli spoken Hebrew (similar to English colloquial use of 'chicken' to denote cowardice).

A Korean myth similar to the Japanese counterpart presents rabbits living on the moon making rice cakes (Tteok in Korean).

In Native American Ojibwe mythology, Nanabozho, or Great Rabbit, is an important deity related to the creation of the world.

A Vietnamese mythological story portrays the rabbit of innocence and youthfulness. The Gods of the myth are shown to be hunting and killing rabbits to show off their power.

'Taushan Tepe' (Rabbit Hill) was the Turkish name of Kabile, Bulgaria.

On the Isle of Portland in Dorset, UK, the rabbit is said to be unlucky and speaking its name can cause upset with older residents. This is thought to date back to early times in the quarrying industry, where piles of extracted stone (not fit for sale) were built into tall rough walls (to save space) directly behind the working quarry face; the rabbit's natural tendency to burrow would weaken these 'walls' and cause collapse, often resulting in injuries or even death. The name rabbit is often substituted with words such as 'long ears' or 'underground mutton', so as not to have to say the actual word and bring bad luck to oneself. It is said that a public house (on the island) can be cleared of people by calling out the word rabbit and while this was very true in the past, it has gradually become more fable than fact over the past 50 years.

Other Fictional Rabbits

The rabbit as trickster appears in American popular culture; for example the Br'er Rabbit character from African-American folktales and Disney animation; and the Warner Bros. cartoon character Bugs Bunny.

Anthropomorphized rabbits have appeared in a host of works of film, literature, and technology, notably the White Rabbit and the March Hare in Lewis Carroll's *Alice's Adventures in Wonderland*; in the popular novels *Watership Down,* by Richard Adams (which has also been made into a movie) and *Rabbit Hill* by Robert Lawson, as well as in Beatrix Potter's Peter Rabbit stories.

Urban Legends

It was commonly believed that pregnancy tests were based on the idea that a rabbit would die if injected with a pregnant woman's urine. This is not true. However, in the 1920s it was discovered that if the urine contained the hCG, a hormone found in the bodies of pregnant women, the rabbit would display ovarian changes.

The rabbit would then be killed to have its ovaries inspected, but the death of the rabbit was not the indicator of the results. Later revisions of the test allowed technicians to inspect the ovaries without killing the animal. A similar test involved injecting Xenopus frogs to make them lay eggs, but animal tests for pregnancy have been made obsolete by faster, cheaper, and simpler modern methods.

6 Deer

Deer (singular and plural) are the ruminant mammals forming the family Cervidae. Species in the Cervidae family include White-tailed deer, Elk, Moose, Red Deer, Reindeer, Roe and Chital. Male deer of all species, except the Chinese Water deer, and female Reindeer grow and shed new antlers each year. In this they differ from permanently horned animals such as antelope; these are in the same order as deer and may bear a superficial resemblance. The musk deer of Asia and Water Chevrotain (or Mouse Deer) of tropical African and Asian forests are not usually regarded as true deer and form their own families, Moschidae and Tragulidae, respectively.

The word 'deer' was originally broad in meaning, but became more specific over time. In Middle English *der* (Old English *deor*) meant a wild animal of any kind (as opposed to *cattle*, which then meant any domestic livestock, from the idea of ownership and related to *chattel* and *capital*). This general sense gave way to the modern sense by the end of the Middle English period around 1500. Cognates of Old English *deor* in other dead Germanic languages have the general sense of 'animal', such as Old High German *tior*, Old Norse *djur* or *d?r*, Gothic *dius*, Old Saxon *dier*, and Old Frisian *diar*. All modern Germanic languages save English and Scots retain this sense — for example, German *Tier*, Alemannic *Diere* or *Tiere*, Pennsylvania Dutch *Gedier*, Dutch *dier*, Afrikaans *dier*, Limburgish *diere*, Norwegian *dyr*, Swedish *djur*, Danish *dyr*, Icelandic *dýr*, Faroese *dýr*, West Frisian *dier*, and North Frisian *diarten*, all of which mean 'animal'. 'Deer' is the same in the plural as in the singular, a convention which stretches back to Old English.

For most deer the male is called a 'buck' and the female is a 'doe', but the terms vary with dialect, and especially according to the size of the species. For many larger deer the male is a 'stag', while for other larger deer the same words are used as for cattle: 'bull' and 'cow'. The male Red Deer is a 'hart', and the female is a 'hind'. Terms for young deer vary similarly, with that of most being called a 'fawn' and that of the larger species 'calf'; young of the smallest kinds may be a *kid.* A group of deer of any kind is a 'herd'. The adjective of relation pertaining to deer is *cervine*; like the family name '*Cervidae*', this is from Latin: *cervus*, 'deer'.

Deer are widely distributed, and hunted, with indigenous representatives in all continents except Antarctica and Australia, though Africa has only one native species, the Red Deer, confined to the Atlas Mountains in the northwest of the continent.

Deer live in a variety of biomes ranging from tundra to the tropical rainforest. While often associated with forests, many deer are ecotone species that live in transitional areas between forests and thickets (for cover) and prairie and savanna (open space). The majority of large deer species inhabit temperate mixed deciduous forest, mountain mixed coniferous forest, tropical seasonal/dry forest, and savanna habitats around the world. Clearing open areas within forests to some extent may actually benefit deer populations by exposing the understory and allowing the types of grasses, weeds, and herbs to grow that deer like to eat. Additionally, access to adjacent croplands may also benefit deer. However, adequate forest or brush cover must still be provided for populations to grow and thrive.

Small species of brocket deer and pudús of Central and South America, and muntjacs of Asia generally occupy dense forests and are less often seen in open spaces, with the possible exception of the Indian Muntjac. There are also several species of deer that are highly specialized, and live almost exclusively in mountains, grasslands, swamps, and 'wet' savannas, or riparian corridors surrounded by deserts. Some deer have a circumpolar distribution in both North America and Eurasia. Examples include the caribou that live in Arctic tundra and taiga (boreal forests) and moose that inhabit taiga and adjacent areas. Huemul Deer (taruca and Chilean Huemul) of South America's Andes fill an ecological niche of the ibex or Wild Goat, with the fawns behaving more like goat kids.

The highest concentration of large deer species in temperate North America lies in the Canadian Rocky Mountain and Columbia Mountain Regions between Alberta and British Columbia where all five North American deer species (White-tailed deer, Mule deer, Caribou, Elk, and Moose) can be found. This region has several clusters of national parks including Mount Revelstoke National Park, Glacier National Park (Canada), Yoho National Park, and Kootenay National Park on the British Columbia side, and Banff National Park, Jasper National Park, and Glacier National Park (U.S.) on the Alberta and Montana sides. Mountain slope habitats vary from moist coniferous/mixed forested habitats to dry subalpine/pine forests with alpine meadows higher up. The foothills and river valleys between the mountain ranges provide a mosaic of cropland and deciduous parklands. The rare woodland caribou have the most restricted range living at higher altitudes in the subalpine meadows and alpine tundra areas of some of the mountain ranges. Elk and Mule Deer both migrate between the alpine meadows and lower coniferous forests and tend to be most common in this region. Elk also inhabit river valley bottomlands, which they share with White-tailed deer. The White-tailed deer have recently expanded their range within the foothills and river valley bottoms of the Canadian Rockies owing to conversion of land to cropland and the clearing of coniferous forests allowing more deciduous vegetation to grow up the mountain slopes. They also live in the aspen parklands north of Calgary and Edmonton, where they share habitat with the moose. The adjacent Great Plains grassland habitats are left to herds of Elk, American Bison, and pronghorn antelope.

The Eurasian Continent (including the Indian Subcontinent) boasts the most species of deer in the world, with most species being found in Asia. Europe, in comparison, has lower diversity in plant and animal species. However, many national parks and protected reserves in Europe do have populations of Red Deer, Roe Deer, and Fallow Deer.

These species have long been associated with the continent of Europe, but also inhabit Asia Minor, the Caucasus Mountains, and Northwestern Iran. 'European' Fallow Deer historically lived over much of Europe during the Ice Ages, but afterwards became restricted primarily to the Anatolian Peninsula, in present-day Turkey. Present-day Fallow deer populations in Europe are a result of historic man-made introductions of this species first to the Mediterranean regions of Europe, then eventually to the rest of Europe. They were initially park animals that later escaped and reestablished themselves in the wild. Historically, Europe's deer species shared their deciduous forest habitat with other herbivores such as the extinct tarpan (forest horse), extinct aurochs (forest ox), and the endangered wisent (European bison). Good places to see deer in Europe include the Scottish Highlands, the Austrian Alps, and the wetlands between Austria, Hungary, and Czech Republic. Some fine National Parks include Doñana National Park in Spain, the Veluwe in the Netherlands, the Ardennes in Belgium, and Bialowieza National Park of Poland. Spain, Eastern Europe, and the Caucasus Mountains still have virgin forest areas that are not only home to sizable deer populations but also for other animals that were once abundant such as the wisent, Eurasian Lynx, Spanish lynx, wolves, and Brown Bears.

The highest concentration of large deer species in temperate Asia occurs in the mixed deciduous forests, mountain coniferous forests, and taiga bordering North Korea, Manchuria (Northeastern China), and the Ussuri Region (Russia). These are among some of the richest deciduous and coniferous forests in the world where one can find Siberian Roe Deer, Sika Deer, Elk, and Moose. Asian Caribou occupy the northern fringes of this region along the Sino-Russian border.

Deer such as the Sika Deer, Thorold's deer, Central Asian Red Deer, and Elk have historically been farmed for their antlers by Han Chinese, Turkic peoples, Tungusic peoples, Mongolians, and Koreans. Like the Sami people of Finland and Scandinavia, the Tungusic peoples, Mongolians, and Turkic peoples of Southern Siberia, Northern Mongolia, and the Ussuri Region have also taken to raising semi-domesticated herds of Asian Caribou.

The highest concentration of large deer species in the tropics occurs in Southern Asia in Northern India's Indo-Gangetic Plain Region and Nepal's Terai Region. These fertile plains consist of tropical seasonal moist deciduous, dry deciduous forests, and both dry and wet savannas that are home to Chital, Hog Deer, Barasingha, Indian Sambar, and Indian Muntjac. Grazing species such as the endangered Barasingha and very common Chital are gregarious and live in large herds. Indian Sambar can be gregarious but are usually solitary or live in smaller herds. Hog Deer are solitary and have lower densities than Indian Muntjac. Deer can be seen in several national parks in India, Nepal, and Sri Lanka of which Kanha National Park, Dudhwa National Park, and Chitwan National Park are most famous. Sri Lanka's Wilpattu National Park and Yala National Park have large herds of Indian Sambar and Chital. The Indian sambar are more gregarious in Sri Lanka than other parts of their range and tend to form larger herds than elsewhere.

The Chao Praya River Valley of Thailand was once primarily tropical seasonal moist deciduous forest and wet savanna that hosted populations of Hog Deer, the now-extinct Schomburgk's Deer, the Eld's Deer, Indian Sambar, and Indian Muntjac. Both the Hog Deer and Eld's Deer are rare, whereas Indian Sambar and Indian Muntjac thrive in protected national parks such as Khao Yai.

Many of these South Asian and Southeast Asian deer species also share their habitat with various herbivores such as Asian Elephants, various Asian rhinoceros species, various antelope species (such as nilgai, Four-horned Antelope, blackbuck, and Indian gazelle in India), and wild oxen (such as Wild Asian Water Buffalo, gaur, banteng, and kouprey). How different herbivores can survive together in a given area is each species have different food preferences, although there may be some overlap.

Australia has six introduced species of deer that have established sustainable wild populations from acclimatisation society releases in the 19th century. These are Fallow Deer, Red Deer, Sambar Deer, Hog Deer, Rusa deer, and Chital. Red Deer introduced into New Zealand in 1851 from English and Scottish stock were domesticated in deer farms by the late 1960s and are common farm animals there now. Seven other species of deer were introduced into New Zealand but none are as widespread as Red Deer.

Deer weights generally range from 30 to 250 kilograms (70 to 600 lb), though the Northern Pudu averages 10 kilograms (20 lb) and the Moose averages 431 kilograms (1,000 lb). They generally have lithe, compact bodies and long, powerful legs suited for rugged woodland terrain. Deer are also excellent jumpers and swimmers. Deer are ruminants, or cud-chewers, and have a four-chambered stomach. The teeth of deer are adapted to feeding on vegetation, and like other ruminants, they lack upper incisors, instead having a tough pad at the front of their upper jaw. Some deer, such as those on the island of Rùm, do consume meat when it is available. The Chinese water deer, Tufted deer and muntjac have enlarged upper canine teeth forming sharp tusks, while other species often lack upper canines altogether. The cheek teeth of deer have crescent ridges of enamel, which enable them to grind a wide variety of vegetation.

Nearly all deer have a facial gland in front of each eye. The gland contains a strongly scented pheromone, used to mark its home range. Bucks of a wide range of species open these glands wide when angry or excited. All deer have a liver without a gallbladder. Deer also have a tapetum lucidum which gives them sufficiently good night vision.

Nearly all cervids are so-called uniparental species: the fawns are cared for by the mother only. A doe generally has one or two fawns at a time (triplets, while not unknown, are uncommon). The gestation period is anywhere up to ten months for the European Roe Deer. Most fawns are born with their fur covered with white spots, though in many species they lose these spots by the end of their first winter. In the first twenty minutes of a fawn's life, the fawn begins to take its first steps. Its mother licks it clean until it is almost free of scent, so predators will not find it. Its mother leaves often, and the fawn does not like to be left behind. Sometimes its mother must gently push it down with her foot. The fawn stays hidden in the grass for one week until it is strong enough to walk with its mother. The fawn and its mother stay together for about one year. A male usually never sees his mother again, but females sometimes come back with their own fawns and form small deer are selective feeders. They are usually browsers, and primarily feed on leaves. They have small, unspecialized stomachs by ruminant standards, and high nutrition requirements. Rather than attempt to digest vast quantities of low-grade, fibrous food as, for example, sheep and cattle do, deer select easily digestible shoots, young leaves, fresh grasses, soft twigs, fruit, fungi, and lichens.

With the exception of the Chinese Water Deer, which have tusks, all male deer have antlers. Sometimes a female will have a small stub. The only female deer with antlers are Reindeer (Caribou). Antlers grow as highly vascular spongy tissue covered in a skin called velvet. Before the beginning of a species' mating season, the antlers calcify under the velvet and become hard bone. The velvet is then rubbed off leaving dead bone which forms the hard antlers. After the mating season, the pedicle and the antler base are separated by a layer of softer tissue, and the antler falls off.

One way that many hunters are able to track main paths that the deer travel on is because of their 'rubs'. A rub is used to deposit scent from glands near the eye and forehead and physically mark territory.

During the mating season, bucks use their antlers to fight one another for the opportunity to attract mates in a given herd. The two bucks circle each other, bend back their legs, lower their heads, and charge.

Each species has its own characteristic antler structure — for example white-tailed deer antlers include a series of tines sprouting upward from a forward-curving main beam, while Fallow Deer and Moose antlers are *palmate*, with a broad central portion. Mule deer (and Black-tailed Deer), species within the same genus as the white-tailed deer, instead have bifurcated (or branched) antlers—that is, the main beam splits into two, each of which may split into two more. Young males of many deer, and the adults of some species, such as brocket deer and pudus, have antlers which are single spikes.

Piebald Deer

A piebald deer is a deer with a brown and white spotting pattern which is not caused by parasites or diseases. They can appear to be almost entirely white. In addition to the non-standard colouration, other differences have been observed: bowing or Roman nose, overly arched spine (scoliosis), long tails, short legs, and underbites.

White Deer

Seneca County, New York maintains the largest herd of white deer. White pigmented White-tailed Deer began populating the deer population in the area now known as the Conservation Area of the former Seneca Army Depot. The U.S. Army gave the white deer protection while managing the normal coloured deer through hunting. The white deer colouration is the result of a recessive gene.

The earliest fossil deer including *Heteroprox* date from the Oligocene of Europe, and resembled the modern muntjacs. Later species were often larger, with more impressive antlers. They rapidly spread to the other continents, even for a time occupying much of northern Africa, where they are now almost wholly absent. Some extinct deer had huge antlers, larger than those of any living species. Examples include *Eucladoceros*, and the giant deer *Megaloceros*, whose antlers stretched to 3.5 metres across.

Deer have long had economic significance to humans. Deer meat, for which they are hunted and farmed, is called venison. Deer organ meat is called *humble*. See humble pie.

The Sami of Scandinavia and the Kola Peninsula of Russia and other nomadic peoples of northern Asia use reindeer for food, clothing, and transport.

The caribou in North America is not domesticated or herded as is the case of reindeer (the same species), reindeer are often found in colder regions in Europe, but is important as a quarry animal to the Inuit. Most commercial venison in the United States is imported from New Zealand.

Deer were originally brought to New Zealand by European settlers, and the deer population rose rapidly. This caused great environmental damage and was controlled by hunting and poisoning until the concept of deer farming developed in the 1960s. Deer farming has advanced into a significant economic activity in New Zealand with more than 3,000 farms running over 1 million deer in total. Deer products are exported to over 50 countries around the world, with New Zealand becoming well recognised as a source of quality venison and co-products.

Automobile collisions with deer can impose a significant cost on the economy. In the U.S., about 1.5 million deer-vehicle collisions occur each year, according to the National Highway Traffic Safety Administration. Those accidents cause about 150 human deaths and $1.1 billion in property damage annually.

Deer hunting is a popular activity in the U.S. that generates revenue for states and the federal government from the sales of licenses, permits and tags. The 2006 survey by the U.S. Fish and Wildlife Service estimates that licence sales generate approximately $700 million annually. This revenue generally goes to support conservation efforts in the states where the licences are purchased. Overall, the U.S. Fish and Wildlife Service estimates that big game hunting for deer and elk generates approximately $11.8 billion annually in hunting-related travel, equipment and related expenditures.

Hybrid Deer

In *On the Origin of Species* (1859), Charles Darwin wrote "Although I do not know of any thoroughly well-authenticated cases of perfectly fertile hybrid animals, I have some reason to believe that the hybrids from Cervulus vaginalis and Reevesii [...] are perfectly fertile." These two varieties of muntjac are currently considered the same species.

A number of deer hybrids are bred to improve meat yield in farmed deer. American Elk (or Wapiti) and Red Deer from the Old World can produce fertile offspring in captivity, and were once considered one species. Hybrid offspring, however, must be able to escape and defend themselves against predators, and these hybrid offspring are unable to do so in the wild state. Recent DNA, animal behaviour studies, and morphology and antler characteristics have shown there are not one but three species of Red Deer: European Red Deer, Central Asian Red Deer, and American Elk or Wapiti. The European Elk is a different species and is known as moose in North America. The hybrids are about 30 per cent more efficient in producing antlers by comparing velvet to body weight. Wapiti have been introduced into some European Red Deer herds to improve the Red Deer type, but not always with the intended improvement.

In New Zealand, where deer are introduced species, there are hybrid zones between Red Deer and North American Wapiti populations and also between Red Deer and Sika Deer populations. In New Zealand, Red Deer have been artificially hybridized with Pere David Deer in order to create a farmed deer which gives birth in spring. The initial hybrids were created by artificial insemination and back-crossed to Red Deer. However, such hybrid offspring can only survive in captivity free of predators.

In Canada, the farming of European Red Deer and Red Deer hybrids is considered a threat to native Wapiti. In Britain, the introduced Sika Deer is considered a threat to native Red Deer. Initial Sika Deer/Red Deer hybrids occur when young Sika stag expand their range into established red deer areas and have no Sika hinds to mate with. They mate instead with young Red hinds and produce fertile hybrids. These hybrids mate with either Sika or Red Deer (depending which species is prevalent in the area), resulting in mongrelization. Many of the Sika Deer which escaped from British parks were probably already hybrids for this reason. These hybrids do not properly inherit survival strategies and can only survive in either a captive state or when there are no predators.

In captivity, Mule Deer have been mated to White-tail Deer. Both male Mule Deer/female White-tailed Deer and male White-tailed Deer/female Mule Deer matings have produced hybrids. Less than 50 per cent of the hybrid fawns survived their first few months. Hybrids have been reported in the wild but are disadvantaged because they don't properly inherit survival strategies. Mule Deer move with bounding leaps (all 4 hooves hit the ground at once, also called 'stotting') to escape predators. Stotting is so specialized that only 100 per cent genetically pure Mule Deer seem able to do it. In captive hybrids, even a one-eighth White-tail/seven-eighths Mule Deer hybrid has an erratic escape behaviour and would be unlikely to survive to breeding age. Hybrids do survive on game ranches where both species are kept and where predators are controlled by man.

CULTURAL SIGNIFICANCE

Heraldry

Deer are represented in heraldry by the *stag* or *hart*, or less often, by the *hind*, and the *brocket* (a young stag up to two years), respectively. Stag's heads and antlers also appear as charges. The old name for deer was simply cerf, and it is chiefly the head which appears on the ancient arms. Examples of deer in heraldry can be found in the arms of Hertfordshire, England, and its county town of Hertford; both are examples of canting arms.

Several Norwegian municipalities have a stag or stag's head in their arms: Gjemnes, Hitra, Hjartdal, Rendalen and Voss. A deer appears on the arms of the Israeli Postal Authority.

Reindeer

The reindeer (*Rangifer tarandus*), also known as the caribou in North America, is a deer from the Arctic and Subarctic, including both resident and migratory populations. While overall widespread and numerous, some of its subspecies are rare and one (or two, depending on taxonomy) has already gone extinct.

Reindeer vary considerably in colour and size, and both sexes grow antlers, though these are larger in the males and there are a few populations where females lack them completely.

Hunting of wild reindeer and herding of semi-domesticated reindeer (for meat, hides, antlers, milk and transportation) is important to several Arctic and Subarctic people. Even far outside its range, the reindeer is well known due to the myth, probably originating in early 19th century America, in which Santa Claus's sleigh is pulled by flying reindeer, a popular secular element of Christmas. In Lapland, reindeer pull pulks.

The reindeer is a widespread and numerous species in the northern Holarctic, being present in both tundra and taiga (boreal forest). Originally, the reindeer was found in Scandinavia, eastern Europe, Russia, Mongolia, and northern China north of the 50th latitude. In North America, it was found in Canada, Alaska (USA), and the northern conterminous USA from Washington to Maine. In the 19th century, it was apparently still present in southern Idaho. It also occurred naturally on Sakhalin, Greenland, and probably even in historical times in Ireland. During the late Pleistocene era, reindeer were found as far south as Nevada and Tennessee in North America and Spain in Europe. Today, wild reindeer have disappeared from many areas within this large historical range, especially from the southern parts, where it vanished almost everywhere. Large populations of wild reindeer are still found in Norway, Finland, Siberia, Greenland, Alaska, and Canada.

Domesticated reindeer are mostly found in northern Fennoscandia and Russia, with a herd of approximately 150-170 reindeer living around the Cairngorms region in Scotland. The last remaining wild tundra reindeer in Europe are found in portions of southern Norway.

A few reindeer from Norway were introduced to the South Atlantic island of South Georgia in the beginning of the 20th century. Today, there are two distinct herds still thriving there, permanently separated by glaciers. Their total numbers are no more than a few thousand. The flag and the coat of arms of the territory contain an image of a reindeer. Around 4000 reindeer have been introduced into the French sub-Antarctic archipelago of Kerguelen Islands. East Iceland has a small herd of about 2500-3000 animals.

Caribou and reindeer numbers have fluctuated historically, but many herds are in decline across their range. This global decline is linked to climate change for northern, migratory caribou and reindeer herds and industrial disturbance of caribou habitat for sedentary, non-migratory herds.

Size

The females usually measure 162-205 cm (64-81 in) in length and weigh 79-120 kg (170-260 lb). The males (or 'bulls') are typically larger (although the extent to which varies in the different subspecies), measuring 180-214 cm (71-84 in) in length and usually weighing 92-210 kg (200-460 lb), though exceptionally large males have weighed as much as 318 kg (700 lb). Shoulder height typically measure from 85 to 150 cm (33 to 59 in), and the tail is 14 to 20 cm (5.5 to 7.9 in) long. The subspecies *R. t. platyrhynchus* from Svalbard island is very small compared to other subspecies (a phenomenon known as insular dwarfism), with females having a length of approximately 150 cm (59 in), and a weight around 53 kg (120 lb) in the spring and 70 kg (150 lb) in the autumn. Males are approximately 160 cm (63 in) long, and weigh around 65 kg (140 lb) in the spring and 90 kg (200 lb) in the autumn. The reindeer from Svalbard are also relatively short-legged and may have a shoulder height of as little as 80 cm (31 in), thereby following Allen's rule.

Fur

The colour of the fur varies considerably, both individually, and depending on season and subspecies. Northern populations, which usually are relatively small, are whiter, while southern populations, which typically are relatively large, are darker. This can be seen well in North America, where the northermost subspecies, the Peary Caribou, is the whitest and smallest subspecies of the continent, while the southermost subspecies, the Woodland Caribou, is the darkest and largest. The coat has two layers of fur, a dense woolly undercoat and longer-haired overcoat consisting of hollow, air-filled hairs.

In most populations both sexes grow antlers, which (in the Scandinavian variety) for old males fall off in December, for young males in the early spring, and for females in the summer. The antlers typically have two separate groups of points, a lower and upper. Domesticated reindeer are shorter-legged and heavier than their wild counterparts. There is considerable subspecific variation in the size of the antlers (*e.g.*, rather small and spindly in the northernmost subspecies), but in some subspecies the bull reindeer's antlers are the second largest of any extant deer, after the moose, and can range up to 100 cm (39 in) in width and 135 cm (53 in) in beam length. They have the largest antlers relative to body size among deer.

Nose and Hooves

Reindeer have specialized noses featuring nasal turbinate bones that dramatically increase the surface area within the nostrils. Incoming cold air is warmed by the animal's body heat before entering the lungs, and water is condensed from the expired air and captured before the deer's breath is exhaled, used to moisten dry incoming air and possibly absorbed into the blood through the mucous membranes.

Reindeer hooves adapt to the season: in the summer, when the tundra is soft and wet, the footpads become sponge-like and provide extra traction. In the winter, the pads shrink and tighten, exposing the rim of the hoof, which cuts into the ice and crusted snow to keep it from slipping. This also enables them to dig down (an activity known as 'cratering') through the snow to their favourite food, a lichen known as reindeer moss. The knees of many species of reindeer are adapted to produce a clicking sound as they walk.

Reindeer are ruminants, having a four-chambered stomach. They mainly eat lichens in winter, especially reindeer moss. However, they also eat the leaves of willows and birches, as well as sedges and grasses. There is some evidence to suggest that on occasion, they will also feed on lemmings, arctic char, and bird eggs. Reindeer herded by the Chukchis have been known to devour mushrooms enthusiastically in late summer.

Reproduction

Mating occurs from late September to early November. Males battle for access to females. Two males will lock each other's antlers together and try to push each other away. The most dominant males can collect as many as 15-20 females to mate with. A male will stop eating during this time and lose much of its body reserves.

Calves may be born the following May or June. After 45 days, the calves are able to graze and forage but continue suckling until the following autumn and become independent from their mothers.

Migration

Some populations of the North American caribou migrate the furthest of any terrestrial mammal, travelling up to 5,000 km (3,100 mi) a year, and covering 1,000,000 km^2 (390,000 sq mi). Other populations (*e.g.*, in Europe) have a shorter migration, and some, for example the subspecies *R. t. pearsoni* and *R. t. platyrhynchus* (both restricted to islands), are residents that only make local movements.

Normally travelling about 19-55 km (12-34 mi) a day while migrating, the caribou can run at speeds of 60-80 km/h (37-50 mph). During the spring migration smaller herds will group together to form larger herds of 50,000 to 500,000 animals but during autumn migrations, the groups become smaller, and the reindeer begin to mate. During the winter, reindeer travel to forested areas to forage under the snow. By spring, groups leave their winter grounds to go to the calving grounds. A reindeer can swim easily and quickly, normally at 6.5 km/h (4.0 mph) but if necessary at 10 km/h (6.2 mph), and migrating herds will not hesitate to swim across a large lake or broad river.

Predators

There are a variety of predators that prey heavily on reindeer. Golden Eagles prey on calves and are the most prolific hunter on calving grounds. Wolverine will take newborn calves or birthing cows, as well as (less commonly) infirm adults. Brown Bears and (in the rare cases where they encounter each other) polar bears prey on reindeer of all ages but (as with the wolverine) are most likely to attack weaker animals such as calves and sick deer. The Gray Wolf is the most effective natural predator of adult reindeer, especially during the winter. As carrion, caribou are fed on by foxes, ravens and hawks. Blood-sucking insects, such as black flies and mosquitoes, are a plague to reindeer during the summer and can cause enough stress to inhibit feeding and calving behaviors. In one case, the entire body of a reindeer was found in a Greenland shark (possibly a case of scavenging), a species found in the far northern Atlantic. The population numbers of some of these predators is influenced by the migration of reindeer. During the Ice Ages, they faced Dire wolves, Cave lions, American lions, Short-faced bears, Cave hyenas, Smilodons, Jaguars, Cougars, and possibly the ground sloth.

Since 1961, reindeer have been divided into two major groups, the tundra reindeer with six subspecies and the woodland reindeer with three subspecies. Among the tundra subspecies are small-bodied, high-Arctic island forms. These island subspecies are probably not closely related, since the Svalbard Reindeer seems to have evolved from large European Reindeer, whereas Peary Caribou and the extinct Arctic Reindeer are closely related and probably evolved in high-Arctic North America.

The following list is partial, as four subspecies which are restricted to Russia and neighbouring regions have been left out. These are *R. tarandus buskensis*, *R. tarandus pearsoni* (Novaya Zemlya Reindeer), *R. tarandus phylarchus* (Kamchatka/Okhotsk Reindeer) and *R. tarandus sibiricus* (Siberian Tundra Reindeer).

Tundra Reindeer

Arctic Reindeer (*R. tarandus eogroenlandicus*), an extinct subspecies found until 1900 in eastern Greenland.

Peary Caribou (*R. tarandus pearyi*), found in the northern islands of the Nunavut and the Northwest Territories of Canada.

Svalbard Reindeer (*R. tarandus platyrhynchus*), found on the Svalbard islands of Norway, is the smallest subspecies of reindeer.

Mountain/Wild Reindeer (*R. tarandus tarandus*), found in the Arctic tundra of Eurasia, including the Fennoscandia peninsula of northern Europe.

Porcupine Caribou or Grant's Caribou (*R. tarandus granti*), which are found in Alaska, the Yukon, and the Northwest Territories of Canada. Very similar to *R. tarandus groenlandicus*, and probably better regarded as a junior synonym of that subspecies.

Approximate range of caribou subspecies in North America. Overlap is possible for ontiguous range. Subspecies *groenlandicus* and *pearyi* mix on some arctic islands, and *granti* is probably a synonym of *groenlandicus*. Populations here included in *caribou* are sometimes divided into four separate subspecies.

Barren-ground Caribou (*R. tarandus groenlandicus*), found in Nunavut and the Northwest Territories of Canada and in western Greenland.

Finnish Forest Reindeer (*R. tarandus fennicus*), found in the wild in only two areas of the Fennoscandia peninsula of Northern Europe, in Finnish/Russian Karelia, and a small population in central south Finland. The Karelia population reaches far into Russia, however, so far that it remains an open question whether reindeer further to the east are *R. t. fennicus* as well.

Migratory Woodland Caribou (*R. tarandus caribou*), or Forest Caribou, once found in the North American taiga (boreal forest) from Alaska to Newfoundland and Labrador and as far south as New England, Idaho, and Washington. Woodland Caribou have disappeared from most of their original southern range and are considered threatened where they remain, with the notable exception of the Migratory Woodland Caribou of northern Quebec and Labrador, Canada. The name of the Cariboo district of central British Columbia relates to their once-large numbers there, but they have almost vanished from that area in the last century. A herd is protected in the Caribou Mountains in Alberta. The above quoted range includes *R. tarandus caboti* (Labrador Caribou), *R. tarandus osborni* (Osborn's Caribou – from British Columbia) and *R. tarandus terraenovae* (Newfoundland Caribou). Based on a review in 1961, these were considered invalid and included in *R. tarandus caribou*, but some recent authorities have considered them all valid, even suggesting that they are quite distinct. An analysis of mtDNA in 2005 found differences between the caribous from Newfoundland, Labrador, south-western Canada and south-eastern Canada, but maintained all in *R. tarandus caribou*.

Queen Charlotte Islands Caribou (*R. tarandus dawsoni*) from the Queen Charlotte Islands was believed to represent a distinct subspecies. It became extinct at the beginning of the 20th century. However, recent DNA analysis from mitochondrial DNA of the remains from those reindeer suggest that the animals from the Queen Charlotte Islands were not genetically distinct from the Canadian mainland reindeer subspecies.

REINDEER AND HUMANS

Hunting

Reindeer hunting by humans has a very long history, and caribou/ wild reindeer "may well be the species of single greatest importance in the entire anthropological literature on hunting".

Humans started hunting reindeer in the Mesolithic and Neolithic periods, and humans are today the main predator in many areas. Norway and Greenland have unbroken traditions of hunting wild reindeer from the ice age until the present day. In the non-forested mountains of central Norway, such as Jotunheimen, it is still possible to find remains of stone-built trapping pits, guiding fences, and bow rests, built especially for hunting reindeer. These can, with some certainty, be dated to the Migration Period, although it is not unlikely that they have been in use since the Stone Age.

Norway is now preparing to apply for nomination as a World Heritage Site for areas with traces and traditions of reindeer hunting in Dovrefjell-Sunndalsfjella National Park, Reinheimen National Park and Rondane National Park in Central Sør-Norge (Southern Norway). There is in these parts of Norway an unbroken tradition of reindeer hunting from post-glacial stone age until today.

Wild caribou are still hunted in North America and Greenland. In the traditional lifestyle of the Inuit people, Northern First Nations people, Alaska Natives, and the Kalaallit of Greenland, the caribou is an important source of food, clothing, shelter, and tools. Many Gwich'in people, who depend on the Porcupine caribou, still follow traditional caribou management practices that include a prohibition against selling caribou meat and limits on the number of caribou to be taken per hunting trip.

The blood of the caribou was supposedly mixed with alcohol as drink by hunters and loggers in colonial Quebec to counter the cold. This drink is now enjoyed without the blood as a wine and whiskey drink known as *Caribou*.

Reindeer Husbandry

Reindeer have been herded for centuries by several Arctic and Subarctic people including the Sami and the Nenets. They are raised for their meat, hides, antlers and, to a lesser extent, for milk and transportation. Reindeer are not considered fully domesticated, as they generally roam free on pasture grounds. In traditional nomadic herding, reindeer herders migrate with their herds between coast and inland areas according to an annual migration route, and herds are keenly tended. However, reindeer were not bred in captivity, though they were tamed for milking as well as for use as draught animals or beasts of burden.

The use of reindeer as semi-domesticated livestock in Alaska was introduced in the late 19th century by the U.S. Revenue Cutter Service, with assistance from Sheldon Jackson, as a means of providing a livelihood for Native peoples there. Reindeer were imported first from Siberia, and later also from Norway. A regular mail run in Wales, Alaska, used a sleigh drawn by reindeer. In Alaska, reindeer herders use satellite telemetry to track their herds, using online maps and databases to chart the herd's progress.

Economy

The reindeer has (or has had) an important economic role for all circumpolar peoples, including the Saami, Nenets, Khants, Evenks, Yukaghirs, Chukchi, and Koryaks in Eurasia. It is believed that domestication started between the Bronze and Iron Ages. Siberian deer owners also use the reindeer to ride on (Siberian reindeer are larger than their Scandinavian relatives). For breeders, a single owner may own hundreds or even thousands of animals. The numbers of Russian herders have been drastically reduced since the fall of the Soviet Union. The fur and meat is sold, which is an important source of income. Reindeer were introduced into Alaska near the end of the 19th century; they interbreed with native caribou subspecies there. Reindeer herders on the Seward Peninsula have experienced significant losses to their herds from animals (such as wolves) following the wild caribou during their migrations.

Reindeer meat is popular in the Scandinavian countries. Reindeer meatballs are sold canned. Sautéed reindeer is the best-known dish in Lapland. In Alaska and Finland, reindeer sausage is sold in supermarkets and grocery stores. Reindeer meat is very tender and lean. It can be prepared fresh, but also dried, salted, hot-and cold-smoked. In addition to meat, almost all internal organs of reindeer can be eaten, some being traditional dishes. Furthermore, *Lapin Poron liha* fresh Reindeer meat completely produced and packed in Finnish Lapland is protected in Europe with PDO classification.

Reindeer antler is powdered and sold as an aphrodisiac, nutritional or medicinal supplement to Asian markets.

Caribou have been a major source of subsistence for Canadian Inuit.

Both Aristotle and Theophrastus have short accounts — probably based on the same source - of an ox-sized deer species, named *tarandos*, living in the land of the Bodines in Scythia, which was able to change the colour of its fur to obtain camouflage. The latter is probably a misunderstanding of the seasonal change in reindeer fur colour. The descriptions have been interpreted as being of reindeer living in the southern Ural Mountains at c. 350 BC.

A deer-like animal described by Julius Caesar in his *Commentarii de Bello Gallico* (chapter 6.26) from the Hercynian Forest in the year 53 BC is most certainly to be interpreted as reindeer:

There is an ox shaped like a stag. In the middle of its forehead a single horn grows between its ears, taller and straighter than the animal horns with which we are familiar. At the top this horn spreads out like the palm of a hand or the branches of a tree. The females are of the same form as the males, and their horns are the same shape and size.

According to Olaus Magnus's Historia de Gentibus Septentrionalibus - printed in Rome in 1555 — Gustav I of Sweden sent 10 reindeer to Albert I, Duke of Prussia, in the year 1533. It may be these animals that Conrad Gessner had seen or heard of.

Name Etymology

The name rangifer, which Linnaeus chose as the name for the reindeer genus, was used by Albertus Magnus in his *De animalibus*, fol. Liber 22, Cap. 268: "Dicitur Rangyfer quasi ramifer". This word may go back to a Saami word *raingo*. For the origin of the word tarandus, which Linnaeus chose as the species epithet, he made reference to Ulisse Aldrovandi's *Quadrupedum omnium bisulcorum historia* fol. 859-863, Cap. 30: De Tarando (1621). However, Aldrovandi — and before him Konrad Gesner thought that *rangifer* and *tarandus* were two separate animals. In any case, the *tarandos* name goes back to Aristotle and Theophrastus.

Local Names

The name *rein* (-deer) is of Norse origin (Old Norse *hreinn*, which again goes back to Proto-Germanic *hraina and Proto-Indo-European *kroino meaning 'horned animal'). In the Finno-Permic languages, Sami *poatsu* (in Northern Sami *boazu*, in Lule Sami *boatsoj*, in Pite Sami *båtsoj*, in Southern Sami *bovtse*), Mari *puc?* and Udmurt *pud•ej*, all referring to domesticated reindeer, go back to *pocaw, an Iranian loanword deriving from Proto-Indo-European *pe?u-, meaning 'cattle'. The Finnish name *poro* may also stem from the same. The name *caribou* comes, through French, from Mi'kmaq *qalipu*, meaning 'snow shoveler', referring to its habit of pawing through the snow for food. In Inuktitut, the caribou is known by the name *tuttuk* (Labrador dialect). In Cree-Montagnais-Naskapi dialects the caribou is called *atihkw*.

Several Norwegian municipalities have one or more reindeer depicted in their coats-of-arms: Eidfjord, Porsanger, Rendalen, Tromsø, Vadsø, and Vågå. The historic province of Västerbotten in Sweden has a reindeer in its coat of arms. The present Västerbotten County has very different borders and uses the reindeer combined with other symbols in its coat-of-arms. The city of Piteå also has a reindeer. The logo for Umeå University features three reindeer.

The Canadian 25-cent coin, or 'quarter' features a depiction of a caribou on one face. The caribou is the official provincial animal of Newfoundland and Labrador, Canada, and appears on the coat of arms of Nunavut. A caribou statue was erected at the center of the Beaumont-Hamel Newfoundland Memorial, marking the spot in France where hundreds of soldiers from Newfoundland were killed and wounded in the First World War and there is a replica in Bowring Park, in St. John's, Newfoundland's capital city.

Two municipalities in Finland have reindeer motifs in their coats-of-arms: Kuusamo has a running reindeer and Inari a fish with reindeer antlers.

7 Sheep Husbandry

Sheep husbandry is practised throughout the majority of the inhabited world, and has been fundamental to many civilizations. In the modern era, Australia, New Zealand, the southern and central South American nations, and the British Isles are most closely associated with sheep production.

Sheep-raising has a large lexicon of unique terms which vary considerably by region and dialect. Use of the word *sheep* began in Middle English as a derivation of the Old English word *sceap*; it is both the singular and plural name for the animal. A group of sheep is called a flock, herd or mob. Adult female sheep are referred to as ewes, intact males as rams or occasionally tups, castrated males as wethers, and younger sheep as lambs. Many other specific terms for the various life stages of sheep exist, generally related to lambing, shearing, and age.

Being a key animal in the history of farming, sheep have a deeply entrenched place in human culture, and find representation in much modern language and symbology. As livestock, sheep are most-often associated with pastoral, Arcadian imagery. Sheep figure in many mythologies—such as the Golden Fleece—and major religions, especially the Abrahamic traditions. In both ancient and modern religious ritual, sheep are used as sacrificial animals.

Like all ruminants, sheep are members of the order Artiodactyla, the even-toed ungulates. Although the name 'sheep' applies to many species in the genus *Ovis*, in everyday usage it almost always refers to *Ovis aries*. Numbering a little over one billion, domestic sheep are also the most numerous species of sheep.

Sheep are most likely descended from the wild mouflon of Europe and Asia. One of the earliest animals to be domesticated for agricultural purposes, sheep are raised for fleece, meat (lamb, hogget or mutton) and milk. A sheep's wool is the most widely used animal fiber, and is usually harvested by shearing. Ovine meat is called lamb when from younger animals and mutton when from older ones. Sheep continue to be important for wool and meat today, and are also occasionally raised for pelts, as dairy animals, or as model organisms for science.

Domestic sheep are relatively small ruminants, usually with a crimped hair called wool and often with horns forming a lateral spiral. Domestic sheep differ from their wild relatives and ancestors in several respects, having become uniquely neotenic as a result of selective breeding by humans. A few primitive breeds of sheep retain some of the characteristics of their wild cousins, such as short tails. Depending on breed, domestic sheep may have no horns at all (polled), or horns in both sexes (as in wild sheep), or in males only. Most horned breeds have a single pair, but a few breeds may have several.

Another trait unique to domestic sheep (as compared to wild ovines, not other livestock) is their wide variation in colour. Wild sheep are largely variations of brown hues, and variation with species is extremely limited. Colours of domestic sheep range from pure white to dark chocolate brown and even spotted or piebald. Selection for easily dyeable white fleeces began early in sheep domestication, and as white wool is a dominant trait it spread quickly. However, coloured sheep do appear in many modern breeds, and may even appear as a recessive trait in white flocks. While white wool is desirable for large commercial markets, there is a niche market for coloured fleeces, mostly for handspinning. The nature of the fleece varies widely among the breeds, from dense and highly crimped, to long and hair-like. There is variation of wool type and quality even among members of the same flock, so wool classing is a step in the commercial processing of the fibre.

Depending on breed, sheep show a range of heights and weights. Their rate of growth and mature weight is a heritable trait that is often selected for in breeding. Ewes typically weigh between 45 and 100 kilograms (99 and 220 lb), and rams between 45 and 160 kilograms (99 and 350 lb). Mature sheep have 32 teeth. As with other ruminants, the front teeth in the lower jaw bite against a hard, toothless pad in the upper jaw. These are used to pick off vegetation, then the rear teeth grind it before it is swallowed. There are eight lower front teeth in ruminants, but there is some disagreement as to whether these are eight incisors, or six incisors and two incisor-shaped canines. This means that the dental formula for sheep is either I:0/4 C:0/0 P:3/3 M:3/3, or I:0/3 C:0/1 P:3/3 M:3/3. There is a large toothless gap between the front 'biting' teeth and the rear 'grinding' teeth.

For the first few years of life it is possible to calculate the age of sheep from their front teeth, as a pair of milk teeth is replaced by larger adult teeth each year, the full set of eight adult front teeth being complete at about four years of age. The front teeth are then gradually lost as sheep age, making it harder for them to feed and hindering the health and productivity of the animal. For this reason, domestic sheep on normal pasture begin to slowly decline from four years on, and the average life expectancy of a sheep is 10 to 12 years, though some sheep may live as long as 20 years.

Sheep have good hearing, and are sensitive to noise when being handled. Sheep have horizontal slit-shaped pupils, possessing excellent peripheral vision; with visual fields of approximately 270° to 320°, sheep can see behind themselves without turning their heads. However, sheep have poor depth perception; shadows and dips in the ground may cause sheep to baulk. In general, sheep have a tendency to move out of the dark and into well-lit areas, and prefer to move uphill when disturbed. Sheep also have an excellent sense of smell, and, like all species of their genus, have scent glands just in front of the eyes, and interdigitally on the feet. The purpose of these glands is uncertain, but those on the face may be used in breeding behaviours. The foot glands might also be related to reproduction, but alternative reasons, such as secretion of a waste product or a scent marker to help lost sheep find their flock, have also been proposed.

Sheep and goats are closely related as both are in the subfamily Caprinae. However, they are separate species, so hybrids rarely occur, and are always infertile. A hybrid of a ewe and a buck (a male goat) is called a sheep-goat hybrid (only a single such animal has been confirmed), and is not to be confused with the genetic chimera called a geep. Visual differences between sheep and goats include the beard and divided upper lip unique to goats. Sheep tails also hang down, even when short or docked, while the short tails of goats are held upwards. Sheep breeds are also often naturally polled (either in both sexes or just in the female), while naturally polled goats are rare (though many are polled artificially). Males of the two species differ in that buck goats acquire a unique and strong odor during the rut, whereas rams do not.

The domestic sheep is a multi-purpose animal, and the more than 200 breeds now in existence were created to serve these diverse purposes. Some sources give a count of a thousand or more breeds, but these numbers cannot be verified. Almost all sheep are classified as being best suited to furnishing a certain product: wool, meat, milk, hides, or a combination in a dual-purpose breed. Other features used when classifying sheep include face colour (generally white or black), tail length, presence or lack of horns, and the topography for which the breed has been developed. This last point is especially stressed in the UK, where breeds are described as either upland (hill or mountain) or lowland breeds. A sheep may also be of a fat-tailed type, which is a dual-purpose sheep common in Africa and Asia with larger deposits of fat within and around its tail.

Breeds are also grouped based on how well they are suited to producing a certain type of breeding stock. Generally, sheep are thought to be either 'ewe breeds' or 'ram breeds'. Ewe breeds are those that are hardy, and have good reproductive and mothering capabilities – they are for replacing breeding ewes in standing flocks. Ram breeds are selected for rapid growth and carcase quality, and are mated with ewe breeds to produce meat lambs. Lowland and upland breeds are also crossed in this fashion, with the hardy hill ewes crossed with larger, fast-growing lowland rams to produce ewes called mules, which can then be crossed with meat-type rams to produce prime market lambs. Many breeds, especially rare or primitive ones, fall into no clear category.

Breeds are categorized by the type of their wool. Fine wool breeds are those that have wool of great crimp and density, which are preferred for textiles. Most of these were derived from Merino sheep, and the breed continues to dominate the world sheep industry. Downs breeds have wool between the extremes, and are typically fast-growing meat and ram breeds with dark faces. Some major medium wool breeds, such as the Corriedale, are dual-purpose crosses of long and fine-wooled breeds and were created for high-production commercial flocks. Long wool breeds are the largest of sheep, with long wool and a slow rate of growth. Long wool sheep are most valued for crossbreeding to improve the attributes of other sheep types. For example: the American Columbia breed was developed by crossing Lincoln rams (a long wool breed) with fine-wooled Rambouillet ewes.

Coarse or carpet wool sheep are those with a medium to long length wool of characteristic coarseness. Breeds traditionally used for carpet wool show great variability, but the chief requirement is a wool that will not break down under heavy use (as would that of the finer breeds). As the demand for carpet-quality wool declines, some breeders of this type of sheep are attempting to use a few of these traditional breeds for alternative purposes. Others have always been primarily meat-class sheep.

A minor class of sheep are the dairy breeds. Dual-purpose breeds that may primarily be meat or wool sheep are often used secondarily as milking animals, but there are a few breeds that are predominantly used for milking. These sheep do produce a higher quantity of milk and have slightly longer lactation curves. In the quality of their milk, fat and protein content percentages of dairy sheep vary from non-dairy breeds but lactose content does not.

A last group of sheep breeds is that of fur or hair sheep, which do not grow wool at all. Hair sheep are similar to the early domesticated sheep kept before woolly breeds were developed, and are raised for meat and pelts. Some modern breeds of hair sheep, such as the Dorper, result from crosses between wool and hair breeds. For meat and hide producers, hair sheep are cheaper to keep, as they do not need shearing. Hair sheep are also more resistant to parasites and hot weather.

With the modern rise of corporate agribusiness and the decline of localized family farms, many breeds of sheep are in danger of extinction. The Rare Breeds Survival Trust of the UK lists 22 native breeds as having only 3,000 registered animals (each), and the American Livestock Breeds Conservancy lists 14 as having fewer than 10,000. Preferences for breeds with uniform characteristics and fast growth have pushed heritage (or heirloom) breeds to the margins of the sheep industry. Those that remain are maintained through the efforts of conservation organizations, breed registries, and individual farmers dedicated to their preservation.

Sheep are exclusively herbivorous mammals. Most breeds prefer to graze on grass and other short roughage, avoiding the taller woody parts of plants that goats readily consume. Both sheep and goats use their lips and tongues to select parts of the plant that are easier to digest or higher in nutrition. Sheep, however, graze well in monoculture pastures where most goats fare poorly. Like all ruminants, sheep have a complex digestive system composed of four chambers, allowing them to break down cellulose from stems, leaves, and seed hulls into simpler carbohydrates. When sheep graze, vegetation is chewed into a mass called a bolus, which is then passed into the first chamber: the rumen. The rumen is a 19 to 38-litre (5 to 10 gal) organ in which feed is fermented via a symbiotic relationship with the bacteria, protozoa, and yeasts of the gut flora. The bolus is periodically regurgitated back to the mouth as cud for additional chewing and salivation. Cud chewing is an adaptation allowing ruminants to graze more quickly in the morning, and then fully chew and digest feed later in the day. This is beneficial as grazing, which requires lowering the head, leaves sheep vulnerable to predators, while cud chewing does not.

During fermentation, the rumen produces gas that must be expelled; disturbances of the organ, such as sudden changes in a sheep's diet, can cause the potentially fatal condition of bloat, when gas becomes trapped in the rumen. After fermentation in the rumen, feed passes in to the reticulum and the omasum; special feeds such as grains may bypass the rumen altogether. After the first three chambers, food moves in to the abomasum for final digestion before processing by the intestines. The abomasum is the only one of the four chambers analogous to the human stomach (being the only one that absorbs nutrients for use as energy), and is sometimes called the 'true stomach'.

Sheep follow a diurnal pattern of activity, feeding from dawn to dusk, stopping sporadically to rest and chew their cud. Ideal pasture for sheep is not lawn-like grass, but an array of grasses, legumes and forbs. Types of land where sheep are raised vary widely, from pastures that are seeded and improved intentionally to rough, native lands. Common plants toxic to sheep are present in most of the world, and include (but are not limited to) oak and acorns, tomato, yew, rhubarb, potato, and rhododendron.

Sheep are largely grazing herbivores, unlike browsing animals such as goats and deer that prefer taller foliage. With a much narrower face, sheep crop plants very close to the ground and can overgraze a pasture much faster than cattle. For this reason, many shepherds use managed intensive rotational grazing, where a flock is rotated through multiple pastures, giving plants time to recover. Paradoxically, sheep can both cause and solve the spread of invasive plant species. By disturbing the natural state of pasture, sheep and other livestock can pave the way for invasive plants. However, sheep also prefer to eat invasives such as cheatgrass, leafy spurge, kudzu and spotted knapweed over native species such as sagebrush, making grazing sheep effective for conservation grazing. Research conducted in Imperial County, California compared lamb grazing with herbicides for weed control in seedling alfalfa fields. Three trials demonstrated that grazing lambs were just as effective as herbicides in controlling winter weeds. Entomologists also compared grazing lambs to insecticides for insect control in winter alfalfa. In this trial, lambs provided insect control as effectively as insecticides.

Other than forage, the other staple feed for sheep is hay, often during the winter months. The ability to thrive solely on pasture (even without hay) varies with breed, but all sheep can survive on this diet. Also included in some sheep's diets are minerals, either in a trace mix or in licks.

Naturally, a constant source of potable water is also a fundamental requirement for sheep. The amount of water needed by sheep fluctuates with the season and the type and quality of the food they consume. When sheep feed on large amounts of new growth and there is precipitation (including dew, as sheep are dawn feeders), sheep need less water. When sheep are confined or are eating large amounts of cured hay, more water is typically needed. Sheep also require clean water, and may refuse to drink water that is covered in scum or algae.

Sheep are one of the few livestock animals raised for meat today that have never been widely raised in an intensive, confined animal feeding operation (CAFO). Although there is a growing movement advocating alternative farming styles, a large percentage of beef cattle, pigs, and poultry are still produced under such conditions. In contrast, only some sheep are regularly given high-concentration grain feed, much less kept in confinement. Especially in industrialized countries, sheep producers may fatten market lambs before slaughter (called 'finishing') in feedlots. Many sheep breeders flush ewes and rams with a daily ration of grain during breeding to increase fertility. Ewes are also flushed during pregnancy to increase birth weights, as 70 per cent of a lamb's growth occurs in the last five to six weeks of gestation. Otherwise, only lactating ewes and especially old or infirm sheep are commonly provided with grain. Feed provided to sheep must be specially formulated, as most cattle, poultry, pig, and even some goat feeds contain levels of copper that are lethal to sheep. The same danger applies to mineral supplements such as salt licks.

Sheep are prey animals with a strong gregarious instinct, and a majority of sheep behaviors can be understood in these terms. The dominance hierarchy of *Ovis aries* and its natural inclination to follow a leader to new pastures were the pivotal factors in it being one of the first domesticated livestock species. All sheep have a tendency to congregate close to other members of a flock, although this behaviour varies with breed. Farmers exploit this behavior to keep sheep together on unfenced pastures and to move them more easily. Shepherds may also use herding dogs in this effort, whose highly bred herding ability can assist in moving flocks. Sheep are also extremely food-oriented, and association of humans with regular feeding often results in sheep soliciting people for food. Those who are moving sheep may exploit this behavior by leading sheep with buckets of feed, rather than forcing their movements with herding.

In regions where sheep have no natural predators, none of the native breeds of sheep exhibit a strong flocking behaviour. Sheep can also become hefted to one particular local pasture (heft) so they do not roam freely in unfenced landscapes. Ewes teach the heft to their lambs, and if whole flocks are culled it must be retaught to the replacement animals.

Flock dynamics in sheep are, as a rule, only exhibited in a group of four or more sheep. Fewer sheep may not react as normally expected when alone or with few other sheep. For sheep, the primary defense mechanism is simply to flee from danger when their flight zone is crossed. Secondly, cornered sheep may charge or threaten to do so through hoof stamping and aggressive posture. This is particularly true for ewes with newborn lambs.

In displaying flocking, sheep have a strong lead-follow tendency, and a leader often as not is simply the first sheep to move. However, sheep do establish a pecking order through physical displays of dominance. Dominant animals are inclined to be more aggressive with other sheep, and usually feed first at troughs. Primarily among rams, horn size is a factor in the flock hierarchy. Rams with different size horns may be less inclined to fight to establish pecking order, while rams with similarly sized horns are more so.

Sheep can become stressed when separated from their flock members. Sheep can recognize individual human and ovine faces, and remember them for years. Relationships in flocks tend to be closest among related sheep: in mixed-breed flocks same-breed subgroups tend to form, and a ewe and her direct descendants often move as a unit within large flocks.

Sheep are frequently thought of as extremely unintelligent animals. A sheep's herd mentality and quickness to flee and panic in the face of stress often make shepherding a difficult endeavor for the uninitiated. Despite these perceptions, a University of Illinois monograph on sheep found them to be just below pigs and on par with cattle in IQ, and some sheep have shown problem-solving abilities; a flock in West Yorkshire, England allegedly found a way to get over cattle grids by rolling on their backs, although documentation of this has relied on anecdotal accounts. In addition to long-term facial recognition of individuals, sheep can also differentiate emotional states through facial characteristics. If worked with patiently, sheep may learn their names, and many sheep are trained to be led by halter for showing and other purposes. Sheep have also responded well to clicker training. Very rarely, sheep are used as pack animals. Tibetan nomads distribute baggage equally throughout a flock as it is herded between living sites.

Sheep follow a similar reproductive strategy to other herd animals. A group of ewes is generally mated by a single ram, who has either been chosen by a breeder or has established dominance through physical contest with other rams (in feral populations). Most sheep are seasonal breeders, although some are able to breed year-round. Ewes generally reach sexual maturity at six to eight months of age, and rams generally at four to six months. Ewes have estrus cycles about every 17 days, during which they emit a scent and indicate readiness through physical displays towards rams. A minority of sheep display a preference for homosexuality (8% on average) or are freemartins (female animals that are behaviourally masculine and lack functioning ovaries).

In feral sheep, rams may fight during the rut to determine which individuals may mate with ewes. Rams, especially unfamiliar ones, will also fight outside the breeding period to establish dominance; rams can kill one another if allowed to mix freely. During the rut, even normally friendly rams may become aggressive towards humans due to increases in their hormone levels.

After mating, sheep have a gestation period of about five months, and normal labour take one to three hours. Although some breeds regularly throw larger litters of lambs, most produce single or twin lambs. During or soon after labour, ewes and lambs may be confined to small lambing jugs, small pens designed to aid both careful observation of ewes and to cement the bond between them and their lambs.

Ovine obstetrics can be problematic. By selectively breeding ewes that produce multiple offspring with higher birth weights for generations, sheep producers have inadvertently caused some domestic sheep to have difficulty lambing; balancing ease of lambing with high productivity is one of the dilemmas of sheep breeding. In the case of any such problems, those present at lambing may assist the ewe by extracting or repositioning lambs. After the birth, ewes ideally break the amniotic sac (if it is not broken during labour), and begin licking clean the lamb. Most lambs will begin standing within an hour of birth. In normal situations, lambs nurse after standing, receiving vital colostrum milk. Lambs that either fail to nurse or that are rejected by the ewe require aid to live, such as bottle-feeding or fostering by another ewe.

After lambs are several weeks old, lamb marking (the process of ear tagging, docking, and castrating) is carried out. Vaccinations are usually carried out at this point as well. Ear tags with numbers are attached, or ear marks are applied for ease of later identification of sheep. Castration is performed on ram lambs not intended for breeding, although some shepherds choose to avoid the procedure for ethical, economic or practical reasons. Ram lambs that will either be slaughtered or separated from ewes before sexual maturity are not usually castrated. Docking, which is the shortening of a lamb's tail, is practised for health reasons. Objections to all these procedures have been raised by animal rights groups, but farmers defend them by saying they solve many practical and veterinary problems, and inflict only temporary pain.

Sheep may fall victim to poisons, infectious diseases, and physical injuries. As a prey species, a sheep's system is adapted to hide the obvious signs of illness, to prevent being targeted by predators. However, there are some obvious signs of ill health, with sick sheep eating little, vocalizing excessively, and being generally listless. Throughout history, much of the money and labour of sheep husbandry has aimed to prevent sheep ailments. Historically, shepherds often created remedies by experimentation on the farm. In some developed countries, including the United States, sheep lack the economic importance for drugs companies to perform expensive clinical trials required to approve drugs for ovine use. In such instances, shepherds resort to illegal, extra-label usage of drugs approved for other animals. In the 20th and 21st centuries, a minority of sheep owners have turned to alternative treatments such as homoeopathy, herbalism and even traditional Chinese medicine to treat sheep veterinary problems. Despite some favourable anecdotal evidence, the effectiveness of alternative veterinary medicine has been met with skepticism in scientific journals. The need for traditional anti-parasite drugs and antibiotics is widespread, and is the main impediment to certified organic farming with sheep.

Many breeders take a variety of preventive measures to ward off problems. The first is to ensure that all sheep are healthy when purchased. Many buyers avoid outlets known to be clearing houses for animals culled from healthy flocks as either sick or simply inferior. This can also mean maintaining a closed flock, and quarantining new sheep for a month. Two fundamental preventive programmes are maintaining good nutrition and reducing stress in the sheep. Handling sheep in loud, erratic ways causes them to produce cortisol, a stress hormone. This can lead to a weakened immune system, thus making sheep far more vulnerable to disease. Signs of stress in sheep include: excessive panting, teeth grinding, restless movement, wool eating, and wood chewing. Avoiding poisoning is also important; common poisons are pesticide sprays, inorganic fertilizer, motor oil, as well as radiator coolant (the ethylene glycol antifreeze is sweet-tasting).

Common forms of preventive medication for sheep are vaccinations and treatments for parasites. Both external and internal parasites are the most prevalent malady in sheep, and are either fatal, or reduce the productivity of flocks. Worms are the most common internal parasites. They are ingested during grazing, incubate within the sheep, and are expelled through the digestive system (beginning the cycle again). Oral anti-parasitic medicines, known as drenches, are given to a flock to treat worms, sometimes after worm eggs in the feces has been counted to assess infestation levels. Afterwards, sheep may be moved to a new pasture to avoid ingesting the same parasites. External sheep parasites include: lice (for different parts of the body), sheep keds, nose bots, sheep itch mites, and maggots. Keds are blood-sucking parasites that cause general malnutrition and decreased productivity, but are not fatal. Maggots are those of the bot fly and the blow-fly. Fly maggots cause the extremely destructive condition of flystrike. Flies lay their eggs in wounds or wet, manure-soiled wool; when the maggots hatch they burrow into a sheep's flesh, eventually causing death if untreated. In addition to other treatments, crutching (shearing wool from a sheep's rump) is a common preventive method. Nose bots are flies that inhabit a sheep's sinuses, causing breathing difficulties and discomfort. Common signs are a discharge from the nasal passage, sneezing, and frantic movement such as head shaking. External parasites may be controlled through the use of backliners, sprays or immersive sheep dips.

A wide array of bacterial diseases affect sheep. Diseases of the hoof, such as foot rot and foot scald may occur, and are treated with footbaths and other remedies. These painful conditions cause lameness and hinder feeding. Ovine Johne's disease is a wasting disease that affects young sheep. Bluetongue disease is an insect-borne illness causing fever and inflammation of the mucous membranes. Ovine rinderpest (or *peste des petits ruminants*) is a highly contagious and often fatal viral disease affecting sheep and goats.

A few sheep conditions are transmissible to humans. Orf (also known as scabby mouth, contagious ecthyma or soremouth) is a skin disease leaving lesions that is transmitted through skin-to-skin contact. Cutaneous anthrax is also called woolsorter's disease, as the spores can be transmitted in unwashed wool. More seriously, the organisms that can cause spontaneous enzootic abortion in sheep are easily transmitted to pregnant women. Also of concern are the prion disease scrapie and the virus that causes foot-and-mouth disease (FMD), as both can devastate flocks. The latter poses a slight risk to humans. During the 2001 FMD pandemic in the UK, hundreds of sheep were culled and some rare British breeds were at risk of extinction due to this.

Other than parasites and disease, predation is a threat to sheep and the profitability of sheep raising. Sheep have little ability to defend themselves, compared with other species kept as livestock. Even if sheep survive an attack, they may die from their injuries, or simply from panic. However, the impact of predation varies dramatically with region. In Africa, Australia, the Americas, and parts of Europe and Asia predators are a serious problem. In the United States, for instance, over one third of sheep deaths in 2004 were caused by predation. In contrast, other nations are virtually devoid of sheep predators, particularly islands known for extensive sheep husbandry. Worldwide, canids—including the domestic dog—are responsible for most sheep deaths. Other animals that occasionally prey on sheep include: felines, bears, birds of prey, ravens and feral hogs.

Sheep producers have used a wide variety of measures to combat predation. Pre-modern shepherds used their own presence, livestock guardian dogs, and protective structures such as barns and fencing. Fencing (both regular and electric), penning sheep at night and lambing indoors all continue to be widely used. More modern shepherds used guns, traps, and poisons to kill predators, causing significant decreases in predator populations. In the wake of the environmental and conservation movements, the use of these methods now usually falls under the purview of specially designated government agencies in most developed countries.

The 1970s saw a resurgence in the use of livestock guardian dogs and the development of new methods of predator control by sheep producers, many of them non-lethal. Donkeys and guard llamas have been used since the 1980s in sheep operations, using the same basic principle as livestock guardian dogs. Interspecific pasturing, usually with larger livestock such as cattle or horses, may help to deter predators, even if such species do not actively guard sheep. In addition to animal guardians, contemporary sheep operations may use non-lethal predator deterrents such as motion-activated lights and noisy alarms.

Sheep were among the first animals to be domesticated by humankind; sources provide a domestication date between nine and eleven thousand years ago in Mesopotamia. Their wild relatives have several characteristics—such as a relative lack of aggression, a manageable size, early sexual maturity, a social nature, and high reproduction rates—which made them particularly suitable for domestication. Today, *Ovis aries* is an entirely domesticated animal that is largely dependent on man for its health and survival. Feral sheep do exist, but exclusively in areas devoid of large predators (usually islands) and not on the scale of feral horses, goats, pigs, or dogs, although some feral populations have remained isolated long enough to be recognized as distinct breeds.

The exact line of descent between domestic sheep to their wild ancestors is presently unclear. The most common hypothesis states that *Ovis aries* is descended from the Asiatic (*O. orientalis*) species of mouflon. It has been proposed that the European mouflon (*O. musimon*) is an ancient breed of domestic sheep turned feral rather than an ancestor, despite it commonly being cited as ancestor in past literature. A few breeds of sheep, such as the Castlemilk Moorit from Scotland, were formed through crossbreeding with wild European mouflon.

The urial (*O. vignei*) was once thought to have been a forebear of domestic sheep, as they occasionally interbreed with mouflon in the Iranian part of their range. However, the urial, argali (*O. ammon*), and snow sheep (*O. nivicola*) have a different number of chromosomes than other Ovis species, making a direct relationship implausible, and phylogenetic studies show no evidence of urial ancestry. Further studies comparing European and Asian breeds of sheep showed significant genetic differences between the two. Two explanations for this phenomenon have been posited. The first is that there is a currently unknown species or subspecies of wild sheep that contributed to the formation of domestic sheep. A second hypothesis suggests that this variation is the result of multiple waves of capture from wild mouflon, similar to the known development of other livestock.

Initially, sheep were kept solely for meat, milk and skins. Archaeological evidence from statuary found at sites in Iran suggests that selection for woolly sheep may have begun around 6000 BC, but the earliest woven wool garments have only been dated to two to three thousand years later. By that span of the Bronze Age, sheep with all the major features of modern breeds were widespread throughout Western Asia. However, one chief difference between ancient sheep and modern breeds is the technique by which wool could be collected. Primitive sheep cannot be shorn, and must have their wool plucked out by hand in a process called 'rooing'. This is because fibres called kemps are still longer than the soft fleece. The fleece may also be collected from the field after it falls out. This trait survives today in unrefined breeds such as the Soay and many Shetlands. Indeed, the Soay, along with other Northern European breeds with short tails, unshearable fleece, diminutive size, and horns in both sexes, are closely related to ancient sheep. Originally, weaving and spinning wool was a handicraft practiced at home, rather than an industry. Babylonians, Sumerians, and Persians all depended on sheep; and although linen was the first fabric to be fashioned in to clothing, wool was a prized product. The raising of flocks for their fleece was one of the earliest industries, and flocks were a medium of exchange in barter economies. Numerous biblical figures kept large flocks, and subjects of the king of Israel were taxed according to the number of rams they owned.

Sheep entered the African continent not long after their domestication in western Asia. A minority of historians once posited a contentious African theory of origin for *Ovis aries*. This theory is based primarily on rock art interpretations, and osteological evidence from Barbary sheep. The first sheep entered North Africa via Sinai, and were present in ancient Egyptian society between eight and seven thousand years ago. Sheep have always been part of subsistence farming in Africa, but today the only country that keeps an influential number of commercial sheep is South Africa. South African sheep producers, in an attempt to deal with the numerous predators of Africa, invented the livestock protection collar, which holds poison at the jugular to sicken or kill predators.

Sheep husbandry spread quickly in Europe. Excavations show that In about 6000 BC, during the Neolithic period of prehistory, the Castelnovien people, living around Chateauneuf-les-Martigues near present-day Marseille in the south of France, were among the first in Europe to keep domestic sheep. Practically from its inception, ancient Greek civilization relied on sheep as primary livestock, and were even said to name individual animals. Scandinavian sheep of a type seen today—with short tails and multi-coloured fleece—were also present early on. Later, the Roman Empire kept sheep on a wide scale, and the Romans were an important agent in the spread of sheep raising throughout the continent. Pliny the Elder, in his Natural History (*Naturalis Historia*), speaks at length about sheep and wool. Declaring "Many thanks, too, do we owe to the sheep, both for appeasing the gods, and for giving us the use of its fleece", he goes on to detail the breeds of ancient sheep and the many colours, lengths and qualities of wool. Romans also pioneered the practice of blanketing sheep, in which a fitted coat (today usually of nylon) is placed over the sheep to improve the cleanliness and luster of its wool.

During the Roman occupation of the British Isles, a large wool processing factory was established in Winchester, England in about 50 AD. By 1000 AD, England and Spain were recognized as the twin centres of sheep production in the Western world. As the original breeders of the fine-wooled merino sheep that have historically dominated the wool trade, the Spanish gained great wealth. Wool money largely financed Spanish rulers and thus the voyages to the New World by conquistadors. The powerful *Mesta* (its full title was *Honrado Concejo de la Mesta*, the Honourable Council of the Mesta) was a corporation of sheep owners mostly drawn from Spain's wealthy merchants, Catholic clergy and nobility that controlled the merino flocks. By the 17th century, the *Mesta* held in upwards of two million head of merino sheep.

Mesta flocks followed a seasonal pattern of transhumance across Spain. In the spring, they left the winter pastures (*invernaderos*) in Extremadura and Andalusia to graze on their summer pastures (*agostaderos*) in Castile, returning again in the autumn. Spanish rulers eager to increase wool profits gave extensive legal rights to the *Mesta*, often to the detriment of local peasantry. The huge merino flocks had a lawful right of way for their migratory routes (*cañadas*). Towns and villages were obliged by law to let the flocks graze on their common land, and the Mesta had its own sheriffs that could summon offending individuals to its own tribunals.

Exportation of merinos without royal permission was also a punishable offence, thus ensuring a near-absolute monopoly on the breed until the mid-18th century. After the breaking of the export ban, fine wool sheep began to be distributed worldwide. The export to Rambouillet by Louis XVI in 1786 formed the basis for the modern Rambouillet (or French Merino) breed. After the Napoleonic Wars and the global distribution of the once-exclusive Spanish stocks of Merinos, sheep raising in Spain reverted to hardy coarse-wooled breeds such as the Churra, and was no longer of international economic significance.

The sheep industry in Spain was an instance of migratory flock management, with large homogenous flocks ranging over the entire nation. The management model used in England was quite different but had a similar importance to economy of the British Empire. Up until the early 20th century, owling (the smuggling of sheep or wool out of the country) was a punishable offence, and to this day the Lord Speaker of the House of Lords sits on a cushion known as the Woolsack.

The high concentration and more sedentary nature of shepherding in the UK allowed sheep especially adapted to their particular purpose and region to be raised, thereby giving rise to an exceptional variety of breeds in relation to the land mass of the country. This greater variety of breeds also produced a valuable variety of products to compete with the superfine wool of Spanish sheep. By the time of Elizabeth I's rule, sheep and wool trade was the primary source of tax revenue to the Crown of England and the country was a major influence in the development and spread of sheep husbandry.

An important event not only in the history of domestic sheep, but of all livestock, was the work of Robert Bakewell in the 18th century. Before his time, breeding for desirable traits was often based on chance, with no scientific process for selection of breeding stock. Bakewell established the principles of selective breeding—especially line breeding—in his work with sheep, horses and cattle; his work later influenced Gregor Mendel and Charles Darwin. His most important contribution to sheep was the development of the Leicester Longwool, a quick-maturing breed of blocky conformation that formed the basis for many vital modern breeds. Today, the sheep industry in the UK has diminished significantly, though pedigreed rams can still fetch around 100,000 Pounds sterling at auction.

No ovine species native to the Americas has ever been domesticated, despite being closer genetically to domestic sheep than many Asian and European species. The first domestic sheep in North America—most likely of the Churra breed—arrived with Christopher Columbus' second voyage in 1493. The next transatlantic shipment to arrive was with Hernán Cortés in 1519, landing in Mexico. No export of wool or animals is known to have occurred from these populations, but flocks did disseminate throughout what is now Mexico and the Southwest United States with Spanish colonists. Churras were also introduced to the Navajo tribe of Native Americans, and became a key part of their livelihood and culture. The modern presence of the Navajo-Churro breed is a result of this heritage.

The next transport of sheep to North America was not until 1607, with the voyage of the *HMS Susan Conant* to Virginia. However, the sheep that arrived in that year were all slaughtered because of a famine, and a permanent flock was not to reach the colony until two years later in 1609. In two decades time, the colonists had expanded their flock to a total of 400 head. By the 1640s there were about 100,000 head of sheep in the 13 colonies, and in 1662, a woolen mill was built in Watertown, Massachusetts Especially during the periods of political unrest and civil war in Britain spanning the 1640s and 50s which disrupted maritime trade, the colonists found it pressing to produce wool for clothing. Many islands off the coast were cleared of predators and set aside for sheep: Nantucket, Long Island, Martha's Vineyard and small islands in Boston Harbour were notable examples. There remain some rare breeds of American sheep—such as the Hog Island sheep—that were the result of island flocks. Placing semi-feral sheep and goats on islands was common practice in colonization during this period. Early on, the British government banned further export of sheep to the Americas, or wool from it, in an attempt to stifle any threat to the wool trade in the British Isles. One of many restrictive trade measures that precipitated the American Revolution, the sheep industry in the Northeast grew despite the bans.

Gradually, beginning in the 19th century, sheep production in the U.S. moved westward. Today, the vast majority of flocks reside on Western range lands. During this westward migration of the industry, competition between sheep (sometime called 'range maggots') and cattle operations grew more heated, eventually erupting into range wars. Other than simple competition for grazing and water rights, cattlemen believed that the secretions of the foot glands of sheep made cattle unwilling to graze on places where sheep had stepped. As sheep production centered on the U.S. western ranges, it became associated with other parts of Western culture, such as the rodeo. In modern America, a minor event in rodeos is mutton busting, in which children compete to see who can stay atop a sheep the longest before falling off. Another effect of the westward movement of sheep flocks in North America was the decline of wild species such as Bighorn sheep (*O. canadesis*). Most diseases of domestic sheep are transmittable to wild ovines, and such diseases, along with overgrazing and habitat loss, are named as primary factors in the plummeting numbers of wild sheep. Sheep production peaked in North America during 1940s and 50s at more than 55 million head. Henceforth and continuing today, the number of sheep in North America has steadily declined with wool prices and the lessening American demand for sheep meat.

In South America, especially in Patagonia, there is an active modern sheep industry. Sheep keeping was largely introduced through immigration to the continent by Spanish and British peoples, for whom sheep were a major industry during the period. South America has a large number of sheep, but the highest-producing nation (Brazil) kept only just over 15 million head in 2004, far fewer than most centers of sheep husbandry. The primary challenges to the sheep industry in South America are the phenomenal drop in wool prices in the late 20th century and the loss of habitat through logging and overgrazing. The most influential region internationally is that of Patagonia, which has been the first to rebound from the fall in wool prices. With few predators and almost no grazing competition (the only large native grazing mammal is the guanaco), the region is prime land for sheep raising. The most exceptional area of production is surrounding the La Plata river in the Pampas region. Sheep production in Patagonia peaked in 1952 at more than 21 million head, but has steadily fallen to fewer than ten today. Most operations focus on wool production for export from Merino and Corriedale sheep; the economic sustainability of wool flocks has fallen with the drop in prices, while the cattle industry continues to grow.

Australia and New Zealand are crucial players in the contemporary sheep industry, and sheep are an iconic part of both countries' culture and economy. New Zealand has the highest density of sheep per capita (sheep outnumber the human population 12 to 1), and Australia is the world's indisputably largest exporter of sheep and cattle. In 2007, New Zealand even declared 15 February their official National Lamb Day to celebrate the country's history of sheep production.

The First Fleet brought the initial population of 70 sheep from the Cape of Good Hope to Australia in 1788. The next shipment was of 30 sheep from Calcutta and Ireland in 1793. All of the early sheep brought to Australia were exclusively used for the dietary needs of the penal colonies. The beginnings of the Australian wool industry were due to the efforts of Captain John Macarthur. At Macarthur's urging 16 Spanish merinos were imported in 1797, effectively beginning the Australian sheep industry. By 1801 Macarthur had 1,000 head of sheep, and in 1803 he exported 111 kilograms (245 lb) of wool to England. Today, Macarthur is generally thought of as the father of the Australian sheep industry.

The growth of the sheep industry in Australia was explosive. In 1820, the continent held 100,000 sheep, a decade later it had one million. By 1840, New South Wales alone kept 4 million sheep; flock numbers grew to 13 million in a decade. While much of the growth in both nations was due to the active support of Britain in its desire for wool, both worked independently to develop new high-production breeds: the Corriedale, Coolalee, Coopworth, Perendale, Polwarth, Booroola Merino, Peppin Merino, and Poll Merino were all created in New Zealand or Australia. Wool production was a fitting industry for colonies far from their home nations.

Before the advent of fast air and maritime shipping, wool was one of the few viable products that was not subject to spoiling on the long passage back to British ports. The abundant new land and milder winter weather of the region also aided the growth of the Australian and New Zealand sheep industries.

Flocks in Australia have always been largely range bands on fenced land, and are aimed at production of medium to superfine wool for clothing and other products as well as meat. New Zealand flocks are kept in a fashion similar to English ones, in fenced holdings without shepherds. Although wool was once the primary income source for New Zealand sheep owners (especially during the New Zealand wool boom), today it has shifted to meat production for export.

Animal Welfare Concerns

The Australian sheep industry is the only sector of the industry to receive international criticism for its practices. Sheep stations in Australia are cited in *Animal Liberation*, the seminal book of the animal rights movement, as the author's primary evidence in his argument against retaining sheep as a part of animal agriculture. The practice of mulesing, in which skin is cut away from an animal's perineal area to prevent cases of the fatal condition flystrike, has been condemned by PETA as being painful and unnecessary. In response, a programme of phasing out mulesing is currently being implemented, and some mulesing operations are being carried out with the use of anaesthetic. The Animal Welfare Advisory Committee to the New Zealand Ministry of Agriculture *Code of recommendations and minimum standards for the welfare of Sheep*, considers mulesing a 'special technique' which is performed on some Merino sheep at a small number of farms in New Zealand.

Most of the sheep meat exported from Australia is either frozen carcases to the UK or is live export to the Middle East. Shipped on livestock carriers in what has been called crowded, unsafe conditions by critics, live sheep are desired by Middle Eastern nations to meet the requirements of ritual halal slaughter. Opponents of the export—such as PETA—say that sheep exported to countries outside the jurisdiction of Australia's animal cruelty laws are treated with horrendous brutality and that halal facilities exist in Australia to make export of live animals redundant. A few celebrities and companies have pledged to boycott all Australian sheep products in protest.

Sheep are an important part of the global agricultural economy. However, their once-vital status has been largely replaced by other livestock species, especially the pig, chicken, and cow. China, Australia, India, and Iran have the largest modern flocks, and serve both local and exportation needs for wool and mutton. Other countries such as New Zealand have smaller flocks but retain a large international economic impact due to their export of sheep products. Sheep also play a major role in many local economies, which may be niche markets focused on organic or sustainable agriculture and local food customers. Especially in developing countries, such flocks may be a part of subsistence agriculture rather than a system of trade. Sheep themselves may be a medium of trade in barter economies.

Domestic sheep provide a wide array of raw materials. Wool was one of the first textiles, although in the late 20th century wool prices began to fall dramatically as the result of the popularity and cheap prices for synthetic fabrics. For many sheep owners, the cost of shearing is greater than the possible profit from the fleece, making subsisting on wool production alone practically impossible without farm subsidies. Fleeces are used as material in making alternative products such as wool insulation. In the 21st century, the sale of meat is the most profitable enterprise in the sheep industry, even though far less sheep meat is consumed than chicken, pork or beef.

Sheepskin is likewise used for making clothes, footwear, rugs, and other products. Byproducts from the slaughter of sheep are also of value: sheep tallow can be used in candle and soap making, sheep bone and cartilage has been used to furnish carved items such as dice and buttons as well as rendered glue and gelatin. Sheep intestine can be formed into sausage casings, and lamb intestine has been formed into surgical sutures, as well as strings for musical instruments and tennis rackets. Sheep droppings, which are high in cellulose, have even been sterilized and mixed with traditional pulp materials to make paper. Of all sheep byproducts, perhaps the most valuable is lanolin: the water-proof, fatty substance found naturally in sheep's wool and used as a base for innumerable cosmetics and other products.

Some farmers who keep sheep also make a profit from live sheep. Providing lambs for youth programmes such as 4-H and competition at agricultural shows is often a dependable avenue for the sale of sheep. Farmers may also choose to focus on a particular breed of sheep in order to sell registered purebred animals, as well as provide a ram rental service for breeding. The most valuable sheep ever sold to date was a purebred Texel ram that fetched £231,000 at auction. The previous record holder was a Merino ram sold for £205,000 in 1989. A new option for deriving profit from live sheep is the rental of flocks for grazing; these 'mowing services' are hired in order to keep unwanted vegetation down in public spaces and to lessen fire hazard.

Despite the falling demand and price for sheep products in many markets, sheep have distinct economic advantages when compared with other livestock. They do not require the expensive housing, such as that used in the intensive farming of chickens or pigs. They are an efficient use of land; roughly six sheep can be kept on the amount that would suffice for a single cow or horse. Sheep can also consume plants, such as noxious weeds, that most other animals will not touch, and produce more young at a faster rate. Also, in contrast to most livestock species, the cost of raising sheep is not necessarily tied to the price of feed crops such as grain, soybeans and corn. Combined with the lower cost of quality sheep, all these factors combine to equal a lower overhead for sheep producers, thus entailing a higher profitability potential for the small farmer. Sheep are especially beneficial for independent producers, including family farms with limited resources, as the sheep industry is one of the few types of animal agriculture that has not been vertically integrated by agribusiness.

Sheep meat and milk were one of the earliest staple proteins consumed by human civilization after the transition from hunting and gathering to agriculture. Sheep meat prepared for food is known as either mutton or lamb. 'Mutton' is derived from the Old French *moton*, which was the word for sheep used by the Anglo-Norman rulers of much of the British Isles in the Middle Ages. This became the name for sheep meat in English, while the Old English word *sceap* was kept for the live animal. Throughout modern history, 'mutton' has been limited to the meat of mature sheep usually at least two years of age; 'lamb' is used for that of immature sheep less than a year.

In the 21st century, the nations with the highest consumption of sheep meat are the Persian Gulf states, New Zealand, Australia, Greece, Uruguay, the United Kingdom and Ireland. These countries eat 14-40 lbs (3-18 kg) of sheep meat per capita, per annum. Sheep meat is also popular in France, Africa (especially the Maghreb), the Caribbean, the rest of the Middle East, India, and parts of China. This often reflects a past history of sheep production. In these countries in particular, dishes comprising alternative cuts and offal may be popular or traditional. Sheep testicles—called animelles or lamb fries—are considered a delicacy in many parts of the world. Perhaps the most unusual dish of sheep meat is the Scottish haggis, composed of various sheep innards cooked along with oatmeal and chopped onions inside its stomach. In comparison, countries such as the U.S. consume only a pound or less (under 0.5 kg), with Americans eating 50 pounds (22 kg) of pork and 65 pounds (29 kg) of beef. In addition, such countries rarely eat mutton, and may favour the more expensive cuts of lamb: mostly lamb chops and leg of lamb.

Though sheep's milk may be drunk rarely in fresh form, today it is used predominantly in cheese and yogurt making. Sheep have only two teats, and produce a far smaller volume of milk than cows. However, as sheep's milk contains far more fat, solids, and minerals than cow's milk, it is ideal for the cheese-making process. It also resists contamination during cooling better because of its much higher calcium content. Well-known cheeses made from sheep milk include the Feta of Bulgaria and Greece, Roquefort of France, Manchego from Spain, the Pecorino Romano (the Italian word for sheep is *pecore*) and Ricotta of Italy. Yogurts, especially some forms of strained yogurt, may also be made from sheep milk. Many of these products are now often made with cow's milk, especially when produced outside their country of origin. Sheep milk contains 4.8 per cent lactose, which may affect those who are intolerant.

Sheep are generally too large and reproduce too slowly to make ideal research subjects, and thus are not a common model organism. They have, however, played an influential role in some fields of science. In particular, the Roslin Institute of Edinburgh, Scotland used sheep for genetics research that produced groundbreaking results. In 1995, two ewes named Megan and Morag were the first mammals cloned from differentiated cells. A year later, a Finnish Dorset sheep named Dolly, dubbed "the world's most famous sheep" in *Scientific American*, was the first mammal to be cloned from an adult somatic cell. Following this, Polly and Molly were the first mammals to be simultaneously cloned and transgenic. As of 2008, the sheep genome has not been fully sequenced, although a detailed genetic map has been published, and a draft version of the complete genome produced by assembling sheep DNA sequences using information given by the genomes of other mammals.

In the study of natural selection, the population of Soay sheep that remain on the island of Hirta have been used to explore the relation of body size and colouration to reproductive success. Soay sheep come in several colours, and researchers investigated why the larger, darker sheep were in decline; this occurrence contradicted the rule of thumb that larger members of a population tend to be more successful reproductively. The feral Soays on Hirta are especially useful subjects because they are isolated.

Sheep are one of the few animals where the molecular basis of the diversity of male sexual preferences has been examined. However, this research has been controversial, and much publicity has been produced by a study at the Oregon Health and Science University that investigated the mechanisms that produce homosexuality in rams. Organizations such as PETA campaigned against the study, accusing scientists of trying to cure homosexuality in the sheep. OHSU and the involved scientists vehemently denied such accusations.

Domestic sheep are sometimes used in medical research, particularly for researching cardiovascular physiology, in areas such as hypertension and heart failure. Pregnant sheep are also a useful model for human pregnancy, and have been used to investigate the effects on fetal development of malnutrition and hypoxia. In behavioural sciences, sheep have been used in isolated cases for the study of facial recognition, as their mental process of recognition is qualitatively similar to humans.

Sheep have had a strong presence in many cultures, especially in areas where they form the most common type of livestock. In the English language, to call someone a sheep or ovine may allude that they are timid and easily led, if not outright stupid. In contradiction to this image, male sheep are often used as symbols of virility and power, such as for the St. Louis Rams and the Dodge Ram. Sheep are key symbols in fables and nursery rhymes like *The Wolf in Sheep's Clothing*, *Little Bo Peep*, *Baa, Baa, Black Sheep*, and *Mary Had a Little Lamb*. Novels such as George Orwell's *Animal Farm*, Haruki Murakami's *A Wild Sheep Chase*, Thomas Hardy's *Far from the Madding Crowd* and *Three Bags Full: A Sheep Detective Story* utilize sheep as characters or plot devices. Poems like William Blake's 'The Lamb', songs such as Pink Floyd's *Sheep* and Bach's aria *Sheep may safely graze* (*Schafe können sicher weiden*) use sheep for metaphorical purposes. In more recent popular culture, the 2007 film *Black Sheep* exploits sheep for horror and comedic effect, ironically turning them into blood-thirsty killers.

Counting sheep is popularly said to be an aid to sleep, and some ancient systems of counting sheep persist today. Sheep also enter in colloquial sayings and idiom frequently with such phrases as 'black sheep'. To call an individual a black sheep implies that they are an odd or disreputable member of a group. This usage derives from the recessive trait that causes an occasional black lamb to be born in to an entirely white flock. These black sheep were considered undesirable by shepherds, as black wool is not as commercially viable as white wool. Citizens who accept overbearing governments have been referred to by the Portmanteau neologism of sheeple. Somewhat differently, the adjective 'sheepish' is also used to describe embarrassment.

In antiquity, symbolism involving sheep cropped up in religions in the ancient Near East, the Mideast, and the Mediterranean area: Çatalhöyük, ancient Egyptian religion, the Cana'anite and Phoenician tradition, Judaism, Greek religion, and others. Religious symbolism and ritual involving sheep began with some of the first known faiths: skulls of rams (along with bulls) occupied central placement in shrines at the Çatalhöyük settlement in 8,000 BCE. In Ancient Egyptian religion, the ram was the symbol of several gods: Khnum, Heryshaf and Amun (in his incarnation as a god of fertility). Other deities occasionally shown with ram features include:

the goddess Ishtar, the Phoenician god Baal-Hamon, and the Babylonian god Ea-Oannes. In Madagascar, sheep were not eaten as they were believed to be incarnations of the souls of ancestors.

There are also many ancient Greek references to sheep: that of Chrysomallos, the golden-fleeced ram, continuing to be told through into the modern era. Astrologically, *Aries*, the ram, is the first sign of the classical Greek zodiac and the sheep is also the eighth of the twelve animals associated with the 12-year cycle of in the Chinese zodiac, related to the Chinese calendar. n Mongolia, shagai are an ancient form of dice made from the cuboid bones of sheep that are often used for fortunetelling purposes.

Sheep play an important role in all the Abrahamic faiths; Abraham, Isaac, Jacob, Moses, King David and the Islamic prophet Muhammad were all shepherds. According to the Biblical story of the Binding of Isaac, a ram is sacrificed as a substitute for Isaac after an angel stays Abraham's hand (in the Islamic tradition, Abraham was about to sacrifice Ishmael). Eid al-Adha is a major annual festival in Islam in which sheep (or other animals) are sacrificed in remembrance of this act. Sheep are also occasionally sacrificed to commemorate important secular events in Islamic cultures. Greeks and Romans also sacrificed sheep regularly in religious practice, and Judaism also once sacrificed sheep as a Korban (sacrifice), such as the Passover lamb . Ovine symbols—such as the ceremonial blowing of a shofar—still find a presence in modern Judaic traditions. Followers of Christianity are collectively often referred to as a flock, with Christ as the Good Shepherd, and sheep are an element in the Christian iconography of the birth of Jesus. Some Christian saints are considered patrons of shepherds, and even of sheep themselves. Christ is also portrayed as the Sacrificial lamb of God (*Agnus Dei*) and Easter celebrations in Greece and Romania traditionally feature a meal of Paschal lamb.

8 Domestic Asian Water Buffalo

The water buffalo or domestic Asian water buffalo (*Bubalus bubalis*) is a large bovine animal, frequently used as livestock in southern Asia, and also widely in South America, southern Europe, north Africa, and elsewhere.

In 2000, the United Nations Food and Agriculture Organization estimated that there were approximately 158 million water buffalo in the world, and that 97 per cent of them (approximately 153 million animals) were in Asia. There are established feral populations in northern Australia, but the dwindling true wild populations are thought to survive in India, Bangladesh, Pakistan, Nepal, Bhutan, and Thailand. All the domestic varieties and breeds descend from one common ancestor, the wild water buffalo, which is now an endangered species. The domestic water buffalo, although derived from the wild water buffalo, is the product of thousands of years of selective breeding in either South Asia or Southeast Asia.

Buffalo are used as draft, meat, and dairy animals. Their dung is used as a fertilizer and as a fuel when dried. In Chonburi, Thailand, Pakistan and in southwestern region of Karnataka, India, there are annual water buffalo races known as Kambala. A few have also found use as pack animals carrying loads even for special forces.

American bison are known as buffalo in parts of North America, but not normally in other usages; bison are more closely related to cattle, gaur, banteng, and yaks than to Asian buffalo. The water buffalo genus includes water buffalo, tamaraw and anoas—all Asian species. The ancestry of the African buffalo is unclear, but it is not believed to be closely related to the water buffalo.

True wild water buffalo are thought to survive in Pakistan, Bangladesh, India, Nepal, Bhutan, and Thailand.

The IUCN Red List of threatened species classifies wild water buffalo (*Bubalis arnee*) as an endangered species in Southeast Asia. They run rampant as a wild animal in Western Australia, which is the only part of the world where they are legally hunted, and because of their large numbers there, encouraged to do so by the government, in their original range. The total number of wild water buffalo left in Southeast Asia is thought to be less than 4,000, which suggests that the number of mature individuals will be less than 2,500, and an estimated continuing decline of at least 20 per cent within 14 years (ca. 2 generations) and at least 50 per cent within 21 years seems likely given the severity of the threats, especially hybridization with the abundant domestic Asian water buffalo, leading to genetic pollution.

Adult water buffalo range in size from 400 to 900 kg (880 to 2,000 lb) for the domestic breeds, while the wild animals are nearly 3 m (9.8 ft) long and 2 m (6.6 ft) tall, weighing up to 1,200 kg (2,600 lb); females are about two-thirds this size.

River buffalo are usually black, have curled horns, and are native to the western half of Asia, whereas swamp buffalo can be black, white or both, with long, gently curved, swept back horns; they are native to the eastern half of Asia from India to Taiwan. The largest recorded horns are just under 2 metres long.

The rumen (the first chamber of the digestive system of a ruminant) of the water buffalo has important differences from that of other ruminants.

The water buffalo rumen has been found to contain a larger population of bacteria, particularly the cellulolytic bacteria, lower protozoa and higher fungi zoospores. In addition, higher rumen ammonia nitrogen (NH_4-N) and higher pH have been found as compared to those in cattle.

Taxonomy

The classification of the water buffalo is uncertain. Some authorities list a single species, *Bubalus bubalis* with three subspecies, the river buffalo (*B. bubalis bubalis*) of South Asia, the carabao or swamp buffalo (*B. bubalis carabanesis*) of the Philippines and Southeast Asia, and the arni, or wild water buffalo (*B. bubalis arnee*). Others regard these as closely related but separate species.

The swamp buffalo has 48 chromosomes; the river buffalo has 50 chromosomes. The two types do not readily interbreed, but fertile offspring can occur. Buffalo-cattle hybrids have not been observed to occur, and the embryos of such hybrids do not reach maturity in laboratory experiments.

The fossil forms of the buffalo provide a definite link between the Indian type and their present extreme representatives and their extinct allies. All Asiatic buffaloes seem to form a closely allied group of species which represent more or less a passage from one variety to another.

Type Locality: "Habitat in Asia, cultus in Italia". Restricted by Thomas (1911a:154) to Italy, Rome, but Linnaeus' (1758) comment indicates Asia (India?).

Distribution: Bangladesh, Myanmar, Cambodia, India (survives in Assam and Orissa), Nepal, northern Thailand, Vietnam, and possibly at least formerly in Laos; domesticated in North Africa, southern Europe, and even England, east to Indonesia and in eastern South America; supposedly feral populations in Sri Lanka, Sumatra, Java, Borneo, Philippines and other parts of SE Asia; feral populations resulting from introductions in New Britain and New Ireland (Bismarck Arch., Papua New Guinea), and Australia. Status.

The average lifespan in captivity is up to 25 years.

Asia is the native home of the water buffalo, with 95 per cent of the world population of water buffalo, with about half of the total in India. Many Asian countries depend on the water buffalo as its primary bovine species. It is valuable for its meat and milk, as well as the labour it performs. As of 1992, the Asian population was estimated at 141 million. The fat content of buffalo milk is the highest amongst farm animals and the butterfat is a major source of ghee in some Asian countries. Its success in Asia is evident by its extensive range. Both variants occur in Asia. River buffalo are found in elevations of 2,800 m in Nepal, and swamp buffalo are found throughout the lowland tropics. Part of their success is due to their ability to thrive on poor foodstuffs and yet be valuable economically. Moreover, they are much better suited to plough the muddy paddy fields, as they are better adapted than common cattle (*Bos taurus*) to move in swamps.

In India, buffalo populations are thriving because they are considered to be similar to the cow, which is sacred to the Hindus. Some ethnic groups, such as Batak and Toraja in Indonesia and the Derung in China, use water buffalo or 'Kerbau' (called 'Horbo' in Batak or 'Tedong' in Toraja) as sacrificial animals at several festivals. Especially in the Tana Toraja Regency, a local variety of water buffalo (called 'Tedong Bonga') features a unique black and white colouration.

Swamp buffalo were introduced into the Northern Territory from Timor early in the 19th century as a food source and a beast of burden. They escaped, thrived and became feral, causing significant environmental damage. Buffalo are also found in Arnhem Land and the Top End. An estimated 350,000 buffalo were living on the floodplains of Arnhem Land and the Katherine region in the 1980s. As a result, they were hunted in the Top End from 1885 until 1980. The commencement of the Brucellosis and Tuberculosis Campaign (BTEC) resulted in a huge culling programme to reduce buffalo herds to a fraction of the numbers that were reached in the 1980s. The BTEC was finished when the Northern Territory was declared free of the disease in 1997.

During the 1950s, buffalo were hunted for their skins, and meat which was exported and used in the local trade. In the late 1970s, live exports were made to Cuba and continued later into other countries. Buffalo are now crossed with riverine buffalo in artificial breeding (AI) programmes and may be found in many areas of Australia. Some of these crossbreds are used for milk production.

Melville Island is a popular hunting location, where a steady population of up to 4,000 individuals exist. Safari outfits run out of Darwin to Melville Island and other locations in the Top End, often with the use of bush pilots. The horns, which can measure up to a record of 3.1 metres tip to tip, are a prized hunting trophy.

The buffalo have developed a different appearance from the Indonesian buffalo from which they descend. They live mainly in freshwater marshes and billabongs, and their territory range can be quite expansive during the wet season. Their only natural predator in Australia are large adult saltwater crocodiles, with whom they share the billabongs.

Europe and Middle East

Introduced into North Africa and the Near East by 600 AD, the water buffalo was brought to Europe with returning Crusaders in the Middle Ages, and herds can be found in Turkey, Bulgaria, Romania, Albania, Hungary, Serbia, Austria and Italy. As in Asia, buffalo of the Middle East and Europe live on coarse vegetation on the marginal land traditionally available to peasants. They are an economic asset by serving as a protein source, draft animal, and storage of family or household wealth. In some areas, they also provide occasional recreation at annual racing festivals. These buffalo are mostly river buffalo; due to genetic isolation, they have adopted a distinct appearance. Buffalo milk is used for the production of buffalo mozzarella in Campania and many other locations around the world.

Water buffalo are a traditional farm animal in Egypt, which has a large number of them. They are used as the main source of red meat in Egypt. Cattle have been introduced in modern farms, yet water buffalo remain as the more widespread type of cattle in Egypt.

North America

There are very limited commercial herds in North America, for yogurt and cheese products. In Gainesville, Florida, a University of Florida professor, Hugh Popenoe, has raised water buffalo from young obtained from zoo overflow. He uses them primarily for meat production (frequently sold as hamburger), although other local ranchers use them for production of high-quality mozzarella cheese.

South America

Water buffalo were introduced into the Amazon River basin in 1895. They are now extensively used there for meat and dairy production. In 2005, the buffalo herd in the Brazilian Amazon stood at approximately 1.6 million head, of which approximately 460,000 were located in the lower Amazon floodplain. Breeds used include Mediterranean (from Italy), Murrah (India), Jafarabadi (India) and Carabao (Philippines).

Water buffalo have been domesticated for 5,000 years and have become economically important animals. They provide more than 5 per cent of the world's milk supply and 20 per cent to 30 per cent of the farm power in Southeast Asia. Milk from these animals is used by many human populations, and is the traditional raw material for mozzarella cheese and curd due to its higher fat content. In Africa and other locations, water buffalo milk is used for yogurt, as in Vermont, USA. The chief dairy breed of buffalo is the Murrah breed. Buffalo meat, sometimes called 'carabeef', is often passed off as beef in certain regions, and is also a major source of export revenue for India, which has the largest population of buffalo in the world. In many Asian regions, buffalo meat is less preferred due to its toughness; however, recipes have evolved (Rendang for example) where the slow cooking process and spices not only makes the meat palatable, but also preserves it, an important factor in hot climates where refrigeration is not always available. Water buffalo horns are used for the embouchure of musical instruments such as ney and kaval. Water buffalo hide provides a tough and useful leather, often used for shoes and motorcycle helmets. The bones and horns are often made into jewellry, especially earrings.

The water buffalo has promise as a major source of meat, even the milking ones. The water buffalo also is the classic work animal in Asia, an integral part of that continent's traditional village farming structure and also used for hauling cotton, pumping water in Pakistan and hauling logs in Turkey. The domesticated water buffalo is often referred to as "the living tractor of the East", as it is relied upon for ploughing and transportation in many parts of Asia.

Water buffalo spend much of their day submerged in the muddy waters of Asia's tropical and subtropical forests. They have wide-splayed hooved feet which are used to prevent them from sinking too deeply in the mud. These adaptations allow them to move in wetlands and swamps. Water buffalo also prefer to feed in grasslands on grass and forbs.

Water buffalo behaviour sometimes differs from cattle. For example, most water buffalo are not trained to be driven. Instead, the herdsman must walk alongside or ahead of them. They then instinctively follow. They also rub against trees more often than cattle do, and they sometimes debark the trees, causing them to die.

Reproduction

The water buffalo has a reputation for being a sluggish breeder. Without reasonable nutrition, the animals cannot reach puberty as early in life as genetic capability would normally allow. Females normally produce calves every other year after gestation of 9 to 11 months. Young bulls typically remain with maternal herds, which consist of around 30 buffalo, for three years after birth. They then go on to form small all-male herds.

Environmental Effects

The water buffalo may affect the environment in either positive or negative ways.

Wildlife and conservation scientists have started to recommend and use introduced populations of feral water buffalo to manage uncontrolled vegetation growth in and around natural wetlands. Introduced Asian water buffalo at home in such environs provide cheap service by regularly grazing uncontrolled vegetation and opening up clogged water bodies for waterfowl, wetland birds and other wildlife. Grazing water buffalo are sometimes used in Great Britain for conservation grazing, for example to manage Chippenham Fen NNR. These buffalo have been found to be better suited to the wet conditions and poor-quality vegetation than many cattle.

Currently, research is being conducted at the Lyle Centre for Regenerative Studies to determine the levels of nutrients removed and returned to wetlands when water buffalo are used for wetland vegetation management.

However, in uncontrolled circumstances, water buffalo can cause environmental damage, such as trampling vegetation, disturbing bird and reptile nesting sites, and spreading exotic weeds.

First Cloned Buffalo

The world's first cloned buffalo was developed by Indian scientists from National Dairy Research Institute, Karnal. The buffalo calf was named

Samrupa. The calf did not survive more than a week, and died due to some genetic disorders. So, the scientists created another cloned buffalo a few months later, and named it as Garima.

On 15 September 2007, the Philippines announced its development of Southeast Asia's first cloned buffalo. The Philippine Council for Agriculture, Forestry and Natural Resources Research and Development (PCARRD), under the Department of Science and Technology in Los Baños, Laguna approved this project. The Department of Agriculture's Philippine Carabao Center (PCC) will implement "Cloning through somatic cell nuclear transfer as a tool for genetic improvement in water buffaloes". 'Super buffalo calves' will be produced. There will be no modification or alteration of the genetic materials, as in genetically modified organisms (GMOs).

The Yoruban Orisha Oya (goddess of change) takes the form of a water buffalo.

Legend has it that the Chinese philosophical sage Lao Tzu left China through the Han Gu Pass riding a water buffalo.

According to Hindu lore, the god of death Yama, rides on a male water buffalo.

The carabao variant is considered as a national symbol in the Philippines.

In Vietnam, water buffalo are often the most valuable possession of poor farmers. They are treated as a member of the family. The husband ploughs, the wife sows, water buffalo draws the rake and are friends of the children. Children talk to their water buffalo. Vietnamese children are responsible for grazing water buffalo. They will feed them a lot of grasses if they work laboriously for men. In the old days, West Lake, Hà N had the name of Kim Nguu - Golden Water Buffalo.

'*Moh juj*': Water Buffalo fighting in Bhogali Bihu of Assam *Moh juj* is held every year in Bhogali Bihu in Assam. Ahotguri in Nagaon is famous for it.

'*Do Son*': Water Buffalo Fighting Festival of Vietnam is held each year on the 9th day of the 8th month of the lunar calendar at Do Son Township, Haiphong City in Vietnam. It is one of the most popular Vietnam festivals and events in Haiphong City. The preparations for this buffalo fighting festival begin right from the 5th and the 6th lunar month itself. The competing buffalo are selected and methodically trained months in advance. It is a traditional festival of Vietnam attached to a Water God worshipping ceremony and the 'Hien Sinh' custom to show martial spirit of the local people of Do Son, Haiphong.

'*Hai Luu*': Water Buffalo Fighting Festival of Vietnam According to ancient records, the buffalo fighting in Hai Luu Commune has existed from the 2nd century B.C. General Lu Gia at that time, had the buffalo slaughtered to give a feast to the local people and the warriors, and organized buffalo fighting for amusement. Eventually, all the fighting buffalo will be slaughtered as tributes to the deities.

'*Ko Samui*': Water Buffalo Fighting Festival of Thailand is a very popular event held on special occasions such as New Year's Day in January, and Songkran in mid-April, this festival features head-wrestling bouts in which two male Asian water buffalo are pitted against one another. Unlike in Spanish Bullfighting, wherein bulls get killed while fighting sword-wielding men, Buffalo Fighting Festival held at Ko Samui, Thailand is fairly harmless contest. The fighting season varies according to ancient customs and ceremonies. The first Buffalo to turn and run away is considered the loser, the winning buffalo becomes worth several million baht. Ko Samui is an island in the Gulf of Thailand in the South China Sea, it is 700 km from Bangkok and is connected to it by regular flights.

'*Ma'Pasilaga Tedong*': Water Buffalo Fighting Festival in Tana Toraja Regency of Sulawesi Island, Indonesia is a very popular event where the Rambu Solo' or a Burial Festival took place in Tana Toraja. It is very attractive moment before the buffalo are being sacrified.

Chon Buri: Water buffalo racing festival, Thailand: Thousands of people flock to this entertainment in downtown Chonburi, 70 km (44 miles) south of Bangkok, at the annual water buffalo festival. About 300 buffalo race in groups of five or six, spurred on by bareback jockeys wielding wooden sticks, as hundreds of spectators cheer. The water buffalo has always played an important role in agriculture in Thailand. For farmers of Chon Buri Province, near Bangkok, it is an important annual festival, beginning in mid-October. It is also a celebration among rice farmers before the rice harvest. At dawn, farmers walk their buffalo through surrounding rice fields, splashing them with water to keep them cool before leading them to the race field. This amazing festival started over a hundred years ago when two men arguing about whose buffalo was the fastest ended up having a race between them. That's how it became a tradition and gradually a social event for farmers who gathered from around the country in Chonburi to trade their goods. The festival also helps a great deal in preserving the number of buffalo, which have been dwindling at quite an alarming rate in other regions. Modern machinery is rapidly replacing buffalo in Thai agriculture. With most of the farm work mechanized, the buffalo-racing tradition has continued. Racing buffalo are now raised just to race; they do not work at all. The few farm buffalo which still do work are much bigger than the racers because of the strenuous work they perform. Farm buffalo are in the 'Buffalo Beauty Pageant', a Miss Farmer beauty contest and a comic buffalo costume contest etc. This festival perfectly exemplifies a favored Thai attitude to life — 'sanuk', meaning fun.

Babulang: Water buffalo racing festival, Sarawak, Malaysia: Babulang is the largest or grandest of the many rituals, ceremonies and festivals of the traditional Bisaya (Borneo) community of Limbang, Sarawak. Highlights are the Ratu Babulang competition and the Water buffalo races which can only be found in this town in Sarawak, Malaysia.

Vihear Suor village: Water buffalo racing festival, Cambodia: Each year, millions of Cambodians visit Buddhist temples across the country to honor their deceased loved ones during a 15-day period commonly known as the Festival of the Dead but in Vihear Suor village, about 22 miles (35 km) northeast of the capital of Cambodia, Phnom Penh, citizens each year wrap up the festival with a water buffalo race to entertain visitors and honour a pledge made hundreds of years ago. There was a time when many village cattle which provide rural Cambodians with muscle power to plough their fields and transport agricultural products died from an unknown disease. The villagers prayed to a spirit to help save their animals from the disease and promised to show their gratitude by holding a buffalo race each year on the last day of 'P'chum Ben' festival as it is known in Cambodian. The race draws hundreds of spectators who come to see riders and their animals charge down the racing field, the racers bouncing up and down on the backs of their buffalo, whose horns were draped with colourful cloth.

Karapan Sapi racing festival, Madura, Indonesia: The Maduranese people of the island of Madura, East Java, Indonesia, race their strongest and fastest buffalo in races hold regularly a few times a year, typically in August, September and October. It is a very popular spectacle in the towns of Pamekasan, Sampang, and Bangkalan. Besides the prize (and the pride that comes with it), buffalo that win a race are regarded very valuable and are a lot more expensive than their peers. This motivates the owners to feed their buffalo unusual cocktails of high calorie food composed of raw eggs, honey, and herbs, in addition to their regular training regimen, to give them the edge.

Kambala races, Karnataka, India: The Kambala water buffalo races of Karnataka, India take place between December and March. The races are conducted by having the water buffalo run in long parallel slushy ditches, where they are driven by men standing on wooden planks drawn by the buffaloes. The objectives of the race are to finish first and to raise the water to the greatest height.

9 Domestic Dog

The dog (*Canis lupus familiaris* and *Canis lupus dingo*) is a domesticated form of the gray wolf, a member of the Canidae family of the order Carnivora. The term is used for both feral and pet varieties. The dog was the first animal to be domesticated, and has been the most widely kept working, hunting, and companion animal in human history. The word 'dog' may also mean the male of a canine species, as opposed to the word 'bitch' for the female of the species.

Dogs were domesticated from gray wolves about 15,000 years ago. They must have been very valuable to early human settlements, for they quickly became ubiquitous across world cultures. Dogs perform many roles for people, such as hunting, herding, pulling loads, protection, assisting police and military, companionship, and, more recently, aiding handicapped individuals. This impact on human society has given them the nickname 'Man's best friend' in the western world. Currently, there are estimated to be 400 million dogs in the world.

Over the 15,000 year span the dog had been domesticated, it diverged into only a handful of landraces, groups of similar animals whose morphology and behaviour have been shaped by environmental factors and functional roles. Through selective breeding by humans, the dog has developed into hundreds of varied breeds, and shows more behavioural and morphological variation than any other land mammal. For example, height measured to the withers ranges from a few inches in the Chihuahua to a few feet in the Irish Wolfhound; colour varies from white through grays (usually called 'blue') to black, and browns from light (tan) to dark ('red' or 'chocolate') in a wide variation of patterns; coats can be short or long, coarse-haired to wool-like, straight, curly, or smooth. It is common for most breeds to shed this coat.

Dog is the common use term that refers to members of the subspecies *Canis lupus familiaris.* The term can also be used to refer to a wider range of related species, such as the members of the genus *Canis*, or 'true dogs', including the wolf, coyote, and jackals; or it can refer to the members of the subfamily Caninae, which would also include the African wild dog; or it can be used to refer to any member of the family Canidae, which would also include the foxes, bush dog, raccoon dog, and others. Some members of the family have 'dog' in their common names, such as the raccoon dog and the African wild dog. A few animals have 'dog' in their common names but are not canids, such as the prairie dog.

The English word *dog* comes from Middle English *dogge*, from Old English *docga*, a 'powerful dog breed'. The term may derive from Proto-Germanic *dukkon*, represented in Old English *finger-docce* ('finger-muscle'). The word also shows the familiar petname diminutive *-ga* also seen in *frogga* 'frog', *picga* 'pig', *stagga* 'stag', *wicga* 'beetle, worm', among others. Due to the archaic structure of the word, the term *dog* may ultimately derive from the earliest layer of Proto-Indo-European vocabulary, reflecting the role of the dog as the earliest domesticated animal.

In 14th century England, *hound* (from Old English: *hund*) was the general word for all domestic canines, and *dog* referred to a subtype of hound, a group including the mastiff. It is believed this 'dog' type of 'hound' was so common it eventually became the prototype of the category 'hound'. By the 16th century, *dog* had become the general word, and hound had begun to refer only to types used for hunting. *Hound*, cognate to German *Hund*, Dutch *hond*, common Scandinavian *hund*, and Icelandic *hundur*, is ultimately derived from the Proto-Indo-European **kwon-* 'dog', found in Welsh *ci* (plural *cwn*), Latin *canis*, Greek *kýon*, Lithuanian *šuõ*.

In breeding circles, a male canine is referred to as a *dog*, while a female is called a *bitch* (Middle English bicche, from Old English bicce, ultimately from Old Norse bikkja). A group of offspring is a *litter*. The father of a litter is called the *sire*, and the mother is called the *dam*. Offspring are generally called *pups* or *puppies*, from French *poupée*, until they are about a year old. The process of birth is *whelping*, from the Old English word *hwelp*, (cf. German Welpe, Dutch welp, Swedish valp, Icelandic hvelpur).

The domestic dog was originally classified as *Canis familiaris* and *Canis familiarus domesticus* by Carolus Linnaeus in 1758, and was reclassified in 1993 as *Canis lupus familiaris*, a subspecies of the gray wolf *Canis lupus*, by the Smithsonian Institution and the American Society of Mammalogists. Overwhelming evidence from behaviour, vocalizations, morphology, and molecular biology led to the contemporary scientific understanding that a single species, the gray wolf, is the common ancestor for all breeds of domestic dogs; however, the timeframe and mechanisms by which dogs diverged are controversial. *Canis lupus familiaris* is listed as the name for the taxon that is broadly used in the scientific community and recommended by ITIS; *Canis familiaris*, however, is a recognised synomym.

Domestic dogs inherited a complex social hierarchy and behaviours from their wolf ancestors. Dogs are pack hunters with a complex set of behaviours related to determining each dog's position in the social hierarchy, and they exhibit various postures and other means of nonverbal communication that reveal their states of mind. These sophisticated forms of social cognition and communication may account for their trainability, playfulness, and ability to fit into human households and social situations, and these attributes have earned dogs a unique relationship with humans, despite being potentially dangerous apex predators.

Although experts largely disagree over the details of dog domestication, it is agreed that human interaction played a significant role in shaping the subspecies. Shortly after domestication, dogs became ubiquitous in human populations, and spread throughout the world. Emigrants from Siberia likely crossed the Bering Strait with dogs in their company, and some experts suggest the use of sled dogs may have been critical to the success of the waves that entered North America roughly 12,000 years ago. Dogs were an important part of life for the Athabascan population in North America, and were their only domesticated animal. Dogs also carried much of the load in the migration of the Apache and Navajo tribes 1,400 years ago. Use of dogs as pack animals in these cultures often persisted after the introduction of the horse to North America.

The current consensus among biologists and archaeologists is that the dating of first domestication is indeterminate. There is conclusive evidence dogs genetically diverged from their wolf ancestors at least 15,000 years ago, but some believe domestication to have occurred earlier. It is not known whether humans domesticated the wolf as such to initiate dog's divergence from its ancestors, or whether dog's evolutionary path had already taken a different course prior to domestication. For example, it is hypothesized that some wolves gathered around the campsites of paleolithic camps to scavenge refuse, and associated evolutionary pressure developed that favoured those who were less frightened by, and keener in approaching, humans.

The bulk of the scientific evidence for the evolution of the domestic dog stems from archaeological findings and mitochondrial DNA studies.

The divergence date of roughly 15,000 years ago is based in part on archaeological evidence that demonstrates the domestication of dogs occurred more than 15,000 years ago, and some genetic evidence indicates the domestication of dogs from their wolf ancestors began in the late Upper Paleolithic close to the Pleistocene/Holocene boundary, between 17,000 and 14,000 years ago. But there is a wide range of other, contradictory findings that make this issue controversial.

Archaeological evidence suggests the latest dogs could have diverged from wolves was roughly 15,000 years ago, although it is possible they diverged much earlier. In 2008, a team of international scientists released findings from an excavation at Goyet Cave in Belgium declaring a large, toothy canine existed 31,700 years ago and ate a diet of horse, musk ox and reindeer.

Prior to this Belgium discovery, the earliest dog fossils were two large skulls from Russia and a mandible from Germany dated from roughly 14,000 years ago. Remains of smaller dogs from Natufian cave deposits in the Middle East, including the earliest burial of a human being with a domestic dog, have been dated to around 10,000 to 12,000 years ago. There is a great deal of archaeological evidence for dogs throughout Europe and Asia around this period and through the next two thousand years (roughly 8,000 to 10,000 years ago), with fossils uncovered in Germany, the French Alps, and Iraq, and cave paintings in Turkey. The oldest remains of a domesticated dog in the Americas were found in Texas and have been dated to about 9,400 years ago.

DNA Studies

DNA studies have provided a wider range of possible divergence dates, from 15,000 to 40,000 years ago, to as much as 100,000 to 140,000 years ago. This evidence depends on a number of assumptions that may be violated. Genetic studies are based on comparisons of genetic diversity between species, and depend on a calibration date. Some estimates of divergence dates from DNA evidence use an estimated wolf-coyote divergence date of roughly 700,000 years ago as a calibration. If this estimate is incorrect, and the actual wolf-coyote divergence is closer to one or two million years ago, or more, then the DNA evidence that supports specific dog-wolf divergence dates would be interpreted very differently.

Furthermore, it is believed the genetic diversity of wolves has been in decline for the last 200 years, and that the genetic diversity of dogs has been reduced by selective breeding. This could significantly bias DNA analyses to support an earlier divergence date. The genetic evidence for the domestication event occurring in East Asia is also subject to violations of assumptions. These conclusions are based on the location of maximal genetic divergence, and assume hybridization does not occur, and that breeds remain geographically localized. Although these assumptions hold for many species, there is good reason to believe that they do not hold for canines.

Genetic analyses indicate all dogs are likely descended from a handful of domestication events with a small number of founding females, although there is evidence domesticated dogs interbred with local populations of wild wolves on several occasions. Data suggest dogs first diverged from wolves in East Asia, and these domesticated dogs then quickly migrated throughout the world, reaching the North American continent around 8000 B.C. The oldest groups of dogs, which show the greatest genetic variability and are the most similar to their wolf ancestors, are primarily Asian and African breeds, including the Basenji, Lhasa Apso, and Siberian Husky. Some breeds thought to be very old, such as the Pharaoh Hound, Ibizan Hound, and Norwegian Elkhound, are now known to have been created more recently.

There is a great deal of controversy surrounding the evolutionary framework for the domestication of dogs. Although it is widely claimed that 'man domesticated the wolf', man may not have taken such a proactive role in the process. The nature of the interaction between man and wolf that led to domestication is unknown and controversial. At least three early species of the *Homo* genus began spreading out of Africa roughly 400,000 years ago, and thus lived for a considerable time in contact with canine species. Despite this, there is no evidence of any adaptation of canine species to the presence of the close relatives of modern man. If dogs were domesticated, as believed, roughly 15,000 years ago, the event (or events) would have coincided with a large expansion in human territory and the development of agriculture. This has led some biologists to suggest one of the forces that led to the domestication of dogs was a shift in human lifestyle in the form of established human settlements. Permanent settlements would have coincided with a greater amount of disposable food and would have created a barrier between wild and anthropogenic canine populations.

Wolves, and their dog descendants, would have derived significant benefits from living in human camps—more safety, more reliable food, lesser caloric needs, and more chance to breed. They would have benefited from humans' upright gait that gives them larger range over which to see potential predators and prey, as well as colour vision that, at least by day, gives humans better visual discrimination. Camp dogs would also have benefitted from human tool use, as in bringing down larger prey and controlling fire for a range of purposes.

Humans would also have derived enormous benefit from the dogs associated with their camps. For instance, dogs would have improved sanitation by cleaning up human waste and food scraps. Dogs may have provided warmth, as referred to in the Australian Aboriginal expression 'three dog night' (an exceptionally cold night), and they would have alerted the camp to the presence of predators or strangers, using their acute hearing to provide an early warning. Anthropologists believe the most significant benefit would have been the use of dogs' sensitive sense of smell to assist with the hunt. The relationship between the presence of a dog and success in the hunt is often mentioned as a primary reason for the domestication of the wolf, and a 2004 study of hunter groups with and without a dog gives quantitative support to the hypothesis that the benefits of cooperative hunting was an important factor in wolf domestication.

The cohabitation of dogs and humans would have greatly improved the chances of survival for early human groups, and the domestication of dogs may have been one of the key forces that led to human success.

"The most widespread form of interspecies bonding occurs between humans and dogs" and the keeping of dogs as companions, particularly by elites, has a long history. However, pet dog populations grew significantly after World War II as suburbanization increased. In the 1950s and 1960s, dogs were kept outside more often than they tend to be today (using the expression 'in the doghouse' to describe exclusion from the group signifies the distance between the doghouse and the home) and were still primarily functional, acting as a guard, children's playmate, or walking companion. From the 1980s, there have have been changes in the role of the pet dog, such as the increased role of dogs in the emotional support of their owners. People and dogs have become increasingly integrated and implicated in each other's lives, to the point where pet dogs actively shape the way a family and home are experienced.

There have been two major trends in the changing status of pet dogs. The first has been the 'commodification' of the dog, shaping it to conform to human expectations of personality and behaviour. The second has been the broadening of the concept of the family and the home to include dogs-as-dogs within everyday routines and practices.

There are a vast range of commodity forms available to transform a pet dog into an ideal companion. The list of goods, services and places available is enormous: from dog perfumes, couture, furniture and housing, to dog groomers, therapists, trainers and care-takers, dog cafes, spas, parks and beaches, and dog hotels, airlines and cemeteries. While dog training as an organized activity can be traced back to the 18th century, in the last decades of the 20th century it became a high profile issue as many normal dog behaviours such as barking, jumping up, digging, rolling in dung, fighting, and urine marking became increasingly incompatible with the new role of a pet dog. Dog training books, classes and television programmes proliferated as the process of commodifying the pet dog continued.

The majority of contemporary dog owners describe their dog as part of the family, although some ambivalence about the relationship is evident in the popular reconceptualisation of the dog-human family as a pack. A dominance model of dog-human relationships has been promoted by some dog trainers, such as on the television programme *Dog Whisperer*, however it has been disputed that 'trying to achieve status' is characteristic of dog–human interactions. Pet dogs play an active role in family life; for example, a study of conversations in dog-human families showed how family members use the dog as a resource, talking to the dog, or talking through the dog, to mediate their interactions with each other. Another study of dogs' roles in families showed many dogs have set tasks or routines undertaken as family members, the most common of which was helping with the washing-up by licking the plates in the dishwasher, and bringing in the newspaper from the lawn. Increasingly, human family members are engaging in activities centred on the perceived needs and interests of the dog, or in which the dog is an integral partner, such as Dog Dancing and Doga.

According to the statistics published by the American Pet Products Manufacturers Association in the National Pet Owner Survey in 2009-2010, it is estimated there are 77.5 million dog owners in the United States. The same survey shows nearly 40 per cent of American households own at least one dog, of which 67 per cent own just one dog, 25 per cent two dogs and nearly 9 per cent more than two dogs. There does not seem to be any gender preference among dogs as pets, as the statistical data reveal an equal number of female and male dog pets. Yet, although several programmes are undergoing to promote pet adoption, only nearly a fifth of the owned dogs come from a shelter.

Dogs have lived and worked with humans in so many roles that they have earned the unique nickname, 'man's best friend', a phrase which is used in other languages as well. They have been bred for herding livestock, hunting (*e.g.* pointers and hounds), rodent control, guarding, helping fishermen with nets, and pulling loads, in addition to their roles as companions.

Service dogs such as guide dogs, utility dogs, assistance dogs, hearing dogs, and psychological therapy dogs provide assistance to individuals with physical or mental disabilities. Some dogs owned by epileptics have been shown to alert their handler when the handler shows signs of an impending seizure, sometimes well in advance of onset, allowing the owner to seek safety, medication, or medical care.

Dogs included in human activities in terms of helping out humans are usually called working dogs. Dogs of several breeds are considered working dogs. Some working dog breeds include Akita, Alaskan Malamute, Anatolian Shepherd Dog, Bernese Mountain Dog, Black Russian Terrier, Boxer, Bullmastiff, Doberman Pinscher, Dogue de Bordeaux, German Pinscher, German Shepherd, Giant Schnauzer, Great Dane, Great Pyrenees, Great Swiss Mountain Dog, Komondor, Kuvasz, Mastiff, Neapolitan Mastiff, Newfoundland, Portuguese Water Dog, Rottweiler, Saint Bernard, Samoyed, Siberian Husky, Standard Schnauzer, and Tibetan Mastiff.

Based on their size and strength, these dogs are more suitable for a wide range of jobs rather than companions for average families. Moreover, most of these dogs have a different type of personality, usually more aggressive, which makes the relationship with their trainer safer when he is a professional and knows what type of behaviour to expect from such a dog. The working dogs are trained properly and accordingly to the activities they will perform. Yet, despite the size of some dogs, they are sometimes used as pets as well. However, they generally require special training and owners might have to learn how to bond with their pets, in these cases.

Some of these dogs are suitable for more than a single activity. For instance, Akita is a popular dog in the show ring, but its qualities make it a reliable animal in therapy work. The Alaskan Malamute is one of the most powerful and strong working dogs, and although some families have this type of breed as a pet, they are more likely to enjoy sledding, and performing different mountainous activities with their owners. The Anatolian Shepherd dog and the Black Russian Terrier are famous for their ability to work as guard dogs, being used to protect livestock. The Swiss Mountain dogs, Bullmastiffs and German Pinschers are suitable for carting, obedience, tracking and even therapy work.

Boxers are commonly used as service dogs for blind people because of their intelligence and alert expression. During war time, this type of dog was also used as a courier. Dobermans have proven themselves as great learners with an amazing capacity of retaining training, and as a result, they are commonly trained and used as police or war dogs. Some other types of breeds are easily trained for hunting or fighting, such as the Dogue de Bordeaux.

Sports and Shows

Owners of dogs often enter them in competitions such as breed conformation shows or sports, including racing and sledding.

In conformation shows, also referred to as breed shows, a judge familiar with the specific dog breed evaluates individual purebred dogs for conformity with their established breed type as described in the breed standard. As the breed standard only deals with the externally observable qualities of the dog (such as appearance, movement, and temperament), separately tested qualities (such as ability or health) are not part of the judging in conformation shows.

As a Food Source

Dog meat is consumed in some East Asian countries, including Korea, China, and Vietnam, a practice that dates back to antiquity. It is estimated that 13-16 million dogs are killed and consumed in Asia every year. The BBC claims that, in 1999, more than 6,000 restaurants served soups made from dog meat in South Korea. In Korea, the primary dog breed raised for meat, the *nureongi* , differs from those breeds raised for pets which Koreans may keep in their homes. The most popular Korean dog dish is *gaejang-guk* (also called *bosintang*), a spicy stew meant to balance the body's heat during the summer months; followers of the custom claim this is done to ensure good health by balancing one's *gi*, or vital energy of the body. A 19th century version of *gaejang-guk* explains that the dish is prepared by boiling dog meat with scallions and chili powder. Variations of the dish contain chicken and bamboo shoots. While the dishes are still popular in Korea with a segment of the population, dog is not as widely consumed as beef, chicken, and pork.

Other cultures, such as Polynesia and pre-Columbian Mexico, also consumed dog meat in their history. However, Western, South Asian, African, and Middle Eastern cultures generally regard consumption of dog meat as taboo. In some places, however, such as in rural areas of Poland, dog fat is believed to have medicinal properties—being good for the lungs for instance.

A CNN reportage in China dated March 2010 interviews a dog meat vendor who states that most of the dogs that are available for selling to restaurant are raised in special farms but that there is always a chance that a sold dog is someone's lost pet, although dog pet breeds are not considered edible.

Health Risks to Humans

In the USA, cats and dogs are a factor in more than 86,000 falls each year. It has been estimated around 2 per cent of dog-related injuries treated in UK hospitals are domestic accidents. The same study found that while dog involvement in road traffic accidents was difficult to quantify, dog-associated road accidents involving injury more commonly involved two-wheeled vehicles.

Toxocara canis (dog roundworm) eggs in dog feces can cause toxocariasis. In the United States, about 10,000 cases of *Toxocara* infection are reported in humans each year, and almost 14 per cent of the US population is infected. In Great Britain, 24 per cent of soil samples taken from public parks contained *T. canis* eggs. Untreated toxocariasis can cause retinal damage and decreased vision. Dog feces can also contain hookworms that cause cutaneous larva migrans in humans.

The incidence of dog bites, and especially fatal dog bites, is extremely rare in America considering the number of pet dogs in the country. Fatalities from dog bites occur in America at the rate of one per four million dogs. A Colorado study found bites in children were less severe than bites in adults. The incidence of dog bites in the US is 12.9 per 10,000 inhabitants, but for boys aged 5 to 9, the incidence rate is 60.7 per 10,000. Moreover, children have a much higher chance to be bitten in the face or neck. Sharp claws with powerful muscles behind them can lacerate flesh in a scratch that can lead to serious infections.

A growing body of research indicates the companionship of a dog can enhance human physical health and psychological well-being. Dog and cat owners have been shown to have better mental and physical health than non-owners, making fewer visits to the doctor and being less likely to be on medication than non-owners. In one study, new pet owners reported a highly significant reduction in minor health problems during the first month following pet acquisition, and this effect was sustained in dog owners through to the end of the study. In addition, dog owners took considerably more physical exercise than cat owners and people without pets. The group without pets exhibited no statistically significant changes in health or behaviour. The results provide evidence that pet acquisition may have positive effects on human health and behaviour, and that for dog owners these effects are relatively long term. Pet ownership has also been associated with increased coronary artery disease survival, with dog owners being significantly less likely to die within one year of an acute myocardial infarction than those who did not own dogs.

The health benefits of dogs can result from contact with dogs, not just from dog ownership. For example, when in the presence of a pet dog, people show reductions in cardiovascular, behavioural, and psychological indicators of anxiety. The benefits of contact with a dog also include social support, as dogs are able to not only provide companionship and social support themselves, but also to act as facilitators of social interactions between humans. One study indicated that wheelchair users experience more positive social interactions with strangers when they are accompanied by a dog than when they are not.

The practice of using dogs and other animals as a part of therapy dates back to the late 18th century, when animals were introduced into mental institutions to help socialize patients with mental disorders. Animal-assisted intervention research has shown that animal-assisted therapy with a dog can increase a person with Alzheimer's disease's social behaviours, such as smiling and laughing. One study demonstrated that children with ADHD and conduct disorders who participated in an education programme with dogs and other animals showed increased attendance, increased knowledge and skill objectives, and decreased antisocial and violent behaviour compared to those who were not in an animal-assisted programme.

Shelters

Every year, between 6 and 8 million dogs and cats enter US animal shelters. The Humane Society of the United States (HSUS) estimates that approximately 3 to 4 million dogs and cats are euthanized yearly in shelters across the United States. However, the percentage of dogs in US animal shelters that are eventually adopted and removed from the shelters by their new owners has increased since the mid 1990s from around 25 per cent up to around 60-75 per cent in the mid first decade of the 21st century.

Pets entering the shelters are euthanized in countries all over the world because of the lack of financial provisions to take care of these animals. Most shelters complain of not having enough resources to feed the pets and by being constrained to kill them, as the likelihood for all of them to find an owner is very small. In poor countries, euthanasia is usually violent.

Biology

Domestic dogs have been selectively bred for millennia for various behaviours, sensory capabilities, and physical attributes. Modern dog breeds show more variation in size, appearance, and behaviour than any other domestic animal. Nevertheless, their morphology is based on that of their wild ancestors, gray wolves. Dogs are predators and scavengers, and like many other predatory mammals, the dog has powerful muscles, fused wrist bones, a cardiovascular system that supports both sprinting and endurance, and teeth for catching and tearing. Dogs are highly variable in height and weight. The smallest known adult dog was a Yorkshire Terrier, that stood only 6.3 centimetres (2.5 in) at the shoulder, 9.5 cm (3.7 in) in length along the head-and-body, and weighed only 113 grams (4.0 oz). The largest known dog was an English Mastiff which weighed 155.6 kilograms (343 lb) and was 250 cm (98 in) from the snout to the tail. The tallest dog is a Great Dane that stands 106.7 cm (42.0 in) at the shoulder.

Like most mammals, dogs are dichromats and have colour vision equivalent to red-green colour blindness in humans (deuteranopia).

The dog's visual system has evolved to aid proficient hunting. While a dog's visual acuity is poor (that of a poodle's has been estimated to translate to a Snellen rating of 20/75), their visual discrimination for moving objects is very high; dogs have been shown to be able to discriminate between humans (e.g. identifying their owner) from distances up to a mile. As crepuscular hunters, dogs often rely on their vision in low light situations: they have very large pupils, a high density of rods in the fovea, an increased flicker rate, and a tapetum lucidum. The tapetum is a reflective surface behind the retina that reflects light back to give the photoreceptors a second chance to catch the photons.

The eyes of different breeds of dogs have different shapes, dimensions, and retina configurations. Many long-nosed breeds have a 'visual streak' — a wide foveal region that runs across the width of the retina and gives them a very wide field of excellent vision. Some long-muzzled breeds, particularly the sighthounds, have a field of vision up to 270° (compared to 180° for humans). Short-nosed breeds, on the other hand, have an 'area centralis': a central patch with up to three times the density of nerve endings as the visual streak, giving them detailed sight much more like a human's. Some broad-headed breeds with short noses have a field of vision similar to that of humans. Most breeds have good vision, but some show a genetic predisposition for myopia — such as Rottweilers, where one out of every two has been found to be myopic.

Hearing

The frequency range of dog hearing is approximately 40 Hz to 60,000 Hz, which means that dogs can detect sounds far beyond the upper limit of the human auditory spectrum. Additionally, dogs have ear mobility which allows them to rapidly pinpoint the exact location of a sound. Eighteen or more muscles can tilt, rotate, raise, or lower a dog's ear. A dog can identify a sound's location much faster than a human can, as well as hear sounds at four times the distance.

Smell

While the human brain is dominated by a large visual cortex, the dog brain is dominated by an olfactory cortex. The olfactory bulb in dogs is roughly forty times bigger than the olfactory bulb in humans, relative to total brain size, with 125 to 220 million smell-sensitive receptors. The bloodhound exceeds this standard with nearly 300 million receptors. Dogs can discriminate odours at concentrations nearly 100 million times lower than humans can. The wet nose is essential for determining the direction of the air current containing the smell. Cold receptors in the skin are sensitive to the cooling of the skin by evaporation of the moisture by air currents.

Physical Characteristics

The coats of domestic dogs are of two varieties: 'double' being common with dogs (as well as wolves) originating from colder climates, made up of a coarse guard hair and a soft down hair, or 'single', with the topcoat only.

Domestic dogs often display the remnants of countershading, a common natural camouflage pattern. A countershaded animal will have dark coloring on its upper surfaces and light coloring below, which reduces its general visibility. Thus many breeds will have an occasional 'blaze', stripe, or 'star' of white fur on their chest or underside.

Tail

There are many different shapes for dog tails: straight, straight up, sickle, curled, or cork-screw. In some breeds, the tail is traditionally docked to avoid injuries (especially for hunting dogs). In some breeds, puppies can be born with a short tail or no tail at all. This occurs more frequently in those breeds that are frequently docked and thus have no breed standard regarding the tail.

While all dogs are genetically very similar, natural selection and selective breeding have reinforced certain characteristics in certain populations of dogs, giving rise to dog types and dog breeds. Dog types are broad categories based on function, genetics, or characteristics. Dog breeds are groups of animals that possess a set of inherited characteristics that distinguishes them from other animals within the same species. Modern dog breeds are non-scientific classifications of dogs kept by modern kennel clubs. Purebred dogs of one breed are genetically distinguishable from purebred dogs of other breeds, but the means by which kennel clubs classify dogs is unsystematic. Systematic analyses of the dog genome has revealed only four major types of dogs that can be said to be statistically distinct. These include the 'old world dogs' (e.g., Malamute and Shar Pei), 'Mastiff'-type (e.g., English Mastiff), 'herding'-type (e.g., Border Collie), and 'all others' (also called 'modern'- or 'hunting'-type).

Dogs are susceptible to various diseases, ailments, and poisons, some of which can affect humans. To defend against many common diseases, dogs are often vaccinated.

Some breeds of dogs are prone to certain genetic ailments such as elbow or hip dysplasia, blindness, deafness, pulmonic stenosis, cleft palate, and trick knees. Two serious medical conditions particularly affecting dogs are pyometra, affecting unspayed females of all types and ages, and bloat, which affects the larger breeds or deep-chested dogs. Both of these are acute conditions, and can kill rapidly. Dogs are also susceptible to parasites such as fleas, ticks, and mites, as well as hookworm, tapeworm, roundworm, and heartworm.

Dogs are highly susceptible to theobromine poisoning, typically from ingestion of chocolate. Theobromine is toxic to dogs because although the dog's metabolism is capable of breaking down the chemical, the process is so slow that even small amounts of chocolate can be fatal, especially dark chocolate.

Dogs are also vulnerable to some of the same health conditions as humans, including diabetes, dental and heart disease, epilepsy, cancer, hypothyroidism, and arthritis.

Mortality

The typical lifespan of dogs varies widely among breeds, but for most the median longevity, the age at which half the dogs in a population have died and half are still alive, ranges from 10 to 13 years. Individual dogs may live well beyond the median of their breed.

The breed with the shortest lifespan (among breeds for which there is a questionnaire survey with a reasonable sample size) is the Dogue de Bordeaux, with a median longevity of about 5.2 years, but several breeds, including Miniature Bull Terriers, Bloodhounds, and Irish Wolfhounds are nearly as short-lived, with median longevities of 6 to 7 years.

The longest-lived breeds, including Toy Poodles, Japanese Spitz, Border Terriers, and Tibetan Spaniels, have median longevities of 14 to 15 years. The median longevity of Mixed-breed dogs, taken as an average of all sizes, is one or more years longer than that of purebred dogs when all breeds are averaged. The dog widely reported to be the longest-lived is 'Bluey', who died in 1939 and was claimed to be 29.5 years old at the time of his death; however, the Bluey record is anecdotal and unverified. The longest verified records are of dogs living for 24 years.

Predation

Although wild dogs, like wolves, are apex predators, they can be killed in territory disputes with wild animals. Furthermore, in areas where both dogs and other large predators live, dogs can be a major food source for big cats or canines. Reports from Croatia indicate that dogs are killed by wolves more frequently than sheep. Wolves in Russia apparently limit feral dog populations. In Wisconsin, more compensation has been paid for dog losses than livestock. Some wolf pairs have been reported to prey on dogs by having one wolf lure the dog out into heavy brush where the second animal waits in ambush. In some instances, wolves have displayed an uncharacteristic fearlessness of humans and buildings when attacking dogs, to the extent that they have to be beaten off or killed. Coyotes and big cats have also been known to attack dogs. Leopards in particular are known to have a predilection for dogs, and have been recorded to kill and consume them regardless of the dog's size or ferocity. Tigers in Manchuria, Indochina, Indonesia, and Malaysia, are reputed to kill dogs with the same vigour as leopards. Striped Hyenas are major predators of village dogs in Turkmenistan, India, and the Caucasus. Reptiles such as alligators and pythons have been known to kill and eat dogs.

Despite their descent from wolves and classification as Carnivora, dogs are variously described in scholarly and other writings as carnivores or omnivores. Unlike obligate carnivores, such as the cat family with its shorter small intestine, dogs can adapt to a wide-ranging diet, and are not dependent on meat-specific protein nor a very high level of protein in order to fulfill their basic dietary requirements. Dogs will healthily digest a variety of foods, including vegetables and grains, and can consume a large proportion of these in their diet.

A number of common human foods and household ingestibles are toxic to dogs, including chocolate solids (theobromine poisoning), onion and garlic (thiosulphate, sulfoxide or disulfide poisoning), grapes and raisins, macadamia nuts, as well as various plants and other potentially ingested materials.

In domestic dogs, sexual maturity begins to happen around age six to twelve months for both males and females, although this can be delayed until up to two years old for some large breeds. This is the time at which female dogs will have their first estrous cycle. They will experience subsequent estrous cycles biannually, during which the body prepares for pregnancy. At the peak of the cycle, females will come into estrus, being mentally and physically receptive to copulation. Because the ova survive and are capable of being fertilized for a week after ovulation, it is possible for a female to mate with more than one male.

Dogs bear their litters roughly 56 to 72 days after fertilization, with an average of 63 days, although the length of gestation can vary. An average litter consists of about six puppies, though this number may vary widely based on the breed of dog. Toy dogs generally produce from one to four puppies in each litter, while much larger breeds may average as many as twelve.

Some dog breeds have acquired traits through selective breeding that interfere with reproduction. Male French Bulldogs, for instance, are incapable of mounting the female. For many dogs of this breed, the female must be artificially inseminated in order to reproduce.

Neutering

Neutering refers to the sterilization of animals, usually by removal of the male's testicles or the female's ovaries and uterus, in order to eliminate the ability to procreate and reduce sex drive. Because of the overpopulation of dogs in some countries, many animal control agencies, such as the American Society for the Prevention of Cruelty to Animals (ASPCA), advise that dogs not intended for further breeding should be neutered, so that they do not have undesired puppies that may have to later be euthanized.

According to the Humane Society of the United States, 3-4 million dogs and cats are put down each year in the United States and many more are confined to cages in shelters because there are many more animals than there are homes. Spaying or castrating dogs helps keep overpopulation down. Local humane societies, SPCAs, and other animal protection organizations urge people to neuter their pets and to adopt animals from shelters instead of purchasing them.

Neutering reduces problems caused by hypersexuality, especially in male dogs. Spayed female dogs are less likely to develop some forms of cancer, affecting mammary glands, ovaries, and other reproductive organs. However, neutering increases the risk of urinary incontinence in female dogs, and prostate cancer in males, as well as osteosarcoma, hemangiosarcoma, cruciate ligament rupture, obesity, and diabetes mellitus in either gender.

The domestic dog has a predisposition to exhibit a social intelligence that is uncommon in the animal world. Dogs are capable of learning in a number of ways, such as through simple reinforcement (*e.g.* classical or operant conditioning) and by observation.

Dogs go through a series of stages of cognitive development. As with humans, the understanding that objects not being actively perceived still remain in existence (called object permanence) is not present at birth. It develops as the young dog learns to interact intentionally with objects around it, at roughly 8 weeks of age.

Puppies learn behaviours quickly by following examples set by experienced dogs. This form of intelligence is not peculiar to those tasks dogs have been bred to perform, but can be generalized to myriad abstract problems. For example, Dachshund puppies who watched an experienced dog pull a cart by tugging on an attached piece of ribbon in order to get a reward from inside the cart learned the task fifteen times faster than those who were left to solve the problem on their own. Dogs can also learn by mimicking human behaviours. In one study, puppies were presented with a box, and shown that when a handler pressed a lever, a ball would roll out of the box. The handler then allowed the puppy to play with the ball, making it an intrinsic reward. The pups were then allowed to interact with the box. Roughly three-quarters of the puppies subsequently touched the lever, and over half successfully released the ball, compared to only 6 per cent in a control group that did not watch the human manipulate the lever. Another study found that handing an object between experimenters who then used the object's name in a sentence successfully taught an observing dog each object's name, allowing the dog to subsequently retrieve the item.

Dogs also demonstrate sophisticated social cognition by associating behavioural cues with abstract meanings. One such class of social cognition involves the understanding that others are conscious agents. Research has shown that dogs are capable of interpreting subtle social cues, and appear to recognize when a human or dog's attention is focussed on them. To test this, researchers devised a task in which a reward was hidden underneath one of two buckets. The experimenter then attempted to communicate with the dog to indicate the location of the reward by using a wide range of signals: tapping the bucket, pointing to the bucket, nodding to the bucket, or simply looking at the bucket. The results showed that domestic dogs were better than chimpanzees, wolves, and human infants at this task, and even young puppies with limited exposure to humans performed well.

Psychology research has shown that human faces are asymmetrical with the gaze instinctively moving to the right side of a face upon encountering other humans to obtain information about their emotions and state. Research at the University of Lincoln (2008) shows that dogs share this instinct when meeting a human being, and only when meeting a human being (*i.e.*, not other animals or other dogs). As such they are the only non-primate species known to do so.

Dr. Stanley Coren, an expert on dog psychology, states that these results demonstrated the social cognition of dogs can exceed that of even our closest genetic relatives, and that this capacity is a recent genetic acquisition which distinguishes the dog from its ancestor, the wolf. Studies have also investigated whether dogs engaged in partnered play change their behaviour depending on the attention-state of their partner. Those studies showed that play signals were only sent when the dog was holding the attention of its partner. If the partner was distracted, the dog instead engaged in attention-getting behaviour before sending a play signal.

Dr. Coren has also argued that dogs demonstrate a sophisticated theory of mind by engaging in deception, which he supports with a number of anecdotes, including one example where a dog hid a stolen treat by sitting on it until the rightful owner of the treat left the room. Although this could have been accidental, Coren suggests that the thief understood that the treat's owner would be unable to find the treat if it were out of view. Together, the empirical data and anecdotal evidence points to dogs possessing at least a limited form of theory of mind.

A study found a third of dogs suffered from anxiety when separated from others.

A Border Collie named Chaser has learned the names for 1,022 toys after three years of training. It is more than Rico done before and also so many that her human handlers had to write on them in marker so that they wouldn't forget.

Although dogs have been the subject of a great deal of behaviourist psychology (*e.g.* Pavlov's dog), they do not enter the world with a psychological 'blank slate'. Rather, dog behaviour is affected by genetic factors as well as environmental factors. Domestic dogs exhibit a number of behaviours and predispositions that were inherited from wolves. The Gray Wolf is a social animal that has evolved a sophisticated means of communication and social structure. The domestic dog has inherited some of these predispositions, but many of the salient characteristics in dog behaviour have been largely shaped by selective breeding by humans. Thus some of these characteristics, such as the dog's highly developed social cognition, are found only in primitive forms in grey wolves.

The existence and nature of personality traits in dogs have been studied (15329 dogs of 164 different breeds) and five consistent and stable 'narrow traits' identified, described as playfulness, curiosity/fearlessness, chase-proneness, sociability and aggressiveness. A further higher order axis for shyness–boldness was also identified.

Dog Growl

A new study in Budapest, Hungary has found that dogs are able to tell how big another dog is just by listening to its growl. A specific growl used by dogs to protect their food. The research also shows that dogs do not lie about their size, and this is the first time research has shown animals can determine another's size by the sound it makes. The test used image of many kind of dogs and together showed a small and big dog and also a growl. The result, showed that 20 of the 24 test dogs looked at the image of the appropriate-sized dog first and looked at it longest.

Compared to equally sized wolves, dogs tend to have 20 per cent smaller skulls, 30 per cent smaller brains, as well as proportionately smaller teeth than other canid species. Dogs require fewer calories to function than wolves. It is thought by certain experts that the dog's limp ears are a result of atrophy of the jaw muscles. The skin of domestic dogs tends to be thicker than that of wolves, with some Inuit tribes favoring the former for use as clothing due to its greater resistance to wear and tear in harsh weather. The paws of a dog are half the size of those of a wolf, and their tails tend to curl upwards, another trait not found in wolves.

Behaviour

Dogs tend to be poorer than wolves at observational learning, being more responsive to instrumental conditioning. Feral dogs show little of the complex social structure or dominance hierarchy present in wolf packs. For example, unlike wolves, the dominant alpha pairs of a feral dog pack do not force the other members to wait for their turn on a meal when scavenging off a dead ungulate as the whole family is free to join in. For dogs, other members of their kind are of no help in locating food items, and are more like competitors. Feral dogs are primarily scavengers, with studies showing that unlike their wild cousins, they are poor ungulate hunters, having little impact on wildlife populations where they are sympatric. However, feral dogs have been reported to be effective hunters of reptiles in the Galápagos Islands, and free ranging pet dogs are more prone to predatory behaviour toward wild animals.

Despite common belief, domestic dogs can be monogamous. Breeding in feral packs can be, but does not have to be restricted to a dominant alpha pair (despite common belief, such things also occur in wolf packs). Male dogs are unusual among canids by the fact that they mostly seem to play no role in raising their puppies, and do not kill the young of other females to increase their own reproductive success. Some sources say that dogs differ from wolves and most other large canid species by the fact that they do not regurgitate food for their young, nor the young of other dogs in the same territory.

However, this difference was not observed in all domestic dogs. Regurgitating of food by the females for the young as well as care for the young by the males has been observed in domestic dogs, dingos as well as in other feral or semi-feral dogs. Regurgitating of food by the females and direct choosing of only one mate has been observed even in those semi-feral dogs of direct domestic dog ancestry. Also regurgitating of food by males has been observed in free-ranging domestic dogs.

Trainability

Dogs display much greater tractability than tame wolves, and are generally much more responsive to coercive techniques involving fear, aversive stimuli, and force than wolves, which are most responsive toward positive conditioning and rewards. Unlike tame wolves, dogs tend to respond more to voice than hand signals.

10 Llama

The llama (*Lama glama*) is a South American camelid, widely used as a pack and meat animal by Andean cultures since pre-hispanic times.

The height of a full-grown, full-size llama is between 1.7 meters (5.5 ft) and 1.8 meters (6 ft) tall at the top of the head. They can weigh between approximately 130 kilograms (280 lb) and 200 kilograms (450 lb). At birth, a baby llama (called a *cria*) can weigh between 9.1 kilograms (20 lb) and 14 kilograms (30 lb). Llamas are very social animals and like to live with other llamas as a herd. Overall, the fibre produced by a llama is very soft and is naturally lanolin free. Llamas are intelligent and can learn simple tasks after a few repetitions. When using a pack, llamas can carry about 25 per cent to 30 per cent of their body weight for several miles.

Llamas appear to have originated from the central plains of North America about 40 million years ago. They migrated to South America about 3 million years ago. By the end of the last ice age (10,000-12,000 years ago) camelids were extinct in North America. As of 2007, there were over 7 million llamas and alpacas in South America and, due to importation from South America in the late 20th century, there are now over 158,000 llamas and 100,000 alpacas in the US and Canada.

Although early writers compared llamas to sheep, their similarity to the camel was soon recognized. They were included in the genus *Camelus* along with alpaca in the *Systema Naturae* (1758) of Linnaeus. They were, however, separated by Cuvier in 1800 under the name of *llama* along with the guanaco. Alpacas and vicuñas are in genus *Vicugna*. The genera *Lama* and *Vicugna* are, with the two species of true camels, the sole existing representatives of a very distinct section of the Artiodactyla or even-toed ungulates, called Tylopoda, or "bump-footed," from the peculiar bumps on the soles of their feet. The Tylopoda consists of a single family, the Camelidae, and shares the order Artiodactyla with the Suina (pigs), the Tragulina (chevrotains), the Pecora (ruminants), and the Cetancodonta (hippos and cetaceans, which belong to Artiodactyla from a cladistic if not traditional standpoint). The Tylopoda have more or less affinity to each of the sister taxa, standing in some respects in a middle position between them, sharing some characteristics from each, but in others showing special modifications not found in any of the other taxa.

The 19th century discoveries of a vast and previously unexpected extinct Tertiary fauna of North America, as interpreted by palaeontologists Leidy, Cope, and Marsh, aided understanding of the early history of this family. Llamas were not always confined to South America; abundant llama-like remains were found in Pleistocene deposits in the Rocky Mountains and in Central America. Some of the fossil llamas were much larger than current forms. Some species remained in North America during the last ice ages. North American llamas are categorized as a single extinct genus, *Hemiauchenia.* Llama-like animals would have been a common sight in 25,000 years ago, in modern-day California, Texas, New Mexico, Utah, Missouri, and Florida.

The camelid lineage has a good fossil record. Camel-like animals have been traced from the thoroughly differentiated modern species back through early Miocene forms. Their characteristics became more general, and they lost those that distinguished them as camelids; hence they were classified as ancestral artiodactyls. No fossils of these earlier forms have been found in the Old World, indicating that North America was the original home of camelids, and that Old World camels crossed over via the Bering land bridge. The formation of the Isthmus of Panama three million years ago allowed camelids to spread to South America as part of the Great American Interchange, where they evolved further. Meanwhile, North American camelids died out at the end of the Pleistocene.

The following characteristics apply especially to llamas.

Dentition of adults: Incisors 1/3 canines 1/1, premolars 2/2, molars 3/2; total 32. In the upper jaw there is a compressed, sharp, pointed laniariform incisor near the hinder edge of the premaxilla, followed in the male at least by a moderate-sized, pointed, curved true canine in the anterior part of the maxilla. The isolated canine-like premolar which follows in the camels is not present. The teeth of the molar series which are in contact with each other consist of two very small premolars (the first almost rudimentary) and three broad molars, constructed generally like those of

Camelus. In the lower jaw, the three incisors are long, spatulate, and procumbent; the outer ones are the smallest. Next to these is a curved, suberect canine, followed after an interval by an isolated minute and often deciduous simple conical premolar; then a contiguous series of one premolar and three molars, which differ from those of *Camelus* in having a small accessory column at the anterior outer edge.

The skull generally resembles that of *Camelus*, the larger brain-cavity and orbits and less developed cranial ridges being due to its smaller size. The nasal bones are shorter and broader, and are joined by the premaxilla.

The ears are rather long and slightly curved inward, characteristically known as 'banana' shaped. There is no dorsal hump. Feet are narrow, the toes being more separated than in the camels, each having a distinct plantar pad. The tail is short, and fibre is long, woolly and soft.

In essential structural characteristics, as well as in general appearance and habits, all the animals of this genus very closely resemble each other, so that whether they should be considered as belonging to one, two, or more species is a matter of controversy among naturalists.

The question is complicated by the circumstance of the great majority of individuals which have come under observation being either in a completely or partially domesticated state. Many are also descended from ancestors which have previously been domesticated; a state which tends to produce a certain amount of variation from the original type. The four forms commonly distinguished by the inhabitants of South America are recognized as distinct species, though with difficulties in defining their distinctive characteristics.

These are:

- the llama, *Lama glama* (Linnaeus);
- the alpaca, *Vicugna pacos* (Linnaeus);
- the guanaco (from the Quechua 'huanaco'), *Lama guanicoe* (Müller); and
- the vicuña, *Vicugna vicugna* (Molina).

The llama and alpaca are only known in the domestic state, and are variable in size and of many colours, being often white, brown, or piebald. Some are grey or black. The guanaco and vicuña are wild, the former being endangered, and of a nearly uniform light-brown colour, passing into white below. They certainly differ from each other, the vicuña being smaller, more slender in its proportions, and having a shorter head than the guanaco. The vicuña lives in herds on the bleak and elevated parts of the mountain range bordering the region of perpetual snow, amidst rocks and precipices, occurring in various suitable localities throughout Peru, in the southern part of Ecuador, and as far south as the middle of Bolivia. Its manners very much resemble those of the chamois of the European Alps; it is as vigilant, wild, and timid. The fiber is extremely delicate and soft, and highly valued for the purposes of weaving, but the quantity which each animal produces is minimal. Alpaca are descended from a wild vicuna ancestor while the domesticated llama is descended from a wild guanaco ancestor, though at this point there has been a considerable amount of hybridization between the two species.

Differentiating characteristics between llamas and alpacas include the llama's larger size and longer head. Alpaca fibre is generally more expensive but not always more valuable. Alpacas tend to have a more consistent colour throughout the body. The most apparent visual difference between llamas and camels is that camels have a hump or humps and llamas do not.

Llamas have an unusual reproductive cycle for a large animal. Female llamas are induced ovulators. Through the act of mating, the female releases an egg and is often fertilized on the first attempt. Female llamas do not go into 'heat' or have an estrus cycle.

Like humans, llama males and females mature sexually at different rates. Females reach puberty at approximately 12 months. However, males do not become sexually mature until approximately 3 years.

Mating

Llamas mate with the female in a kush (lying down) position, which is fairly unusual in a large animal. They mate for an extended period of time (20-45 minutes), also unusual in a large animal.

Gestation

The gestation period of a llama is 11½ months (350 days). Dams (female llamas) do not lick off their babies, as they have an attached tongue which does not reach outside of the mouth more than half an inch. Rather, they will nuzzle and hum to their newborns.

Crias

A cria (from Spanish, pronounced *cree-ah*, meaning 'baby') is the name for a baby llama (also alpaca, vicuña, or guanaco). Crias are typically born with all the females of the herd gathering around, in an attempt to protect against the male llamas and potential predators. Llamas give birth standing. Birth is usually quick and problem free, over in less than 30 minutes. Most births take place between 8 a.m. and noon, during the warmer daylight hours. This may increase cria survival by reducing fatalities due to hypothermia during cold Andean nights. While unproven, it is speculated that this birthing pattern is a continuation of the birthing patterns observed in the wild. Crias are up and standing, walking and attempting to nurse within the first hour after birth. Crias are partially fed with llama milk that is lower in fat and salt and higher in phosphorus and calcium than cow or goat milk. A female llama will only produce about 60 ml (2.1 imp fl oz) of milk at a time when she gives milk. For this reason, the cria must suckle frequently to receive the nutrients it requires.

BREEDING SITUATIONS

Harem Breeding

Male is left with females most of the year.

Field Breeding

A female is turned out into a field with a male llama and left there for some period of time. This is the easiest method in terms of labour, but the least useful in terms of prediction of a likely birth date. An ultrasound test can be performed and together with the exposure dates a better idea when the cria is expected can be determined.

Hand Breeding

This is the most efficient method, but requires the most work on the part of the human involved. A male and female llama are put into the same pen and breeding is monitored. They are then separated and rebred every other day until one or the other refuses the breeding. Usually one can get in two breedings using this method, though some studs have routinely refused to breed a female more than once. The separation presumably helps to keep the sperm count high for each breeding and also helps to keep the condition of the female llama's reproductive tract more sound. If the breeding is not successful within two to three weeks, the female is rebred once again.

Llamas should be tested for pregnancy after breeding at 2-3 weeks, 6 weeks, and at least 12 weeks.

PREGNANCY TESTING

Spit Testing

Bring the potentially pregnant dam to an intact male. If the stud attempts to mate with her and she lies down for him within a fairly short period of time, she is *not* pregnant. If she remains on her feet, spits, attacks him, or otherwise prevents his being able to mate, it is assumed that she is probably pregnant. This test gets its name due to the dam spitting at the male if she is pregnant.

Progesterone Testing

A veterinarian can take a blood sample test for progesterone. A high level can indicate a pregnancy.

Palpation

In this test, the veterinarian or breeder manually feels inside the llama to detect a pregnancy. There are some risks to the llama, but it can be an accurate method for pregnancy detection.

Ultrasound

This is the most accurate method in the hands of an experienced veterinarian. A veterinarian experienced with ultrasound can do an exterior exam and detect a fetus as early as 45 days.

Spit testing with an intact male is generally free and is usually accurate. However, some hormonal conditions in females can make them reject a male when they are in fact not pregnant, and, more rarely, accept a male when they are pregnant. Progesterone tests can give a high reading in some females with a hormonal problem who are in fact not pregnant. Neither of the previous methods, nor palpation, can give you a reasonably accurate idea of the age of the fetus, while an ultrasound procedure can. In addition, an ultrasound procedure can distinguish between pregnancy and misleading physical conditions, or between a live and dead fetus. The big disadvantage of an ultrasound procedure is that some training in the use of ultrasound equipment is required, and not all veterinarians have the equipment needed to perform the examination.

Llamas which are well-socialized and trained to halter and lead after weaning are very friendly and pleasant to be around. They are extremely curious and most will approach people easily. However, llamas that are bottle-fed or over-socialised and over-handled as youngsters will become extremely difficult to handle when mature, when they will begin to treat humans as they treat each other, which is characterized by bouts of spitting, kicking and neck wrestling. Anyone having to bottle-feed a cria should keep contact to a minimum and stop as soon as possible.

When correctly reared spitting at a human is a rare thing. Llamas are very social herd animals, however, and do sometimes spit at each other as a way of disciplining lower-ranked llamas in the herd. A llama's social rank in a herd is never static. They can always move up or down in the social ladder by picking small fights. This is usually done between males to see who will become alpha. Their fights are visually dramatic with spitting, ramming each other with their chests, neck wrestling and kicking, mainly to knock the other off balance. The females are usually only seen spitting as a means of controlling other herd members.

While the social structure might always be changing, they live as a family and they do take care of each other. If one notices a strange noise or feels threatened, a warning bray is sent out and all others come to alert. They will often hum to each other as a form of communication.

The sound of the llama making groaning noises or going 'mwa' is often a sign of fear or anger. If a llama is agitated, it will lay its ears back. One may determine how agitated the llama is by the materials in the spit. The more irritated the llama is, the further back into each of the three stomach compartments it will try to draw materials from for its spit.

An 'orgle' is the mating sound of a llama or alpaca, made by the sexually aroused male. The sound is reminiscent of gargling, but with a more forceful, buzzing edge. Males begin the sound when they become aroused and continue throughout the act of procreation—from 15 minutes to more than an hour.

Using llamas as livestock guards in North America began in the early 1980s and some sheep producers have used llamas successfully for that entire time. The use of guard llamas has greatly increased since a magazine article in 1990, when national attention was drawn to the potential use of llamas for guarding sheep. The ideal guard animal should protect sheep against predation while requiring minimal training, care, and maintenance. It should stay with and not disrupt the flock, and live long enough to be cost effective. A variety of guard animals currently in use include dogs, donkeys, kangaroos, ostriches, and llamas. Of these, guard dogs are still the most common; guard llamas number only in the hundreds. Studies have proven that llamas are successfully being used as guard animals for herds of sheep, goats, alpacas and other livestock throughout North America. Protection of the herd and easy maintenance are the two most commonly cited advantages. Llamas are introduced to a herd and are pastured with them; they do not require separate shelters. Ideally, a llama should be introduced to the sheep while they are in a corral or small pasture rather than on open range or large pasture. The llama should remain in a small area until the sheep and llama seem well-adjusted and attached to each other. This encourages bonding between the sheep and llama. A llama introduced in this manner will be more effective as a guard against predators.

Research suggests the use of multiple guard llamas is not as effective as one llama. Multiple male llamas tend to bond with one another, rather than with the livestock, and may ignore the flock. A gelded male of two years of age bonds closely with its new charges and is instinctively very effective in preventing predation. Some llamas appear to bond more quickly to sheep or goats if they are introduced just prior to lambing. Many sheep and goat producers indicate a special bond quickly develops between lambs and their guard llama and that the llama is particularly protective of the lambs.

Using llamas as guards has eliminated the losses to predators for many producers. The value of the livestock saved each year more than exceeds the purchase cost and annual maintenance of a llama. Although not every llama is suited to the job, most llamas are a viable, non-lethal alternative for reducing predation, requiring no training and little care.

The Moche people frequently placed llamas and llama parts in the burials of important people, as offerings or provisions for the afterlife. The Moche culture of pre-Columbian Peru depicted llamas quite realistically in their ceramics.

Inca Empire

In the Inca empire llamas were the only beasts of burden, and many of the peoples dominated by the Inca had long traditions of llama herding. For the Inca nobility the llama were of symbolical signicance and llama figures were often buried with the dead. In South America llamas are still used as beasts of burden, as well as for the production of fibre and meat.

The Inca deity Urcuchillay was depicted in the form of a multi-coloured llama.

Spanish Empire

One of the main uses for llamas at the time of the Spanish conquest was to bring down ore from the mines in the mountains. Gregory de Bolivar estimated that in his day, as many as three hundred thousand were employed in the transport of produce from the Potosí mines alone, but since the introduction of horses, mules, and donkeys, the importance of the llama as a beast of burden has greatly diminished.

According to Juan Ignacio Molina the Dutch captain Joris van Spilbergen observed the use of chiliquenes (a llama type) by native Mapuches of Mocha Island as plough animals in 1614.

Fibre

Llamas have a fine undercoat which can be used for handicrafts and garments. The coarser outer guard hair is used for rugs, wall-hangings and lead ropes. The fibre comes in many different colours ranging from white, grey, reddish brown, brown, dark brown and black.

11 Donkey

The donkey or ass, *Equus africanus asinus*, is a domesticated member of the Equidae or horse family. The wild ancestor of the donkey is the African Wild Ass, *E. africanus*. In the western United States, a small donkey is sometimes called a *burro* (from the Spanish word for the animal).

A male donkey or ass is called a jack, a female a jenny, and offspring less than one year old, a foal (male: colt, female filly).

While different species of the Equidae family can interbreed, offspring are almost always sterile. Nonetheless, horse/donkey hybrids are popular for their durability and vigour. A mule is the offspring of a jack (male donkey) and a mare (female horse). The much rarer successful mating of a male horse and a female donkey produces a hinny.

Asses were first domesticated around 3000 BC, approximately the same time as the horse, and have spread around the world. They continue to fill important roles in many places today and domesticated species are increasing in numbers, but the African wild ass and another relative, the Onager, are endangered. As 'beasts of burden' and companions, asses and donkeys have worked together with humans for millennia.

Jennies are normally pregnant for about 12 months, though the gestation period varies from 11 to almost 14 months. Jennies usually give birth to a single foal. Twins are very rare: only about 1.7 per cent of donkey pregnancies result in twins, and both twins survive in only about 14 per cent of cases.

Donkeys vary considerably in size, depending on breed and management. Most domestic donkeys range from 9 to 14.2 hands (36 to 58 inches, 91 to 147 cm), though the Mammoth Jack breed is taller, and the Andalucian-Cordobesan breed of southern Spain can reach up to 15.2 hands (62 inches, 157 cm)high. Donkeys have a lifespan of 30 to 50 years.

Donkeys are adapted to marginal desert lands, and have many traits that are unique to the species as a result. Wild donkeys live separated from each other, unlike tight wild horse and feral horse herds. Donkeys have developed very loud vocalizations, which help keep in contact with other donkeys over the wide spaces of the desert. The best-known call is referred to as a 'bray', which can be heard for over three kilometers. Donkeys have larger ears than horses. Their longer ears may pick up more distant sounds, and may help cool the donkey's blood. Donkeys in the wild can defend themselves with a powerful kick of their hind legs as well as by biting and striking with their front hooves.

Braying is the characteristic sound made by an ass, donkey, and most mules. Donkeys use this sound to communicate and will bray more frequently when a new donkey is encountered. The sound typically lasts for twenty seconds. The sound may be rendered onomatapoeically as '*eeyore*' and so this was used as the name of the donkey in Winnie-the-Pooh. Donkeys may be trained to bray or not to bray upon command. This may be used as a form of mockery. Braying may be considered a simile for loud and foolish speech. For example:

> There are braying men in the world as well as braying asses; for what's loud and senseless talking and swearing, any other than braying.
>
> —*Sir Roger L'Estrange*

Nutrition

Donkeys' tough digestive system is somewhat less prone to colic than that of horses, can break down near-inedible vegetation and extract moisture from food very efficiently. As a rule, donkeys need smaller amounts of feed than horses of comparable height and weight. Because they are easy keepers, if overfed, donkeys are also quite susceptible to developing a condition called laminitis.

Donkeys evolved to spend 14-16 hours per day browsing and foraging for food. In their native arid and semi-arid climates this would often be a poor quality, scrubby fibre. Domesticated donkey owners face the challenge of feeding their donkey enough low energy fibre in order to meet their appetite, but in temperate climates the forage available is often too rich and abundant, resulting in weight gain and obesity with further implications including laminitis, hyperlipidemia and gastric ulcers. Although the donkey's gastrointestinal tract has no marked differences in structure to that of the horse, it is well documented that "donkeys are more efficient at digesting food than horses and, as a consequence, can thrive on less forage than a similar sized pony." Donkeys need to eat approximately 1.5 per cent of their body weight per day in dry matter, compared with 2-2.5 per cent for horses. It is not fully understood why donkeys are such efficient digestors but it is thought that they may have a different microbial population in the large intestine than do horses. Another possibility is increased gut retention time compared to ponies.

Donkeys gain most of their daily energy needs from structural carbohydrates. An average, healthy donkey only requires free choice feeding of low-calorie fibre-rich forage such as straw (preferably barley straw), supplemented with controlled grazing in the summer and hay in the winter. A donkey's requirement for protein and fat are so low that in practice once the energy requirements are met so too are the protein and fat requirements. Cereal based feeds designed for horses are often too high in energy levels and will exceed the daily requirements of donkeys. Even a small amount of grazing or fresh fodder during the spring and summer will provide adequate vitamin levels, so for a normal, healthy donkey a diet of straw plus a little grazing or hay meets their nutritional needs without need for concentrated feeds. A low-calorie vitamin and mineral supplement is recommended for donkeys year-round when on a restricted diet, and to all donkeys during the winter months.

Until recently the synonym *ass* was the more common term for *Equus asinus* (as in *jackass,* meaning "male donkey"). The first written use of donkey is as recent as 1785. While the word *ass* has cognates in most other Indo-European languages, *donkey* is an etymologically obscure word for which no credible cognate has been identified. Hypotheses on its derivation include the following:

- Perhaps a diminutive of *dun* (dull grayish-brown), a typical donkey colour;
- Perhaps from the name *Duncan*;
- Perhaps of imitative origin.

The homonymity in the United States with a vulgar term *ass* for 'buttocks' might have influenced its gradual replacement by *donkey* there, though this does not account for the parallel change in Britain and Australia.

Traditionally, the scientific name for the donkey is *Equus asinus asinus* based on the principle of priority used for scientific names of animals.

However, the International Commission on Zoological Nomenclature has ruled in 2003 that if the domestic species and the wild species are considered subspecies of each other, the scientific name of the wild species has priority, even when that subspecies has been described after the domestic subspecies. This means that the proper scientific name for the donkey is *Equus africanus asinus* when it is considered a subspecies, and *Equus asinus* when it is considered a species.

The ancestors of the modern donkey are the Nubian and Somalian subspecies of African wild ass. The African Wild Ass was domesticated around 4000 BC. The donkey became an important pack animal for people living in the Egyptian and Nubian regions as they can easily carry 20 per cent to 30 per cent of their own body weight and can also be used as a farming and dairy animal. By 1800 BC, the ass had reached the Middle East, where the trading city of Damascus was referred to as the 'City of Asses' in cuneiform texts. Syria produced at least three breeds of donkeys, including a saddle breed with a graceful, easy gait. These were favored by women.

For the Greeks, the donkey was associated with Dionysus, the god of wine. The Romans also valued the ass and would use it as a sacrificial animal.

Equines had become extinct in the Western Hemisphere at the end of the last Ice Age. However, horses and donkeys were brought back to the Americas by the Conquistadors. In 1495, the ass first appeared in the New World when Christopher Columbus brought four jacks and two jennys. It is from this bloodline that many of the mules which the Conquistadors used while they explored the Americas were produced. Shortly after the United States became independent, President George Washington imported the first mammoth jack stock into the country. Because the existing Jack donkeys in the New World at the time lacked the size and strength he sought to produce quality work mules, he imported donkeys from Spain and France, some standing over 1.63 m tall. One of the donkeys Washington received from the Marquis de Lafayette, named 'Knight of Malta', stood 1.43 m and thus was regarded as a great disappointment. Viewing this donkey as unfit for producing mules, Washington instead bred Knight of Malta to his jennys and, in doing so, created an American line of Mammoth Jacks (a breed name that includes both males and females).

Despite these early appearances of donkeys in America, the donkey did not find widespread distribution in America until it was found useful as a pack animal by miners, particularly the gold prospectors, of the mid-19th century. Miners preferred this animal due to its ability to carry tools, supplies, and ore. Their sociable disposition and adaptation to human companionship allowed many miners to lead their donkeys without ropes. They simply followed behind their owner. As mining became less an occupation of the individual prospector and more of an industrial underground operation, the miners' donkeys lost their jobs, and many were simply turned loose into the American deserts. Descendants of these donkeys, now feral, can still be seen roaming the Southwest today.

By the early 20th century, donkeys began to be used less as working animals and instead kept as pets in the United States and other wealthier nations, while remaining an important work animal in many poorer regions. The increased popularity of the donkey as a pet was seen in the appearance of the miniature donkey in 1929. Robert Green imported miniature donkeys to the United States and was a lifetime advocate of the breed. Mr. Green is perhaps best quoted when he said, "Miniature donkeys possess the affectionate nature of a Newfoundland, the resignation of a cow, the durability of a mule, the courage of a tiger, and the intellectual capability only slightly inferior to man's." Standing only 32-40 inches, many families recognized the potential of miniature donkeys as pets and companions for their children.

Although the donkey faded from public notice and became viewed as a comical, stubborn beast which was considered 'cute' at best, the donkey has recently regained some popularity in North America as a mount, for pulling wagons, and even as a guard animal. Some standard species are ideal for guarding herds of sheep against predators, since most donkeys have a natural wariness toward coyotes and other canines, and will keep them away from the herd. Donkeys have a notorious reputation for stubbornness, but this has been attributed to a much stronger sense of 'self preservation' than exhibited by horses. Likely based on a stronger prey instinct and a weaker connection with man, it is considerably more difficult to force or frighten a donkey into doing something it perceives to be dangerous for whatever reason.

Although formal studies of their behaviour and cognition are rather limited, donkeys appear to be quite intelligent, cautious, friendly, playful, and eager to learn. They are often pastured or stabled with horses and ponies, and are thought to have a calming effect on nervous horses. If a donkey is introduced to a mare and foal, the foal will often turn to the donkey for support after it has been weaned from its mother.

Once a person has earned their confidence they can be willing and companionable partners and very dependable in work . For this reason, they are now commonly kept as pets in countries where their use as beasts of burden has disappeared. Donkey rides for children are also a popular pastime for children in holiday resorts or other leisure contexts.

Present Status

There are about 44 million donkeys today. China has the most with 11 million, followed by Pakistan, Ethiopia and Mexico. Some researchers believe the actual number is somewhat higher since many donkeys go uncounted.

The vast majority of donkeys are used for the same types of work that they have been doing for 6000 years. Their most common role is for transport, whether riding, pack transport, or pulling carts. They may also be used for farm tillage, threshing, raising water, milling, and other jobs. Other donkeys are used to sire mules, as companions for horses, to guard sheep, and as pets. A few are milked or raised for meat.

The number of donkeys in the world continues to grow, as it has steadily throughout most of history. Some factors contributing to this are increasing human population, progress in economic development and social stability in some poorer nations, conversion of forests to farm and range land, rising prices of motor vehicles and fuel, and donkeys' popularity as pets.

In prosperous countries, the welfare of donkeys both at home and abroad has recently become a concern, and a number of sanctuaries for retired and rescued donkeys have been set up. The largest is the Donkey Sanctuary of England, which also supports donkey welfare projects in Egypt, Ethiopia, India, Kenya, and Mexico.

Feral Donkeys

Donkeys can become feral and cause problems, notably in environments that have been evolutionarily free of any form of equid, such as Hawaii.

Donkeys in Warfare

Donkeys have been used throughout history for transportation of supplies, pulling wagons, and, in a few cases, as riding animals. During World War I a British stretcher bearer, John Simpson Kirkpatrick, serving with the Australian and New Zealand Army Corps, used a donkey named Duffy to rescue wounded soldiers, carrying them to safety in Gallipoli. There is a statue of John Simpson Kirkpatrick and his donkey in his home town, South Shields.

According to British food writer Matthew Fort, donkeys were, until recently, used in the Italian Army. The Mountain Fusiliers each had a donkey to carry their gear, and in extreme circumstances the animal could be eaten. In 2006, security forces in Afghanistan prevented a man from entering a town in Zabul Province with a donkey which he had laden with 30 kg (66 lbs.) of explosives and a number of landmines, which the man had planned to set off with a remote controlled detonator.

The Spanish brought donkeys, called '*burros*' in Spanish, to North America, where they were prized for their hardiness in arid country and became the beast of burden of choice by early prospectors in the Southwest United States. In the western United States the word '*burro*' is often used interchangeably with the word 'donkey' by English speakers. Sometimes the distinction is made with smaller donkeys, descended from Mexican stock, called '*burros*', while those descended from stock imported directly from Europe are called 'donkeys'.

The feral burros on the western rangelands descend from animals that ran away, were abandoned, or were freed. Wild *burros* in the United States were protected by Pub.L. 92-195, the Wild Free-Roaming Horses and Burros Act of 1971 . These animals, considered to be a living legacy, are periodically at risk when severe drought conditions prevail. To reduce herd populations and preserve grazing land, the Bureau of Land Management conducts roundups of burro herds, which are then sold at public auctions.

Wild *burros* can make good pets when treated well and trained properly. They are clever and curious. When trust has been established, they appreciate, and even seek, attention and grooming.

A male donkey (jack) can be crossed with a female horse to produce a mule. A male horse can be crossed with a female donkey (jennet or jenny) to produce a hinny. A female donkey in the UK is called a *mare,* or *jenny.*

Horse-donkey hybrids are almost always sterile because horses have 64 chromosomes whereas donkeys have 62, producing offspring with 63 chromosomes. Mules are much more common than hinnies. This is believed to be caused by two factors, the first being proven in cat hybrids, that when the chromosome count of the male is the higher, fertility rates drop (as in the case of stallion x jennet). The lower progesterone production of the jenny may also lead to early embryonic loss. In addition, there are reasons not directly related to reproductive biology. Due to different mating behaviour, jacks are often more willing to cover mares than stallions are to breed jennys. Further, mares are usually larger than jennys and thus have more room for the ensuing foal to grow in the womb, resulting in a larger animal at birth. It is commonly believed that mules are more easily handled and also physically stronger than hinnies, making them more desirable for breeders to produce, and it is unquestioned that mules are more common in total number.

The offspring of a zebra-donkey cross is called a zonkey, zebroid, zebrass, or zedonk; *zebra mule* is an older term, but still used in some regions today. The foregoing terms generally refer to hybrids produced by breeding a male zebra to a female donkey. *Zebra hinny, zebret* and *zebrinny* all refer to the cross of a female zebra with a male donkey. Zebrinnies are rarer than zedonkies because female zebras in captivity are most valuable when used to produce full-blooded zebras. There are not enough female zebras breeding in captivity to spare them for hybridizing; there is no such limitation on the number of female donkeys breeding.

With domestication of almost all donkeys few species now exist in the wild. Some of them are the African Wild Ass (*Equus africanus*) and its subspecies Somalian wild ass (*Equus africanus somaliensis*). Also the Asiatic wild ass or Onager, *Equus hemionus*, and the kiang, *Equus kiang*, of the Himalayan upland.

There was one other, now extinct species called the European Ass (*Equus hydruntinus*) which became extinct during the Neolithic. In the wild the asses can reach top speeds equalling zebras and even most horses.

There are 68 references to a donkey ('hamor' or 'chamor') in the Old Testament, starting with a gift of some to Abraham by the Pharaoh in Genesis 12:16. A donkey features in the binding of Isaac (Genesis 22:3). Donkeys are again mentioned as a measure of wealth in the story of Jacob's life in Genesis 30:43.

In Genesis the King of Shechem (the modern Nablus), killed by Jacob's sons, is called 'Hamor' - showing that at the time this animal was held in high enough esteem that it was no disrespect for royalty to use its name as their first name. (Shechem, Animal names as first names in Hebrew.)

In Numbers 22: 22-41 "The Lord opened the mouth of the donkey" (*vs.* 28) and it speaks to Balaam. In Judges 15:13-17 where the hero Samson slays Philistines with the jawbone of an ass. Additional references can be found in Deuteronomy 22: 10 Job 11:12, Proverbs 26:3 and elsewhere.

In Jewish Oral Tradition, the son of David was prophesied as riding on a donkey if the tribes of Israel are undeserving of redemption. As noted, in the context of the Torah this connoted wealth and affluence befitting the House of David, as at the time commoners are described as simply going on foot.

The donkey mostly appears reflecting the natural environment and as an aspect of an agricultural economy. The Bible often specifies whether a person rode donkeys, since this was used to indicate a person's wealth in much the same way luxury cars do today. (Horses at that time were used solely for war, powerful kings such as Solomon being the only ones who could afford to import them from Egypt).

In contemporary Israel, the term 'Messiah's Donkey' (Chamoro Shel Mashiach) stands at the centre of a controversial religious-political doctrine, attributed to Rabbi Avraham Yitchak Hacohen Cook, under which it was the Heavenly-imposed 'task' of secular Zionists to build up a Jewish State, but once the state is established they are fated to give place to the Religious who are ordained to lead the state. The secularists in this analogy are 'The Donkey' while the religious who are fated to supplant them are a collective 'Messiach'. A book on the subject, published in 1998 by the militant secularist Sefi Rechlevsky, aroused a major controversy in the Israeli public opinion.

In Hindu Mythology a donkey (in sanskrit) *gardbha* is vahana (*vehicle*) of God Kalaratr.

Greek mythology includes the story of King Midas who judged against Apollo in favour of Pan during a musical contest, and had his ears changed to those of a donkey as punishment.

The ass was a symbol of the Greek god Dionysus, particularly in relationship to his companion, Silenus.

The most common Greek word for ass appears roughly 100 times in the Biblical text. In the Gospels, Jesus rides a donkey into Jerusalem (Mark 11: 1 in which *colt* refers to a donkey colt).

Traditionally, Mary is portrayed as riding a donkey while pregnant. Legend has it that the cross on the donkey's shoulders comes from the shadow of Christ's crucifixion, placing the donkey at the foot of the cross. It was once believed that hair cut from this cross and hung from a child's neck in a bag would prevent fits and convulsions. However, in later times when the aristocracy used horses, depicting the Jesus as riding a donkey came to have an opposite connotation, as indicating a simple, sober way of life and avoiding luxury. The same connotation is evident in the description of saints such as Francis of Assisi as riding donkeys.

Muhammad, the prophet of Islam said that dogs and donkeys, if they pass in front of men in prayer, will void or nullify that prayer. He also said that "when you hear the braying of donkeys, seek Refuge with Allah from Satan for (their braying indicates) that they have seen a devil."

Several were buried in Hor-Aha's tomb.

Fable and Folklore

European folklore claims that the tail of a donkey can be used to combat whooping cough or scorpion stings.

In Panchatantra which is a collection of animal fables, where are two stories of donkey:

1. The Lion and The Foolish Donkey; and
2. The Singing Donkey.

In Hitopadesha there is a story of Donkey named *the Donkey and the Dog.*

One of Aesop's fables has an ass dressed in a lion skin who gives himself away by braying.

La Fontaine's fable about the donkey of a miser who made the donkey work hard and eat less, coming to one day when thieves came and the donkey told his master to run for his life; however, the donkey didn't care about escaping, because one way or another he would continue working hard.

Literature

Any number of donkeys appear in world literary works.

In *The Golden Ass* by Lucius Apuleius Platonicus, the narrator is turned into a donkey by mistake and spends most of the novel in that shape.

In William Shakespeare's *A Midsummer Night's Dream*, the character Bottom has his head turned into that of a donkey by Puck who was told by Oberon, king of the fairies, to change it.

Travels with a Donkey in the Cévennes, is one of Robert Louis Stevenson's earliest published works and is considered a pioneering classic of outdoor literature.

In Don Quixote, Sancho Panza rides a donkey he refers to as 'my *rucio*' or 'the *rucio*', an elegant (and ironic) designation of the texture of the animal's fur.

Eeyore, the gloomy donkey from A.A. Milne's Winnie-the-Pooh books.

In Pinocchio, naughty boys turn into donkeys and are sold off to hard labour by the evil Coachman. In the book, Pinocchio turns into a donkey for a time.

A German proverb claims a donkey can wear a lion suit but its ear will still stick out and give it away. British colloquial expressions include 'donkey's years', a long time or many years, probably a pun on 'donkey's ears', while 'to talk the hind leg off a donkey' means to tire somebody with one's talk. Speed bumps are called in the Rioplatense Spanish of Argentina '*lomos de burro*', that is, 'donkey's backs'. Classical Greek expressions about donkeys included: *onos pros eorten* = 'a donkey at the festival' (gets all the work); *onos hyetai* = 'a donkey is rained on' (*i.e.* he is unaffected or insensitive), *onos pros phatnen* = 'a donkey at a feed trough' (like the English expression 'in clover'). English proverbs include 'better be the head of an ass than the tail of a horse', 'if an ass goes a-travelling, he'll not come back a horse', and 'better ride on an ass that carries me home than a horse that throws me' (though all these are now obsolete).

Horse

The horse (*Equus ferus caballus*) is a hooved (ungulate) mammal, a subspecies of the family Equidae. The horse has evolved over the past 45 to 55 million years from a small multi-toed creature into the large, single-toed animal of today. Humans began to domesticate horses around 4000 BC, and their domestication is believed to have been widespread by 3000 BC. Although most horses today are domesticated, there are still endangered populations of the Przewalski's Horse, the only remaining true wild horse, as well as more common populations of feral horses which live in the wild but are descended from domesticated ancestors. There is an extensive, specialized vocabulary used to describe equine-related concepts, covering everything from anatomy to life stages, size, colours, markings, breeds, locomotion, and behaviour.

Horses' anatomy enables them to make use of speed to escape predators and they have a well-developed sense of balance and a strong fight-or-flight instinct. Related to this need to flee from predators in the wild is an unusual trait: horses are able to sleep both standing up and lying down. Female horses, called mares, carry their young for approximately 11 months, and a young horse, called a foal, can stand and run shortly following birth. Most domesticated horses begin training under saddle or in harness between the ages of two and four. They reach full adult development by age five, and have an average lifespan of between 25 and 30 years.

Horse breeds are loosely divided into three categories based on general temperament: spirited 'hot bloods' with speed and endurance; 'cold bloods', such as draft horses and some ponies, suitable for slow, heavy work; and 'warmbloods', developed from crosses between hot bloods and cold bloods, often focusing on creating breeds for specific riding purposes, particularly in Europe. There are over 300 breeds of horses in the world today, developed for many different uses.

Horses and humans interact in a wide variety of sport competitions and non-competitive recreational pursuits, as well as in working activities such as police work, agriculture, entertainment, and therapy. Horses were historically used in warfare, from which a wide variety of riding and driving techniques developed, using many different styles of equipment and methods of control. Many products are derived from horses, including meat, milk, hide, hair, bone, and pharmaceuticals extracted from the urine of pregnant mares. Humans provide domesticated horses with food, water and shelter, as well as attention from specialists such as veterinarians and farriers.

Depending on breed, management and environment, the domestic horse today has a life expectancy of 25 to 30 years. It is uncommon, but a few animals live into their 40s and, occasionally, beyond. The oldest verifiable record was 'Old Billy', a 19th-century horse that lived to the age of 62. In modern times, Sugar Puff, who had been listed in the Guinness Book of World Records as the world's oldest living pony, died in 2007, aged 56.

Regardless of a horse's actual birth date, for most competition purposes an animal is considered a year older on January 1 of each year in the northern hemisphere and August 1 in the southern hemisphere. The exception is in endurance riding, where the minimum age to compete is based on the animal's calendar age. A very rough estimate of a horse's age can be made from looking at its teeth.

The following terminology is used to describe horses of various ages:

- *Foal:* A horse of either sex less than one year old. A nursing foal is sometimes called a *suckling* and a foal that has been weaned is called a *weanling.* Most domesticated foals are weaned at 5 to 7 months of age, although foals can be weaned at 4 months with no adverse effects.
- *Yearling:* A horse of either sex that is between one and two years old.
- *Colt:* A male horse under the age of four. A common terminology error is to call any young horse a 'colt', when the term actually only refers to young male horses.
- *Filly:* A female horse under the age of four.
- *Mare:* A female horse four years old and older.
- *Stallion:* A non-castrated male horse four years old and older. Some people, particularly in the UK, refer to a stallion as a 'horse'.
- *Gelding:* a castrated male horse of any age.

In horse racing, these definitions may differ: For example, in the British Isles, Thoroughbred horse racing defines colts and fillies as less than five years old. However, for Australian Thoroughbred racing, colts and fillies are less than four years old.

Size and Measurement

The height of horses is measured at the highest point of the withers, where the neck meets the back. This point was chosen as it is a stable point of the anatomy, unlike the head or neck, which move up and down.

The English-speaking world measures the height of horses in hands (abbreviated 'h' or 'hh', for 'hands high') and inches. One hand is equal to 101.6 millimetres (4 in). The height is expressed as the number of full hands, followed by a decimal point, then the number of additional inches. Thus, a horse described as '15.2 h' is 15 hands (60 inches (152.4 cm)) plus 2 inches (5.1 cm), for a total of 62 inches (157.5 cm) in height.

The size of horses varies by breed, but also is influenced by nutrition. Light riding horses usually range in height from 14 to 16 hands (56 to 64 inches, 142 to 163 cm) and can weigh from 380 to 550 kilograms (840 to 1,200 lb). Larger riding horses usually start at about 15.2 hands (62 inches, 157 cm) and often are as tall as 17 hands (68 inches, 173 cm), weighing from 500 to 600 kilograms (1,100 to 1,300 lb). Heavy or draft horses are usually at least 16 to 18 hands (64 to 72 inches, 163 to 183 cm) high and can weigh from about 700 to 1,000 kilograms (1,500 to 2,200 lb).

The largest horse in recorded history was probably a Shire horse named Mammoth, who was born in 1848. He stood 21.2½ hands high (86.5 in/220 cm), and his peak weight was estimated at 1,500 kilograms (3,300 lb). The current record holder for the world's smallest horse is Thumbelina, a fully mature miniature horse affected by dwarfism. She is 17 inches (43 cm) tall and weighs 57 pounds (26 kg).

The general rule for height between a horse and a pony at maturity is 14.2 hands (58 inches, 147 cm). An animal 14.2 h or over is usually considered to be a horse and one less than 14.2 h a pony. However, there are many exceptions to the general rule. In Australia, ponies measure under 14 hands (56 inches, 142 cm). The International Federation for Equestrian Sports, which uses metric measurements, defines the cutoff between horses and ponies at 148 centimetres (58.27 in) (just over 14.2 h) without shoes and 149 centimetres (58.66 in) (just over 14.2½ h) with shoes. Some breeds which typically produce individuals both under and over 14.2 h consider all animals of that breed to be horses regardless of their height. Conversely, some pony breeds may have features in common with horses, and individual animals may occasionally mature at over 14.2 h, but are still considered to be ponies.

The distinction between a horse and pony is not simply a difference in height, but other aspects of *phenotype* or appearance, such as conformation and temperament. Ponies often exhibit thicker manes, tails, and overall coat. They also have proportionally shorter legs, wider barrels, heavier bone, shorter and thicker necks, and short heads with broad foreheads. They may have calmer temperaments than horses and also a high level of equine intelligence that may or may not be used to cooperate with human handlers. In fact, small size, by itself, is sometimes not a factor at all. While the Shetland pony stands on average 10 hands (40 inches, 102 cm), the Falabella and other miniature horses, which can be no taller than 30 inches (76 cm), the size of a medium-sized dog, are classified by their respective registries as very small horses rather than as ponies.

Horses exhibit a diverse array of coat colours and distinctive markings, described with a specialized vocabulary. Often, a horse is classified first by its coat colour, before breed or sex. Horses of the same colour may be distinguished from one another by white markings, which, along with various spotting patterns, are inherited separately from coat colour.

Many genes that create horse coat colours have been identified, although research continues to further identify factors that result in specific traits. One of the first genetic relationships to be understood was that between recessive 'red' (chestnut) and dominant 'black', which is controlled by the 'red factor' or extension gene. Additional alleles control spotting, graying, suppression or dilution of colour, and other effects that create the dozens of possible coat colours found in horses.

Chestnut, bay, and black are the basic equine coat colours. These colours are modified by at least ten other genes to create all other colours, including dilutions such as palomino and spotting patterns such as pinto. Horses which are white in coat colour are often mislabeled as 'white' horses. However, a horse that looks white is usually a middle-aged or older gray. Grays are born a darker shade, get lighter as they age, and usually have black skin underneath their white hair coat (with the exception of pink skin under white markings). The only horses properly called white are born with a white hair coat and have predominantly pink skin, a fairly rare occurrence. There are no truly 'albino' horses having both pink skin and red eyes.

Gestation lasts for approximately 335-340 days and usually results in one foal. Twins are rare. Horses are a precocial species, and foals are capable of standing and running within a short time following birth.

Horses, particularly colts, sometimes are physically capable of reproduction at about 18 months, but domesticated horses are rarely allowed to breed before the age of three, especially females. Horses four years old are considered mature, although the skeleton normally continues to develop until the age of six; maturation also depends on the horse's size, breed, sex, and quality of care. Also, if the horse is larger, its bones are larger; therefore, not only do the bones take longer to actually form bone tissue, but the epiphyseal plates are also larger and take longer to convert from cartilage to bone. These plates convert after the other parts of the bones, and are crucial to development.

Depending on maturity, breed, and work expected, horses are usually put under saddle and trained to be ridden between the ages of two and four. Although Thoroughbred race horses are put on the track at as young as two years old in some countries, horses specifically bred for sports such as dressage are generally not put under saddle until they are three or four years old, because their bones and muscles are not solidly developed. For endurance riding competition, horses are not deemed mature enough to compete until they are a full 60 calendar months (5 years) old.

Horses have a skeleton that averages 205 bones. A significant difference between the horse skeleton and that of a human, is the lack of a collarbone—the horse's forelimbs are attached to the spinal column by a powerful set of muscles, tendons, and ligaments that attach the shoulder blade to the torso. The horse's legs and hooves are also unique structures. Their leg bones are proportioned differently from those of a human. For example, the body part that is called a horse's 'knee' is actually made up of the carpal bones that correspond to the human wrist. Similarly, the hock contains bones equivalent to those in the human ankle and heel. The lower leg bones of a horse correspond to the bones of the human hand or foot, and the fetlock (incorrectly called the 'ankle') is actually the proximal sesamoid bones between the cannon bones (a single equivalent to the human metacarpal or metatarsal bones) and the proximal phalanges, located where one finds the 'knuckles' of a human. A horse also has no muscles in its legs below the knees and hocks, only skin, hair, bone, tendons, ligaments, cartilage, and the assorted specialized tissues that make up the hoof.

Hooves

The critical importance of the feet and legs is summed up by the traditional adage, 'no foot, no horse'. The horse hoof begins with the distal phalanges, the equivalent of the human fingertip or tip of the toe, surrounded by cartilage and other specialized, blood-rich soft tissues such as the laminae. The exterior hoof wall and horn of the sole is made of essentially the same material as a human fingernail. The end result is that a horse, weighing on average 500 kilograms (1,100 lb), travels on the same bones as would a human on tiptoe. For the protection of the hoof under certain conditions, some horses have horseshoes placed on their feet by a professional farrier. The hoof continually grows, and needs to be trimmed (and horseshoes reset, if used) every five to eight weeks.

Teeth

Horses are adapted to grazing. In an adult horse, there are 12 incisors, adapted to biting off the grass or other vegetation, at the front of the mouth. There are 24 teeth adapted for chewing, the premolars and molars, at the back of the mouth. Stallions and geldings have four additional teeth just behind the incisors, a type of canine teeth that are called 'tushes'. Some horses, both male and female, will also develop one to four very small vestigial teeth in front of the molars, known as 'wolf' teeth, which are generally removed because they can interfere with the bit. There is an empty interdental space between the incisors and the molars where the bit rests directly on the bars (gums) of the horse's mouth when the horse is bridled.

The incisors show a distinct wear and growth pattern as the horse ages, as well as change in the angle at which the chewing surfaces meet. The teeth continue to erupt throughout life as they are worn down by grazing, so a very rough estimate of a horse's age can be made by an examination of its teeth, although diet and veterinary care can affect the rate of tooth wear.

Digestion

Horses are herbivores with a digestive system adapted to a forage diet of grasses and other plant material, consumed steadily throughout the day. Therefore, compared to humans, they have a relatively small stomach but very long intestines to facilitate a steady flow of nutrients. A 450-kilogram (990 lb) horse will eat 7 to 11 kilograms (15 to 24 lb) of food per day and, under normal use, drink 38 litres (8.4 imp gal; 10 US gal) to 45 litres (9.9 imp gal; 12 US gal) of water. Horses are not ruminants, so they have only one stomach, like humans, but unlike humans, they can digest cellulose, a major component of grass. Cellulose digestion occurs in the cecum, or 'water gut', which food goes through before reaching the large intestine. Unlike humans, horses cannot vomit, so digestion problems can quickly cause colic, a leading cause of death.

The horse's senses are generally superior to those of a human. As prey animals, they must be aware of their surroundings at all times. They have the largest eyes of any land mammal, and are lateral-eyed, meaning that their eyes are positioned on the sides of their heads. This means that horses have a range of vision of more than 350°, with approximately 65° of this being binocular vision and the remaining 285° monocular vision. Horses have excellent day and night vision, but they have two-colour, or dichromatic vision; their colour vision is somewhat like red-green colour blindness in humans, where certain colours, especially red and related colours, appear more green.

Their hearing is good, and the pinna of each ear can rotate up to 180°, giving the potential for 360° hearing without having to move the head. Their sense of smell, while much better than that of humans, is not their strongest asset; they rely to a greater extent on vision.

Horses have a great sense of balance, due partly to their ability to feel their footing and partly to highly developed proprioceptive abilities (the unconscious sense of where the body and limbs are at all times). A horse's sense of touch is well developed. The most sensitive areas are around the eyes, ears, and nose. Horses sense contact as subtle as an insect landing anywhere on the body.

Horses have an advanced sense of taste that allows them to sort through fodder to choose what they would most like to eat, and their prehensile lips can easily sort even the smallest grains. Horses generally will not eat poisonous plants. However, there are exceptions and horses will occasionally eat toxic amounts of poisonous plants even when there is adequate healthy food.

All horses move naturally with four basic gaits: the four-beat walk, which averages 6.4 kilometres per hour (4.0 mph); the two-beat trot or jog at 13 to 19 kilometres per hour (8.1 to 12 mph) (faster for harness racing horses); the canter or lope, a three-beat gait that is 19 to 24 kilometres per hour (12 to 15 mph); and the gallop. The gallop averages 40 to 48 kilometres per hour (25 to 30 mph), but the world record for a horse galloping over a short, sprint distance is 88 kilometres per hour (55 mph). Besides these basic gaits, some horses perform a two-beat pace, instead of the trot. There also are several four-beat 'ambling' gaits that are approximately the speed of a trot or pace, though smoother to ride. These include the lateral rack, running walk, and tölt as well as the diagonal fox trot. Ambling gaits are often genetic in some breeds, known collectively as gaited horses. Often, gaited horses replace the trot with one of the ambling gaits.

Horses are prey animals with a strong fight-or-flight instinct. Their first response to threat is to startle and usually flee, although they will stand their ground and defend themselves when flight is not possible, or if their young are threatened. They also tend to be curious; when startled, they will often hesitate an instant to ascertain the cause of their fright, and may not always flee from something that they perceive as non-threatening. Most light horse riding breeds were developed for speed, agility, alertness and endurance; natural qualities that extend from their wild ancestors. However, through selective breeding, some breeds of horses are quite docile, particularly certain draft horses. Horses are herd animals, with a clear hierarchy of rank, led by a dominant animal (usually a mare). They are also social creatures who are able to form companionship attachments to their own species and to other animals, including humans. They communicate in various ways, including vocalizations such as nickering or whinnying, mutual grooming, and body language. Many horses will become difficult to manage if they are isolated, but with training, horses can learn to accept a human as a companion, and thus be comfortable away from other horses. However, when confined with insufficient companionship, exercise, or stimulation, individuals may develop stable vices, an assortment of bad habits, mostly psychological in origin, that include wood chewing, wall kicking, 'weaving' (rocking back and forth), and other problems.

Intelligence and Learning

In the past, horses were considered unintelligent, with no abstract thinking ability, unable to generalize, and driven primarily by a herd mentality. However, modern studies show that they perform a number of cognitive tasks on a daily basis, with mental challenges that include food procurement and social system identification. They also have good spatial discrimination abilities. Studies have assessed equine intelligence in the realms of problem solving, learning speed, and knowledge retention. Results show that horses excel at simple learning, but also are able to solve advanced cognitive challenges that involve categorization and concept learning. They learn from habituation, desensitization, Pavlovian conditioning, and operant conditioning. They respond to and learn from both positive and negative reinforcement. Recent studies even suggest horses are able to count if the quantity involved is less than four.

Domesticated horses tend to face greater mental challenges than wild horses, because they live in artificial environments that stifle instinctual behaviour while learning tasks that are not natural. Horses are creatures of habit that respond and adapt well to regimentation, and respond best when the same routines and techniques are used consistently. Some trainers believe that 'intelligent' horses are reflections of intelligent trainers who effectively use response conditioning techniques and positive reinforcement to train in the style that fits best with an individual animal's natural inclinations. Others who handle horses regularly note that personality also may play a role separate from intelligence in determining how a given animal responds to various experiences.

Temperament

Horses are mammals, and as such are 'warm-blooded' creatures, as opposed to cold-blooded reptiles. However, these words have developed a separate meaning in the context of equine terminology, used to describe temperament, not body temperature. For example, the 'hot-bloods', such as many race horses, exhibit more sensitivity and energy, while the 'old-bloods', such as most draft breeds, are quieter and calmer. Sometimes 'hot-bloods' are classified as 'light horses' or 'riding horses', with the 'cold-bloods' classified as 'draft horses' or 'work horses'.

'Hot blooded' breeds include 'oriental horses' such as the Akhal-Teke, Barb, Arabian horse and now-extinct Turkoman horse, as well as the Thoroughbred, a breed developed in England from the older oriental breeds. Hot bloods tend to be spirited, bold, and learn quickly. They are bred for agility and speed. They tend to be physically refined—thin-skinned, slim, and long-legged. The original oriental breeds were brought to Europe from the Middle East and North Africa when European breeders wished to infuse these traits into racing and light cavalry horses.

Muscular, heavy draft horses are known as 'cold bloods', as they are bred not only for strength, but also to have the calm, patient temperament needed to pull a plow or a heavy carriage full of people. They are sometimes nicknamed 'gentle giants'. Well-known draft breeds include the Belgian and the Clydesdale. Some, like the Percheron are lighter and livelier, developed to pull carriages or to plow large fields in drier climates. Others, such as the Shire, are slower and more powerful, bred to plow fields with heavy, clay-based soils. The cold-blooded group also includes some pony breeds.

'Warmblood' breeds, such as the Trakehner or Hanoverian, developed when European carriage and war horses were crossed with Arabians or Thoroughbreds, producing a riding horse with more refinement than a draft horse, but greater size and milder temperament than a lighter breed. Certain pony breeds with warmblood characteristics have been developed for smaller riders. Warmbloods are considered a 'light horse' or 'riding horse'.

Today, the term 'Warmblood' refers to a specific subset of sport horse breeds that are used for competition in dressage and show jumping. Strictly speaking, the term 'warm blood' refers to any cross between cold-blooded and hot-blooded breeds. Examples include breeds such as the Irish Draught or the Cleveland Bay. The term was once used to refer to breeds of light riding horse other than Thoroughbreds or Arabians, such as the Morgan horse.

Horses are able to sleep both standing up and lying down. In an adaptation from life in the wild, horses are able to enter light sleep by using a 'stay apparatus' in their legs, allowing them to doze without collapsing. Horses sleep better when in groups because some animals will sleep while others stand guard to watch for predators. A horse kept alone will not sleep well because its instincts are to keep a constant eye out for danger.

Unlike humans, horses do not sleep in a solid, unbroken period of time, but take many short periods of rest. Horses spend four to fifteen hours a day in standing rest, and from a few minutes to several hours lying down. Total sleep time in a 24-hour period may range from several minutes to a couple of hours, mostly in short intervals of about 15 minutes each.

Horses must lie down to reach REM sleep. They only have to lie down for an hour or two every few days to meet their minimum REM sleep requirements. However, if a horse is never allowed to lie down, after several days it will become sleep-deprived, and in rare cases may suddenly collapse as it involuntarily slips into REM sleep while still standing. This condition differs from narcolepsy, although horses may also suffer from that disorder.

The horse adapted to survive in areas of wide-open terrain with sparse vegetation, surviving in an ecosystem where other large grazing animals, especially ruminants, could not. Horses and other equids are odd-toed ungulates of the order Perissodactyla, a group of mammals that was dominant during the Tertiary period. In the past, this order contained 14 families, but only three—Equidae (the horse and related species), the tapir, and the rhinoceros—have survived to the present day. The earliest known member of the Equidae family was the *Hyracotherium*, which lived between 45 and 55 million years ago, during the Eocene period. It had 4 toes on each front foot, and 3 toes on each back foot. The extra toe on the front feet soon disappeared with the *Mesohippus*, which lived 32 to 37 million years ago. Over time, the extra side toes shrank in size until they vanished. All that remains of them in modern horses is a set of small vestigial bones on the leg below the knee, known informally as splint bones. Their legs also lengthened as their toes disappeared until they were a hooved animal capable of running at great speed. By about 5 million years ago, the modern *Equus* had evolved. Equid teeth also evolved from browsing on soft, tropical plants to adapt to browsing of drier plant material, then to grazing of tougher plains grasses. Thus proto-horses changed from leaf-eating forest-dwellers to grass-eating inhabitants of semi-arid regions worldwide, including the steppes of Eurasia and the Great Plains of North America.

By about 15,000 years ago, *Equus ferus* was a widespread holarctic species. Horse bones from this time period, the late Pleistocene, are found in Europe, Eurasia, Beringia, and North America. Yet between 10,000 and 7,600 years ago, the horse became extinct in North America and rare elsewhere. The reasons for this extinction are not fully known, but one theory notes that extinction in North America paralleled human arrival. Another theory points to climate change, noting that approximately 12,500 years ago, the grasses characteristic of a steppe ecosystem gave way to shrub tundra, which was covered with unpalatable plants.

Wild Species Surviving into Modern Times

A truly wild horse is a species or subspecies with no ancestors that were ever domesticated. Therefore, most "wild" horses today are actually feral horses, animals that escaped or were turned loose from domestic herds and the descendants of those animals. Only one truly wild horse species (*Equus ferus*) with two subspecies, the Tarpan and the Przewalski's Horse, survived into recorded history.

The only true wild horse alive today is the Przewalski's Horse (*Equus ferus przewalskii*), named after the Russian explorer Nikolai Przhevalsky. It is a rare Asian animal, also known as the Mongolian Wild Horse; Mongolian people know it as the *taki*, and the Kyrgyz people call it a *kirtag*. The species was presumed extinct in the wild between 1969 and 1992, while a small breeding population survived in zoos around the world. In 1992, it was reestablished in the wild due to the conservation efforts of numerous zoos. Today, a small wild breeding population exists in Mongolia. There are additional animals still maintained at zoos throughout the world.

The Tarpan or European Wild Horse (*Equus ferus ferus*) was found in Europe and much of Asia. It survived into the historical era, but became extinct in 1909, when the last captive died in a Russian zoo. Thus, the genetic line was lost. Attempts have been made to recreate the Tarpan, which resulted in horses with outward physical similarities, but nonetheless descended from domesticated ancestors and not true wild horses.

Periodically, populations of horses in isolated areas are speculated to be relic populations of wild horses, but generally have been proven to be feral or domestic. For example, the Riwoche horse of Tibet was proposed as such, but testing did not reveal genetic differences with domesticated horses, Similarly, the Sorraia of Spain was proposed as a direct descendant of the Tarpan based on shared characteristics, but genetic studies have shown that the Sorraia is more closely related to other horse breeds and that the outward similarity is an unreliable measure of relatedness.

Besides the horse, there are seven other species of genus *Equus* in the Equidae family. These are the ass or donkey, *Equus asinus*; the mountain zebra, *Equus zebra*; plains zebra, *Equus burchelli*; Grévy's zebra, *Equus grevyi*; the kiang, *Equus kiang*; and the onager, *Equus hemionus*.

Horses can crossbreed with other members of their genus. The most common hybrid is the mule, a cross between a 'jack' (male donkey) and a mare. A related hybrid, a hinny, is a cross between a stallion and a jenny (female donkey). Other hybrids include the zorse, a cross between a zebra and a horse. With rare exceptions, most hybrids are sterile and cannot reproduce.

Domestication

Domestication of the horse most likely took place in central Asia prior to 3500 BC. Two major sources of information are used to determine where and when the horse was first domesticated and how the domesticated horse spread around the world. The first source is based on palaeological and archaeological discoveries, the second source is a comparison of DNA obtained from modern horses to that from bones and teeth of ancient horse remains.

The earliest archaeological evidence for the domestication of the horse comes from sites in Ukraine and Kazakhstan, dating to approximately 3500-4000 BC. By 3000 BC, the horse was completely domesticated and by 2000 BC there was a sharp increase in the number of horse bones found in human settlements in northwestern Europe, indicating the spread of domesticated horses throughout the continent. The most recent, but most irrefutable evidence of domestication comes from sites where horse remains were interred with chariots in graves of the Sintashta and Petrovka cultures c. 2100 BC.

Domestication is also studied by using the genetic material of present day horses and comparing it with the genetic material present in the bones and teeth of horse remains found in archaeological and palaeological excavations. The variation in the genetic material shows that very few wild stallions contributed to the domestic horse, while many mares were part of early domesticated herds. This is reflected in the difference in genetic variation between the DNA that is passed on along the paternal, or sire line (Y-chromosome) versus that passed on along the maternal, or dam line (mitochondrial DNA). There are very low levels of Y-chromosome variability, but a great deal of genetic variation in mitochondrial DNA. There is also regional variation in mitochondrial DNA due to the inclusion of wild mares in domestic herds. Another characteristic of domestication is an increase in coat colour variation. In horses, this increased dramatically between 5000 and 3000 BC.

Before the availability of DNA techniques to resolve the questions related to the domestication of the horse, various hypothesis were proposed. One classification was based on body types and conformation, suggesting the presence of four basic prototypes that had adapted to their environment prior to domestication. Another hypothesis held that the four prototypes originated from a single wild species and that all different body types were entirely a result of selective breeding after domestication. However, the lack of a detectable substructure in the horse has resulted in a rejection of both hypotheses.

Feral Populations

Feral horses are born and live in the wild, but are descended from domesticated animals. Many populations of feral horses exist throughout the world. Studies of feral herds have provided useful insights into the behaviour of prehistoric horses, as well as greater understanding of the instincts and behaviours that drive horses that live in domesticated conditions.

Breeds

Horse breeds are groups of horses with distinctive characteristics that are transmitted consistently to their offspring, such as conformation, colour, performance ability, or disposition. These inherited traits result from a combination of natural crosses and artificial selection methods. Horses have been selectively bred since their domestication. Breeds developed due to a need for 'form to function', the necessity to develop certain characteristics in order to perform a particular type of work. Thus, powerful but refined breeds such as the Andalusian developed as riding horses that also had a great aptitude for dressage, while heavy draft horses such as the Clydesdale developed out of a need to perform demanding farm work and pull heavy wagons. Other horse breeds developed specifically for light agricultural work, carriage and road work, various sport disciplines, or simply as pets. Some breeds developed through centuries of crossings with other breeds, while others, such as Tennessee Walking Horses and Morgans, descended from a single foundation sire. There are more than 300 horse breeds in the world today.

However, the concept of purebred bloodstock and a controlled, written breed registry only became of significant importance in modern times. Sometimes purebred horses are called Thoroughbreds, which is incorrect; 'Thoroughbred' is a specific breed of horse, while a 'purebred' is a horse (or any other animal) with a defined pedigree recognized by a breed registry. An early example of people who practiced selective horse breeding were the Bedouin, who had a reputation for careful practices, keeping extensive pedigrees of their Arabian horses and placing great value upon pure bloodlines. These pedigrees were originally transmitted via an oral tradition. In the 14th century, Carthusian monks of southern Spain kept meticulous pedigrees of bloodstock lineages still found today in the Andalusian horse. One of the earliest formal registries was General Stud Book for Thoroughbreds, which began in 1791 and traced back to the foundation bloodstock for the breed.

Interaction with Humans

Worldwide, horses play a role within human cultures and have done so for millennia. Horses are used for leisure activities, sports, and working purposes. The Food and Agriculture Organization (FAO) estimates that in 2008, there were almost 59,000,000 horses in the world, with around 33,500,000 in the Americas, 13,800,000 in Asia and 6,300,000 in Europe and smaller portions in Africa and Oceania. There are estimated to be 9,500,000 horses in the United States alone. The American Horse Council estimates that horse-related activities have a direct impact on the economy of the United States of over $39 billion, and when indirect spending is considered, the impact is over $102 billion. In a 2004 'poll' conducted by Animal Planet, more than 50,000 viewers from 73 countries voted for the horse as the world's 4th favorite animal.

Communication between human and horse is paramount in any equestrian activity; to aid this process horses are usually ridden with a saddle on their backs to assist the rider with balance and positioning, and a bridle or related headgear to assist the rider in maintaining control. Sometimes horses are ridden without a saddle, and occasionally, horses are trained to perform without a bridle or other headgear. Many horses are also driven, which requires a harness, bridle, and some type of vehicle.

Historically, equestrians honed their skills through games and races. Equestrian sports provided entertainment for crowds and honed the excellent horsemanship that was needed in battle. Many sports, such as dressage, eventing and show jumping, have origins in military training, which were focused on control and balance of both horse and rider. Other sports, such as rodeo, developed from practical skills such as those needed on working ranches and stations. Sport hunting from horseback evolved from earlier practical hunting techniques. Horse racing of all types evolved from impromptu competitions between riders or drivers. All forms of competition, requiring demanding and specialized skills from both horse and rider, resulted in the systematic development of specialized breeds and equipment for each sport. The popularity of equestrian sports through the centuries has resulted in the preservation of skills that would otherwise have disappeared after horses stopped being used in combat.

Horses are trained to be ridden or driven in a variety of sporting competitions. Examples include show jumping, dressage, three-day eventing, competitive driving, endurance riding, gymkhana, rodeos, and fox hunting. Horse shows, which have their origins in medieval European fairs, are held around the world. They host a huge range of classes, covering all of the mounted and harness disciplines, as well as 'In-hand' classes where the horses are led, rather than ridden, to be evaluated on their conformation.

The method of judging varies with the discipline, but winning usually depends on style and ability of both horse and rider. Sports such as polo do not judge the horse itself, but rather use the horse as a partner for human competitors as a necessary part of the game. Although the horse requires specialized training to participate, the details of its performance are not judged, only the result of the rider's actions—be it getting a ball through a goal or some other task. Examples of these sports of partnership between human and horse include jousting, in which the main goal is for one rider to unseat the other, and buzkashi, a team game played throughout Central Asia, the aim being to capture a goat carcass while on horseback.

Horse racing is an equestrian sport and major international industry, watched in almost every nation of the world. There are three types: 'flat' racing; steeplechasing, *i.e.* racing over jumps; and harness racing, where horses trot or pace while pulling a driver in a small, light cart known as a sulky. A major part of horse racing's economic importance lies in the gambling associated with it.

There are certain jobs that horses do very well, and no technology has yet developed to fully replace them. For example, mounted police horses are still effective for certain types of patrol duties and crowd control. Cattle ranches still require riders on horseback to round up cattle that are scattered across remote, rugged terrain. Search and rescue organizations in some countries depend upon mounted teams to locate people, particularly hikers and children, and to provide disaster relief assistance. Horses can also be used in areas where it is necessary to avoid vehicular disruption to delicate soil, such as nature reserves. They may also be the only form of transport allowed in wilderness areas. Horses are quieter than motorized vehicles. Law enforcement officers such as park rangers or game wardens may use horses for patrols, and horses or mules may also be used for clearing trails or other work in areas of rough terrain where vehicles are less effective.

Although machinery has replaced horses in many parts of the world, an estimated 100 million horses, donkeys and mules are still used for agriculture and transportation in less developed areas. This number includes around 27 million working in Africa alone. Some land management practices such as cultivating and logging can be efficiently performed with horses. In agriculture, less fossil fuel is used and increased environmental conservation occurs over time with the use of draft animals such as horses. Logging with horses can result in reduced damage to soil structure and less damage to trees due to more selective logging.

Entertainment and Culture

Modern horses are often used to reenact many of their historical work purposes. Horses are used, complete with equipment that is authentic or a meticulously recreated replica, in various live action historical reenactments of specific periods of history, especially recreations of famous battles. Horses are also used to preserve cultural traditions and for ceremonial purposes. Countries such as the United Kingdom still use horse-drawn carriages to convey royalty and other VIPs to and from certain culturally significant events. Public exhibitions are another example, such as the Budweiser Clydesdales, seen in parades and other public settings, a team of draft horses that pull a beer wagon similar to that used before the invention of the modern motorized truck.

Horses are frequently seen in television and films. They are used both as main characters, in films such as *Seabiscuit*, and *Dreamer*, and as visual elements that assure the accuracy of historical stories. Both live horses and iconic images of horses are used in advertising to promote a variety of products. The horse frequently appears in coats of arms in heraldry. The horse can be represented as standing, walking (passant), trotting, running (courant), rearing (rampant or forcine) or springing (salient). The horse may be saddled and bridled, harnessed, or without any apparel whatsoever. The horse also appears in the 12-year cycle of animals in the Chinese zodiac related to the Chinese calendar. According to Chinese folklore, each animal is associated with certain personality traits, and those born in the year of the horse are intelligent, independent, and free-spirited.

Therapeutic Use

People of all ages with physical and mental disabilities obtain beneficial results from association with horses. Therapeutic riding is used to mentally and physically stimulate disabled persons and help them improve their lives through improved balance and coordination, increased self-confidence, and a greater feeling of freedom and independence. The benefits of equestrian activity for people with disabilities has also been recognized with the addition of equestrian events to the Paralympic Games and recognition of para-equestrian events by the International Federation for Equestrian Sports (FEI). Hippotherapy and therapeutic horseback riding are names for different physical, occupational, and speech therapy treatment strategies that utilize equine movement. In hippotherapy, a therapist uses the horse's movement to improve their patient's cognitive, coordination, balance, and fine motor skills, whereas therapeutic horseback riding uses specific riding skills.

Horses also provide psychological benefits to people whether they actually ride or not. 'Equine-assisted' or 'equine-facilitated' therapy is a form of experiential psychotherapy that uses horses as companion animals to assist people with mental illness, including anxiety disorders, psychotic disorders, mood disorders, behavioural difficulties, and those who are going through major life changes. There are also experimental programmes using horses in prison settings. Exposure to horses appears to improve the behaviour of inmates and help reduce recidivism when they leave.

Warfare

Horses in warfare have been seen for most of recorded history. The first archaeological evidence of horses used in warfare dates to between 4000 to 3000 BC, and the use of horses in warfare was widespread by the end of the Bronze Age. Although mechanization has largely replaced the horse as a weapon of war, horses are still seen today in limited military uses, mostly for ceremonial purposes, or for reconnaissance and transport activities in areas of rough terrain where motorized vehicles are ineffective. Horses have been used in the 21st century by the Janjaweed militias in the War in Darfur.

Products

Horses are raw material for many products made by humans throughout history, including byproducts from the slaughter of horses as well as materials collected from living horses.

Products collected from living horses include mare's milk, used by people with large horse herds, such as the Mongols, who let it ferment to produce kumis. Horse blood was once used as food by the Mongols and other nomadic tribes, who found it a convenient source of nutrition when travelling. Drinking their own horses' blood allowed the Mongols to ride for extended periods of time without stopping to eat. Today, the drug Premarin is a mixture of estrogens extracted from the urine of pregnant mares (pregnant mares' urine). It is a widely used drug for hormone replacement therapy. The tail hair of horses can be used for making bows for string instruments such as the violin, viola, cello, and double bass.

Horse meat has been used as food for humans and carnivorous animals throughout the ages. It is eaten in many parts of the world, though consumption is taboo in some cultures. Horsemeat has been an export industry in the United States and other countries, though legislation has periodically been introduced in the United States Congress which would end export from the United States. Horsehide leather has been used for boots, gloves, jackets, baseballs, and baseball gloves. Horse hooves can also be used to produce animal glue. Horse bones can be used to make implements. Specifically, in Italian cuisine, the horse tibia is sharpened into a probe called a *spinto*, which is used to test the readiness of a (pig) ham as it cures. In Asia, the saba is a horsehide vessel used in the production of kumis.

Horses are grazing animals, and their major source of nutrients is good-quality forage from hay or pasture. They can consume approximately 2 per cent to 2.5 per cent of their body weight in dry feed each day. Therefore, a 450-kilogram (990 lb) adult horse could eat up to 11 kilograms (24 lb) of food. Sometimes, concentrated feed such as grain is fed in addition to pasture or hay, especially when the animal is very active. When grain is fed, equine nutritionists recommend that 50 per cent or more of the animal's diet by weight should still be forage.

Horses require a plentiful supply of clean water, a minimum of 10 US gallons (38 L) to 12 US gallons (45 L) per day. Although horses are adapted to live outside, they require shelter from the wind and precipitation, which can range from a simple shed or shelter to an elaborate stable.

Horses require routine hoof care from a farrier, as well as vaccinations to protect against various diseases, and dental examinations from a veterinarian or a specialized equine dentist. If horses are kept inside in a barn, they require regular daily exercise for their physical health and mental well-being. When turned outside, they require well-maintained, sturdy fences to be safely contained. Regular grooming is also helpful to help the horse maintain good health of the hair coat and underlying skin.

13 American Bison

The American bison (*Bison bison*), also commonly known as the American buffalo, is a North American species of bison that once roamed the grasslands of North America in massive herds. Their range once roughly comprised a triangle between the Great Bear Lake in Canada's far northwest, south to the Mexican states of Durango and Nuevo León, and east along the western boundary of the Appalachian Mountains. Due to commercial hunting and slaughter in the 19th century, the bison nearly went extinct and is today restricted to a few national parks and other reserves.

Two subspecies or ecotypes have been described: the plains bison (*Bison bison bison*), smaller in size and with a more rounded hump, and the wood bison (*Bison bison athabascae*) — the larger of the two and having a taller, square hump. Furthermore, it has been suggested that the plains bison consists of a northern (*Bison bison montanae*) and a southern subspecies, bringing the total to three. However, this is generally not supported. The wood bison is one of the largest species of bovid in the world, surpassed by only the Italian Chianina, the Asian gaur and wild Asian water buffalo. It is the largest extant land animal in North America.

A bison has a shaggy, long, dark brown winter coat, and a lighter weight, lighter brown summer coat. As is typical in ungulates, the male bison are slightly larger than the female. Bison bulls can reach up to 6 feet 6 inches (2 m) tall, 11 feet 6 inches (4 m) long, and weigh up to 2,200 pounds (1,000 kg). The biggest specimens on record have weighed as much as 2,500 pounds (1,130 kg). The heads and forequarters are massive, and both sexes have short, curved horns that can grow up to 2 feet (61 cm) long, which they use in fighting for status within the herd and for defence.

Bison are herbivores, grazing on the grasses and sedges of the North American prairies. Their daily schedule involves two-hour periods of grazing, resting and cud chewing, then moving to a new location to graze again. Bison mate in August and September; gestation is 285 days. A single reddish-brown calf nurses until the next calf is born. If the cow is not pregnant, a calf will nurse for 18 months. Bison cows are mature enough to produce a calf at 3 years of age. Bison bulls may try to mate with cows at 3 years of age, but if more mature bulls are present, they may not be able to compete until they reach 5 years of age. Bison have a life expectancy of approximately 15 years in the wild and up to 25 years in captivity.

For the first two months of life, calves are lighter in colour than mature bison. One very rare condition is the white buffalo, in which the calf turns entirely white. White bison are considered sacred by many Native Americans.

Some consider the term 'buffalo' somewhat of a misnomer for this animal, as it is only distantly related to either of the two 'true buffalo', the Asian water buffalo and the African buffalo. However, 'bison' is a Greek word meaning ox-like animal, while 'buffalo' originated with the French fur trappers who called these massive beasts *bœufs*, meaning ox or bullock — so both names, 'bison' and 'buffalo', have a similar meaning. In reference to this animal, the term 'buffalo', which dates to 1635, has a much longer history than the term 'bison', which was first recorded in 1774. The American bison is more closely related to the wisent or European bison.

Differences from European Bison

Although they are superficially similar, the American and European bison exhibit a number of physical and behavioural differences. The American species has 15 ribs, while the European bison has 14.

The American bison has four lumbar vertebrae, while the European has five Adult American bison are not as rangy in build, and have shorter legs. American bison tend to graze more, and browse less than their European cousins, due to their necks being set differently. Compared to the nose of the American bison, that of the European species is set farther forward than the forehead when the neck is in a neutral position. The body of the American bison is hairier, though its tail has less hair than that of the European bison. The horns of the European bison point forward through the plane of its face, making it more adept at fighting through the interlocking of horns in the same manner as domestic cattle, unlike the American bison which favours charging. American bison are more easily tamed than their European cousins, and breed more readily with domestic cattle.

There are approximately 500,000 bison in captive commercial populations (mostly plains bison) on about 4,000 privately owned ranches. Under the IUCN Red List Guidelines, commercial herds are not eligible for consideration in determining a Red List designation, therefore the total population of bison calculated in conservation herds is approximately 30,000 individuals and the mature population consists of approximately 20,000 individuals. Of the total number presented, only 15,000 total individuals are considered wild bison in the natural range within North America (free-ranging, not confined primarily by fencing).

Bison are now raised for meat and hides. The majority of bison in the world are being raised for human consumption. Bison meat is lower in fat and cholesterol than beef, a fact which has led to the development of beefalo, a fertile crossbreed of bison and domestic cattle. In 2005, about 35,000 bison were processed for meat in the U.S., with the National Bison Association and USDA providing a 'Certified American Buffalo' programme with birth-to-consumer tracking of bison via RFID ear tags. There is even a market for kosher bison meat; these bison are slaughtered at one of the few kosher mammal slaughterhouses in the U.S., and the meat is then distributed nationwide.

Bison are found in both publicly and privately held herds. Custer State Park in South Dakota is home to 1,500 bison, one of the largest publicly held herds in the world. Wildlife officials believe that free roaming and genetically pure herds on public lands in North America can be found only in Yellowstone National Park, Henry Mountains in Utah, Wind Cave National Park in South Dakota, Mackenzie Bison Sanctuary in the Northwest Territories, Elk Island National Park and Wood Buffalo National Park in Alberta, and Prince Albert National Park in Saskatchewan.

Recent genetic studies of privately owned herds of bison show that many of them include animals with genes from domestic cattle. For example, the herd on Santa Catalina Island, isolated since 1924, after being brought there for a movie shoot, were found to be mostly crossbreeds. It is estimated that there are as few as 12,000 to 15,000 pure bison in the world. The numbers are uncertain because the tests used to date — mitochondrial DNA analysis — indicate only if the maternal line (back from mother to mother...) ever included domesticated bovines and thus say nothing about possible male input in the process. It was found that most hybrids look exactly like purebred bison; therefore, appearance is not a good indicator of genetics.

A proposal known as Buffalo Commons has been suggested by a handful of academics and policymakers to restore large parts of the drier portion of the Great Plains to native prairie grazed by bison. Proponents argue that current agricultural use of the shortgrass prairie is not sustainable, pointing to periodic disasters, including the Dust Bowl, and continuing significant human population loss over the last 60 years. However, this plan is opposed by some who live in the areas in question.

Female bison live in maternal herds which include other females and their offspring. Male offspring leave their maternal herd when around three years old and will either live alone or join other males in bachelor herds. Male and female herds do not mingle until the breeding season.

During the breeding season, dominant bulls maintain a small harem of females for mating. Individual bulls 'tend' cows until allowed to mate, by following them around and chasing away rival males. The tending bull will shield the female's vision with his body so she will not see any other challenging males. A challenging bull may bellow or roar to get a female's attention and the tending bull has to bellow/roar back. The most dominant bulls mate in the first 2-3 weeks of the season. More subordinate bulls will mate with any remaining estrous cow that has not mated yet. Male bison play no part in raising the young.

Bison herds have dominance hierarchies that exist for both males and females. A bison's dominance is related to its birth date. Bison born earlier in the breeding season are more likely to be larger and more dominant as adults. Thus bison are able to pass on their dominance to their offspring as dominant bison breed earlier in the season. In addition to dominance, the older bison of a generation also have a higher fertility rate than the younger ones.

Wallowing Behaviour

A bison wallow is a shallow depression in the soil, which is used either wet or dry. Bison roll in these depressions, covering themselves with dust or mud. Past explanations and current hypotheses suggested for wallowing behaviour include grooming behaviour associated with shedding, male-male interaction (typically rutting behaviour), social behaviour for group cohesion, play behaviour, relief from skin irritation due to biting insects; reduction of ectoparasite (tick and lice) load; and thermoregulation.

In some areas, wolves are a major predator of bison. Wolf predation typically peaks in late spring and early summer, with attacks usually being concentrated on cows and calves. Observations have shown that wolves actively target herds with calves over ones with none.

The length of a predation episode varies, ranging from a few minutes to 11 hours. Bison display five apparent defense strategies in protecting calves from wolves: running to a cow, running to a herd, running to the nearest bull, running in the front or center of a stampeding herd, and entering water bodies such as lakes or rivers. When fleeing wolves in open areas, cows with young calves take the lead, while bulls take to the rear of the herds, to guard the cows' escape. Bison typically ignore wolves not displaying hunting behaviour. Wolf packs specializing in bison tend to have a greater number of males, as their superior size compared to the females allows them to wrestle their prey to the ground more effectively.

The American bison is a relative newcomer to North America, having originated in Eurasia and migrated over the Bering Strait. About 10,000 years ago it replaced the steppe bison (*Bison priscus*), a previous immigrant that was much larger. It is thought that the long-horned bison became extinct due to a changing ecosystem and hunting pressure following the development of the Clovis point and related technology, and improved hunting skills. During this same period, other megafauna vanished and were replaced to some degree by immigrant Eurasian animals that were better adapted to predatory humans. The American bison, technically a dwarf form, was one of these animals.

Bison were a keystone species, whose grazing pressure was a force that shaped the ecology of the Great Plains as strongly as periodic prairie fires and which were central to the lifestyle of Native Americans of the Great Plains. However, there is now some controversy over their interaction. "Hernando De Soto's expedition staggered through the Southeast for four years in the early 16th century and saw hordes of people but apparently did not see a single bison," Charles C. Mann wrote in *1491: New Revelations of the Americas Before Columbus.* Mann discussed the evidence that Native Americans not only created (by selective use of fire) the large grasslands that provided the bison's ideal habitat but also kept the bison population regulated. In this theory, it was only when the original human population was devastated by wave after wave of epidemic (from diseases of Europeans) after the 16th century that the bison herds propagated wildly. In such a view, the seas of bison herds that stretched to the horizon were a symptom of an ecology out of balance, only rendered possible by decades of heavier-than-average rainfall. Other evidence of the arrival circa 1550–1600 CE in the savannas of the eastern seaboard includes the lack of places which southeast natives named after buffalo. Bison were the most numerous single species of large wild mammal on Earth.

What is not disputed is that before the introduction of horses, bison were herded into large chutes made of rocks and willow branches and then stampeded over cliffs. These buffalo jumps are found in several places in the U.S. and Canada, such as Head-Smashed-In Buffalo Jump. Large groups of people would herd the bison for several miles, forcing them into a stampede that would ultimately drive many animals over a cliff. The large quantities of meat obtained in this way provided the hunters with surplus, which was used in trade. A similar method of hunting was to drive the bison into natural corrals, such as the Ruby site.

To get the optimum use out of the bison, the Native Americans had a specific method of butchery, first identified at the Olsen-Chubbock archaeological site in Colorado. The method involves skinning down the back to get at the tender meat just beneath the surface, the area known as the "hatched area." After the removal of the hatched area, the front legs are cut off as well as the shoulder blades. Doing so exposes the hump meat (in the wood bison), as well as the meat of the ribs and the bison's inner organs. After everything was exposed, the spine was then severed and the pelvis and hind legs removed. Finally, the neck and head were removed as one. This allowed for the tough meat to be dried and made into pemmican.

Later, when Plains Indians obtained horses, it was found that a good horseman could easily lance or shoot enough bison to keep his tribe and family fed, as long as a herd was nearby. The bison provided meat, leather, sinew for bows, grease, dried dung for fires, and even the hooves could be boiled for glue. When times were bad, bison were consumed down to the last bit of marrow.

19th Century Bison Hunts

Bison were hunted almost to extinction in the late 19th century primarily by market hunters and were reduced to a few hundred by the mid-1880s. They were hunted for their skins, with the rest of the animal left behind to decay on the ground. After the animals rotted, their bones were collected and shipped back east in large quantities.

The US Army sanctioned and actively endorsed the wholesale slaughter of bison herds. The US federal government promoted bison hunting for various reasons, to allow ranchers to range their cattle without competition from other bovines, and primarily to weaken the North American Indian population by removing their main food source and to pressure them onto the reservations. Without the bison, native people of the plains were forced either to leave the land or starve to death.

According to historian Pekka Hämäläinen, Native Americans also contributed to the collapse of the bison. By the 1830s the Comanche and their allies on the southern plains were killing about 280,000 bison a year, which was near the limit of sustainability for that region. Firearms and horses, along with a growing export market for buffalo robes and bison meat had resulted in larger and larger numbers of bison killed each year by the white and half breed market hunters. A long and intense drought hit the southern plains in 1845, lasting into the 1860s, which caused a widespread collapse of the bison herds. In the 1860s, the rains returned and the bison herds recovered to a degree.

The railroad industry also wanted bison herds culled or eliminated. Herds of bison on tracks could damage locomotives when the trains failed to stop in time. Herds often took shelter in the artificial cuts formed by the grade of the track winding through hills and mountains in harsh winter conditions. As a result, bison herds could delay a train for days.

The main or primary reason for the bison's near-demise, much like the actual demise of the passenger pigeon, was commercial market hunting.

Bison skins were used for clothing such as robes, rugs and, most importantly, for industrial machine belts. Prior to electrification factories were usually powered by a centrally located steam engine, with the power carried throughout the factory using an arrangement known as line shaft transmission. Power from the engine was transferred to rods suspended below the ceiling on each floor of the factory, where it was in turn transferred to individual machines on the floor via a leather belt running on two pulleys, one on the rod and the other on the machine. Buffalo leather was the material of choice for this application because of its strength and wear resistance.

There was a huge export trade to Europe of bison hides. Old West bison hunting by white people was very often a big commercial enterprise, involving organized teams of one or two professional market hunters, backed by a team of skinners, gun cleaners, cartridge reloaders, cooks, wranglers, blacksmiths, security guards, teamsters, and numerous horses and wagons. Men were even employed to recover and recast lead bullets taken from the carcasses. Many of these professional [market hunters], such as Buffalo Bill Cody, killed over a hundred animals at a single stand and many thousands in their career. One professional market hunter killed over 20,000 buffalo by his own count. A good hide could bring $3 in Dodge City, Kansas, and a very good one (the heavy winter coat) could sell for $50 in an era when a labourer would be lucky to make a dollar a day.

The market hunter would customarily locate the herd in the early morning, and station himself about 100 metres (109 yd) from it, shooting the animals broadside through the lungs. Head shots were not preferred as the soft lead bullets would often flatten and fail to penetrate the skull, especially if mud was matted on the head of the animal. The bison would drop until either the herd sensed danger and stampeded or perhaps a wounded animal attacked another, causing the herd to disperse. If done properly, a large number of bison would be felled at one time. Following up were the skinners, who would drive a spike through the nose of each dead animal with a sledgehammer, hook up a horse team, and pull the hide from the carcass. The hides were dressed, prepared, and stacked on the wagons by other members of the organization.

For a decade from 1873 on, there were several hundred, perhaps over a thousand, such commercial hide/market hunting outfits harvesting bison at any one time, vastly exceeding the take by American Indians or individual meat hunters. The commercial take arguably was anywhere from 2,000 to 100,000 animals per day depending on the season, though there are no statistics available. It was said that the Big .50s were fired so much that the market hunters needed at least two rifles to let the barrels cool off; The Fireside Book of Guns reports they were sometimes quenched in the winter snow. Dodge City saw railroad cars sent East filled with stacked hides.

The building of the railroads through Colorado and Kansas split the bison herd in two parts, the southern herd and the northern herd. The last refuge of the southern herd was in the Texas Panhandle.

As the great herds began to wane, proposals to protect the bison were discussed. Cody, among others, spoke in favor of protecting the bison because he saw that the pressure on the species was too great. Yet these proposals were discouraged since it was recognized that the Plains Indians, often at war with the United States, depended on bison for their way of life. In 1874, President Ulysses S. Grant 'pocket vetoed' a Federal bill to protect the dwindling bison herds, and in 1875, General Philip Sheridan pleaded to a joint session of Congress to slaughter the herds, to deprive the Indians of their source of food. By 1884, the American bison was close to extinction.

The famous herd of James 'Scotty' Philip in South Dakota was one of the earliest reintroductions of bison to North America. In 1899, Phillip purchased a small herd (five of them, including the female) from Dug Carlin, Pete Dupree's brother-in-law, whose son Fred had roped five calves in the Last Big Buffalo Hunt on the Grand River in 1881 and taken them back home to the ranch on the Cheyenne River. Scotty's goal was to preserve the animal from extinction. At the time of his death in 1911 at 53, Philip had grown the herd to an estimated 1,000 to 1,200 head of bison. A variety of privately owned herds had also been established, starting from this population.

Simultaneously, two Montana ranchers, Michel Pablo and Charles Allard, spent more than 20 years assembling one of the largest collections of purebred bison on the continent (by the time of Allard's death in 1896, the herd numbered 300). In 1907, after U.S. authorities declined to buy the herd, Pablo struck a deal with the Canadian government and shipped most of his bison northward to the newly created Elk Island National Park. Also, in 1907, the New York Zoological Park sent 15 bison to Wichita Mountains Wildlife Refuge in Oklahoma forming the nucleus of a herd that now numbers 650.

An isolated bison herd on Utah's Antelope Island has also been used to improve the genetic diversity of American bison. The current American bison population has been growing rapidly, and is estimated at 350,000, compared to an estimated 60 to 100 million in the mid-19th century. Most current herds, however are genetically polluted or partly crossbred with cattle. Today there are only four genetically unmixed herds and only one that is also free of brucellosis: it roams Wind Cave National Park. A founder population of 16 animals from the Wind Cave herd was established in Montana in 2005 by the American Prairie Foundation. The herd now numbers near 100 and roams a 14,000-acre (57 km^2) grassland expanse on American Prairie Reserve.

One of the largest privately owned herds, numbering 2,500, in the US is on the Tallgrass Prairie Preserve in Oklahoma which is owned by the Nature Conservancy. Ted Turner is the largest private owner of Bison with about 50,000 on several different ranches.

The only continuously wild bison herd in the United States resides within Yellowstone National Park. Numbering between 3,000 and 3,500, this herd is descended from a remnant population of 23 individual mountain bison that survived the mass slaughter of the 1800s by hiding out in the Pelican Valley of Yellowstone Park. In 1902, a captive herd of 21 plains bison was introduced to the Lamar Valley and managed as livestock until the 1960s, when a policy of natural regulation was adopted by the park.

The end of the ranching era and the onset of the natural regulation era set into motion a chain of events that have led to the bison of Yellowstone Park migrating to lower elevations outside the park in search of winter forage. The presence of wild bison in Montana is perceived as a threat to many cattle ranchers, who fear that the small percentage of bison that carry brucellosis will infect livestock and cause cows to abort their first calves. However, there has never been a documented case of brucellosis being transmitted to cattle from wild bison. The management controversy that began in the early 1980s continues to this day, with advocacy groups arguing that the Yellowstone herd should be protected as a distinct population segment under the Endangered Species Act.

Bison Hunting Today

Hunting of wild bison is legal in some states and provinces where public herds require culling to maintain a target population. In Alberta, where one of only two continuously wild herds of bison exist in North America at Wood Buffalo National Park, bison are hunted to protect disease-free public (reintroduced) and private herds of bison.

In Montana, a public hunt was reestablished in 2005, with 50 permits being issued. The Montana Fish, Wildlife, and Parks Commission increased the number of tags to 140 for the 2006/2007 season. Advocacy groups claim that it is premature to reestablish the hunt, given the bison's lack of habitat and wildlife status in Montana.

Bison were also reintroduced to Alaska in 1928, and both domestic and wild herds subsist in a few parts of the state. The state grants limited permits to hunt wild bison each year.

The bison is one of the few North American large game animals that can be hunted year round, though hunters prefer to hunt it at certain times of the year to achieve desired appearances of the coat.

In 2002 the United States government donated some buffalo calfs offspring to reintroduce the Mexican government to its wildlife, these specimens were from South Dakota and Colorado, the reintroduction of the American buffalo in the Mexican nature reserves El Uno Ranch at Janos and Santa Helena Canyon, Chihuahua, and Boquillas del Carmen, Coahuila, is located in the southern shores of the Rio Grande and the grasslands borderline with Texas and New Mexico.

The first thoroughfares of North America, except for the time-obliterated paths of mastodon or muskox and the routes of the Mound Builders, were the traces made by bison and deer in seasonal migration and between feeding grounds and salt licks. Many of these routes, hammered by countless hoofs instinctively following watersheds and the crests of ridges in avoidance of lower places' summer muck and winter snowdrifts, were followed by the Indians as courses to hunting grounds and as warriors' paths. They were invaluable to explorers and were adopted by pioneers.

Bison traces were characteristically north and south, but several key east-west trails were used later as railways. Some of these include the Cumberland Gap through the Blue Ridge Mountains to upper Kentucky. A heavily used trace crossed the Ohio River at the Falls of the Ohio and ran west, crossing the Wabash River near Vincennes, Indiana. In Senator Thomas Hart Benton's phrase saluting these sagacious path-makers, the bison paved the way for the railroads to the Pacific.

The American bison is often used in North America in official seals, flags, and logos. In the United States, the American bison is a popular symbol in the Great Plains states. Kansas, Oklahoma, and Wyoming have adopted the animal as their official state mammal, and many sports teams have chosen the bison as their mascot. In Canada, the bison is the official animal of the province of Manitoba and appears on the Manitoba flag. It is also used in the official coat of arms of the Royal Canadian Mounted Police.

Several American coins feature the bison, most famously on the reverse side of the 'buffalo nickel' from 1913 to 1938. In 2005, the United States Mint coined a nickel with a new depiction of the bison as part of its 'Westward Journey' series. The Kansas and North Dakota state quarters, part of the '50 State Quarter' series, each feature bison. The Kansas state quarter has only the bison and does not feature any writing, while the North Dakota state quarter has two bison.

14 Camel

A camel is an even-toed ungulate within the genus *Camelus*, bearing distinctive fatty deposits, known as humps, on its back. There are two species of camels — the Dromedary or Arabian camel has a single hump, and the Bactrian camel has two humps. Dromedaries are native to the dry desert areas of West Asia, and Bactrian camels are native to Central and East Asia. Both species are domesticated, they provide milk and meat, and are beasts of burden.

The term *camel*, (from the Arabic , *gml*, derived from the triconsonantal root signifying 'beauty'), is also used more broadly to describe any of the six camel-like creatures in the family Camelidae—the two true camels, and the four South American camelids—the llama, alpaca, guanaco, and vicuña.

The average life expectancy of a camel is 40 to 50 years. A fully grown adult camel stands 1.85 m (6 ft 1 in) at the shoulder and 2.15 m (7 ft 1 in) at the hump. The hump rises about 30 in (76.20 cm) out of its body. Camels can run at up to 65 km/h (40 mph) in short bursts and sustain speeds of up to 40 km/h (25 mph).

Fossil evidence indicates that the ancestors of modern camels evolved in North America during the Palaeogene period (see also *Camelops*), and later spread to most parts of Asia. The people of ancient Somalia or the Kingdom of Punt first domesticated camels well before 2000 BC.

14,000 dromedaries alive today are domesticated animals (mostly living in Somalia, the Sahel, Maghreb, Middle East and Indian subcontinent). An estimated quarter of the world's camel population is found in Somalia and in the Somali Region of Ethiopia, where the camel is an important part of nomadic Somali life. They provide the Somali people with milk, food and transportation.

The Bactrian camel is now reduced to an estimated 1.4 million animals, mostly domesticated. It is thought that there are about 1000 wild Bactrian camels in the Gobi Desert in China and Mongolia.

There is a substantial feral population of dromedaries estimated at up to 1,000,000 in central parts of Australia, descended from individuals introduced as transport animals in the 19th century and early 20th century. This population is growing at approximately 18 per cent per year. The government of South Australia has decided to cull the animals using aerial marksmen, because the camels use too much of the limited resources needed by sheep farmers.

A small population of introduced camels, dromedaries and Bactrians survived in the Southwest United States until the second half of the 20th Century. These animals, imported from Turkey, were part of the U.S. Camel Corps experiment and used as draft animals in mines and escaped or were released after the project was terminated. A descendant of one of these was seen by a backpacker in Los Padres National Forest in 1972. Twenty-three Bactrian camels were brought to Canada during the Cariboo Gold Rush.

Camels do not store water in their humps as is commonly believed. The humps are actually a reservoir of fatty tissue. Concentrating body fat in their humps minimizes heat-trapping insulation throughout the rest of their body, which may be an adaptation to living in hot climates. When this tissue is metabolized, it acts as a source of energy, and yields more than 1 g of water for each 1 g of fat converted through reaction with oxygen from air. This process of fat metabolization generates a net loss of water through respiration for the oxygen required to convert the fat.

Their ability to withstand long periods without water is due to a series of physiological adaptations. Their red blood cells have an oval shape, unlike those of other mammals, which are circular. This facilitates their flow in a dehydrated state. These cells are also more stable in order to withstand high osmotic variation without rupturing when drinking large amounts of water (100 litres (22 imp gal; 26 US gal) to 150 litres (33 imp gal; 40 US gal) in one drink). Oval red corpuscles are not found in any other mammal, but are present in reptiles, birds, and fish.

Camels are able to withstand changes in body temperature and water content that would kill most other animals. Their temperature ranges from 34°C (93°F) at night and up to 41°C (106°F) during the day, and only above this threshold will they begin to sweat. The upper body temperature range is often not reached during the day in milder climatic conditions, and therefore, the camel may not sweat at all during the day. Evaporation of their sweat takes place at the skin level, not at the surface of their coat, thereby being very efficient at cooling the body compared to the amount of water lost through perspiration.

A feature of their nostrils is that a large amount of water vapour in their exhalations is trapped and returned to their body fluids, thereby reducing the amount of water lost through respiration.

They can withstand at least 20-25 per cent weight loss due to sweating (most mammals can only withstand about 15 per cent dehydration before cardiac failure results from circulatory disturbance). A camel's blood remains hydrated, even though the body fluids are lost, until this 25 per cent limit is reached.

Camels eating green herbage can ingest sufficient moisture in milder conditions to maintain their bodies' hydrated state without the need for drinking.

A camel's thick coat reflects sunlight, and also insulates it from the intense heat radiated from desert sand. A shorn camel has to sweat 50 per cent more to avoid overheating. Their long legs help by keeping them further from the hot ground. Camels have been known to swim.

Their mouth is very sturdy, able to chew thorny desert plants. Long eyelashes and ear hairs, together with sealable nostrils, form a barrier against sand. Their gait and their widened feet help them move without sinking into the sand.

The kidneys and intestines of a camel are very efficient at retaining water. Urine comes out as a thick syrup, and their feces are so dry that they can fuel fires.

All camelids have an unusual immune system. In all mammals, the Y-shaped antibody molecules consist of two heavy (or long) chains along the length of the Y, and two light (or short) chains at each tip of the Y. Camels also have antibody molecules that have only two heavy chains, which makes them smaller and more durable. These *heavy chain-only* antibodies, which were discovered in 1993, probably developed 50 million years ago, after camelids split from ruminants and pigs, according to biochemist Serge Muyldermans.

The camel is the only animal to have replaced the wheel (mainly in North Africa) where the wheel had already been established. The camel did not lose that distinction until the wheel was combined with the internal combustion engine in the 20th century.

The karyotypes of different camelid species have been studied earlier by many groups, but no agreement on chromosome nomenclature of camelids has been reached. The most recent study used flow-sorted camel chromosomes building undoubtedly the camel's karyotype (2n=74) that consists of one metacentric, three submetacentric and 32 acrocentric autosomes. The Y is a small metacentric chromosome, while the X is a large metacentric chromosome. According to molecular data, the New World and Old World camelids diverged 11 MYA. In spite of this, these species turned out to be conserved sufficiently to hybridize and produce live offspring(cama). The dromedary-guanaco inter-specific hybrid provided the ideal platform to compare the karyotypes of Old World and New World camels.

The cama is a camel/llama hybrid bred by scientists who wanted to see how closely related the parent species were. The dromedary is six times the weight of a llama, hence artificial insemination was required to impregnate the llama female (llama male to dromedary female attempts have proven unsuccessful). Though born even smaller than a llama cria, the cama had the short ears and long tail of a camel, no hump and llama-like cloven hooves rather than the dromedary-like pads. At four years old, the cama became sexually mature and attracted to llama and guanaco females. A second cama (female) has since been produced using artificial insemination. Because camels and llamas both have 74 chromosomes, scientists hope that the cama will be fertile. If so, there is potential for increasing size, meat/wool yield and pack/draft ability in South American camels. The cama apparently inherited the poor temperament of both parents as well as demonstrating the relatedness of the New World and Old World camelids.

Dromedary-Bactrian hybrids are called bukhts, are larger than either parent, have a single hump and are good draft camels. The females can be mated back to a Bactrian to produce ¾-bred riding camels. These hybrids are found in Kazakhstan.

Military Uses

Since at least 1200 BC, the first camel saddles appeared, and Bactrian camels could be ridden. The first Arabian saddle was put way to the back of the camel, and control of the Bactrian camel happened by means of a stick. However it wasn't until between 500-100 BC that Bactrian camels finally attained a military use. These new saddles were put over the humps of the animal, and they were also inflexible and bent, dividing the weight sufficiently over the animal. In the seventh century D.C., the military Arabian saddle then appeared, which improved the saddle design again slightly.

Camel cavalry have been used in wars throughout Africa, the Middle East and into modern-day India. Armies have also used camels as freight animals instead of horses and mules.

In the East Roman Empire the Romans used auxiliary forces known as Dromedarii, whom they recruited in desert provinces. The camels were mostly used in combat because of their ability to scare off horses in close ranges, a quality famously employed by the Achaemenid Persians when fighting Lydia, although the Persians usually used camels as baggage trains for arrows and equipment.

19th and 20th Centuries

The United States Army established the U.S. Camel Corps, which was stationed in California in the 19th century. One may still see brick stables at the Benicia Arsenal in Benicia, California, where they serve as artists' and artisans' studio spaces. During the American Civil War, camels were used at an experimental stage, but were not used any further, as they were unpopular with the men. Some escaped and their descedants roamed the arid parts of the American West until as late as the early 20th century.

France created a méhariste camel corps as part of the Armée d'Afrique in the Sahara from 1902, replacing regular units of Algerian spahis and tirailleurs earlier used to patrol the desert boundaries. The camel-mounted units remained in service until the end of French rule in 1962. The French transferred the French personnel to other units and disbanded the locally recruited méharistes.

In 1916, during World War I, the British created the Imperial Camel Corps, which was a brigade-sized military formation that fought in the Sinai and Palestine Campaign. It comprised infantry mounted on camels for movement across desert. In May 1918 the Corps was reduced in strength to a single battalion and was formally disbanded in May 1919. Also during World War I, the British Army created the Egyptian Camel Transport Corps, which consisted of a group of Egyptian camel drivers and their camels. The Corps supported British war operations in the Sinai desert, Palestine and Syria by transporting supplies to the troops.

The Somaliland Camel Corps was a unit of the British Army based in British Somaliland from the early 20th century until the 1960s.

The Bikaner Camel Corps was a military unit from India that fought for the Allies in World War I and World War II.

The Tropas Nómadas (Nomad Troops) were an auxiliary regiment of Sahrawi tribesmen serving in the colonial army in Spanish Sahara (today Western Sahara). Operational from the 1930s until the end of the Spanish presence in the territory in 1975, the Tropas Nómadas were equipped with small arms and led by Spanish officers. The unit guarded outposts and sometimes conducted patrols on camelback.

Milk

Camel milk is a staple food of desert nomad tribes and is richer in fat and protein than cow milk. It is said to have many healthful properties. It is used as a medicinal product in India and as an aphrodisiac in Ethiopia. Bedouins believe that the curative powers of camel milk are enhanced if the camel's diet consists of certain plants. Camel milk can readily be made into yogurt, but can only be made into butter or cheese with difficulty. Butter or yogurt made from camel milk is said to have a very faint greenish tinge.

Camel milk cannot be made into butter by the traditional churning method. It can be made if it is soured first, churned, and a clarifying agent added, or if it is churned at 24-25°C (75-77°F), but times vary greatly in achieving results. Until recently, camel milk could not be made into cheese because rennet was unable to coagulate the milk proteins to allow the collection of curds. Under the commission of the FAO, Professor J.P. Ramet of the École Nationale Supérieure d'Agronomie et des Industries Alimentaires (ENSAIA) was able to produce curdling by the addition of calcium phosphate and vegetable rennet. The cheese produced from this process has low levels of cholesterol and lactose. The sale of camel cheese is limited owing to the low yield of cheese from milk and the uncertainty of pasteurization levels for camel milk, which makes adherence to dairy import regulations difficult.

Meat

A camel carcass can provide a substantial amount of meat. The male dromedary carcass can weigh 400 kg (900 lb) or more, while the carcass of a male Bactrian can weigh up to 650 kg (1,400 lb). The carcass of a female camel (or she-camel) weighs less than the male, ranging between 250 and 350 kg (550 and 770 lb). The brisket, ribs and loin are among the preferred parts, but the hump is considered a delicacy and is most favoured. It is reported that camel meat tastes like coarse beef, but older camels can prove to be very tough and less flavourful. The meat from older camels is best prepared by slow cooking. Camel meat is low in fat, and can thus taste dry. The Abu Dhabi Officers' Club serves a camel burger, as this allows the meat to be mixed with beef or lamb fat, improving both the texture and taste. In Karachi, Pakistan the exclusive Nihari restaurants prepare this dish from camel meat, while the general restaurants prepare it with either beef or water buffalo meat.

Camel meat has been eaten for centuries. It has been recorded by ancient Greek writers as an available dish in ancient Persia at banquets, usually roasted whole. The ancient Roman emperor Heliogabalus enjoyed camel's heel. Camel meat is still eaten in certain regions including Somalia, where it is called *Hilib geel*, Saudi Arabia, Egypt, Libya, Sudan, Kazakhstan and other arid regions where alternative forms of protein may be limited or where camel meat has had a long cultural history. In the Middle East, camel meat is the rarest and most prized source of pastirma. Not just the meat, but also blood is a consumable item as is the case in northern Kenya, where camel blood is a source of iron, vitamin D, salts and minerals. Camel meat is also occasionally found in Australian cuisine, for example, a camel lasagne is available in Alice Springs.

Domestic Cat

The cat (*Felis catus*), also known as the domestic cat or housecat to distinguish it from other felines and felids, is a small furry domesticated carnivorous mammal that is valued by humans for its companionship and for its ability to hunt vermin and household pests. Cats have been associated with humans for at least 9,500 years, and are currently the most popular pet in the world. Owing to their close association with humans, cats are now found almost everywhere on Earth.

Cats are similar in anatomy to the other felids, with strong, flexible bodies, quick reflexes, sharp retractable claws, and teeth adapted to killing small prey. As nocturnal predators, cats use their acute hearing and ability to see in near darkness to locate prey. Not only can cats hear sounds too faint for human ears, they can also hear sounds higher in frequency than humans can perceive. This is because cats' usual prey (particularly rodents such as mice) make high frequency noises, so cats' hearing has evolved to pinpoint these faint high-pitched sounds. Cats rely more on smell than taste, and have a vastly better sense of smell than humans.

Despite being solitary hunters, cats are a social species and use a variety of vocalizations, pheromones and types of body language for communication. These include meowing, purring, trilling, hissing, growling, and grunting.

Cats have a rapid breeding rate. Under controlled breeding, they can be bred and shown as registered pedigree pets, a hobby known as cat fancy. Failure to control the breeding of pet cats by spaying and neutering and the abandonment of former household pets has resulted in problems caused by large numbers of feral cats worldwide, with a population of up to 60 million of these animals in the United States alone.

As *The New York Times* wrote in 2007, "Until recently the cat was commonly believed to have been domesticated in ancient Egypt, where it was a cult animal", but a study that year revealed that the lines of descent of all house cats probably run through as few as five self-domesticating African Wildcats *(Felis silvestris lybica)* c. 8000 BC, in the Near East. The earliest direct evidence of cat domestication is a kitten that was buried alongside a human 9,500 years ago in Cyprus.

The word *cat* derives from Old English *catt*, which belongs to a group of related words in European languages, including Welsh *cath*, Spanish *gato*, French *chat* (French pronunciation: , Basque *katu*, Byzantine Greek *? kátia*, Old Irish *cat*, Frisian and Dutch *kat*, German *Katze*, Armenian *katu*, and Old Church Slavonic *kotka*. The ultimate source of all these terms is Late Latin *catus, cattus, catta* 'domestic cat', as opposed to *feles* 'European wildcat'. It is unclear whether the Greek or the Latin came first, but they were undoubtedly borrowed from an Afro-Asiatic language akin to Nubian *kadís* and Berber *kaddîska*, both meaning 'wildcat'. The term *puss* (as in pussycat) may come from Dutch *poes* or from Low German *Puuskatte*, dialectal Swedish *kattepus*, or Norwegian *pus*, *pusekatt*, all of which primarily denote a woman and, by extension, a female cat.

While *wildcats* are the ancestral species from which domestic cats are descended, there are several intermediate stages between domestic pet and pedigree cats and these entirely wild cats. The semi-feral cat is a cat that is not owned by any one individual, but is generally friendly to people and may be fed by several households. Feral cats are associated with human habitations and may be fed by people or forage in rubbish, but are wary of human interaction. Pseudo-wildcats are descended from domestic cats, but now tend to live entirely independently from people.

A group of cats is referred to as a 'clowder', a male cat is called a 'tom' (or a 'gib', if neutered), and a female is called a 'molly' or 'queen'. The male progenitor of a cat, especially a pedigreed cat, is its 'sire', and its female progenitor is its 'dam'. An immature cat is called a 'kitten' (which is also an alternative name for young rats, rabbits, hedgehogs, beavers, squirrels and skunks).

In mediaeval Britain, the word *kitten* was interchangeable with the word *catling*. A cat whose ancestry is formally registered is called a pedigreed cat, purebred cat, or a show cat. In strict terms, a pure-bred cat is one whose ancestry contains only individuals of the same breed. A pedigreed cat is one whose ancestry is recorded, but may have ancestors of different breeds. Cats of unrecorded mixed ancestry are referred to as domestic longhairs and domestic shorthairs or commonly as random-bred, moggies, mongrels, or mutt-cats.

The Felids are a rapidly evolving family of mammals that share a common ancestor only 10-15 million years ago, and include, in addition to the domestic cat, lions, tigers, cougars, and many others. Within this family, domestic cats (*Felis catus*) are part of the genus *Felis*, which is a group of small cats containing seven species. Members of the genus are found worldwide and include the Jungle Cat (*Felis chaus*) of southeast Asia, the African Wildcat (*Felis silvestris lybica*), the Chinese Mountain Cat (*Felis silvestris bieti*) and the Arabian Sand Cat (*Felis margarita*).

All the cats in this genus share a common ancestor that probably lived around 6-7 million years ago in Asia. Although the exact relationships within the Felidae are still uncertain, both the Chinese Mountain Cat and the African Wildcat are close relations of the domestic cat and are both classed as subspecies of the Wildcat *Felis silvestris*. As domestic cats are little altered from wildcats, they can readily interbreed. This hybridization may pose a danger to the genetic distinctiveness of wildcat populations, particularly in Scotland and Hungary.

The domestic cat was first classified as *Felis catus* by Carolus Linnaeus in the tenth edition of his *Systema Naturae* of 1758. However, because of modern phylogenetics, domestic cats are now usually regarded as another subspecies of the Wildcat *Felis silvestris*. This has resulted in mixed usage of the terms, as the domestic cat can be called by its subspecies name, *Felis silvestris catus*. Wildcats have also been referred to as various subspecies of *F. catus*, but in 2003 the International Commission on Zoological Nomenclature fixed the name for wildcats as *F. silvestris*. The most common name in use for the domestic cat remains *F. catus*, following a convention for domesticated animals of using the earliest (the senior) synonym proposed. Sometimes the domestic cat is called *Felis domesticus* or *Felis domestica*, the term coined by German naturalist Johann Christian Polycarp Erxleben in 1777. These are not valid taxonomic names, and Linnaeus' binomial takes precedence.

Cats have either a mutualistic or commensal relationship with humans. However, in comparison to dogs, cats have not undergone major changes during the domestication process, as the form and behaviour of the domestic cat are not radically different from those of wildcats, and domestic cats are perfectly capable of surviving in the wild. This limited evolution during domestication means that domestic cats tend to interbreed freely with feral cats, which distinguishes them from other domesticated animals. However, several natural behaviours and characteristics of wildcats may have preadapted them for domestication as pets. These traits include their small size, social nature, obvious body language, love of play and relatively high intelligence; they may also have an inborn tendency towards tameness.

There are two main theories about how cats were domesticated. In one, people deliberately tamed cats in a process of artificial selection, as they were useful predators of vermin. However, this has been criticized as implausible, because there may have been little reward for such an effort: cats do not carry out commands and, although they do eat rodents, other species such as ferrets or terriers may be better at controlling these pests. The alternative idea is that cats were simply tolerated by people and gradually diverged from their 'wild' relatives through natural selection, as they adapted to hunting the vermin found around humans in towns and villages.

The domesticated cat and its closest wild ancestor are both diploid organisms that possess 38 chromosomes and roughly 20,000 genes. About 250 heritable genetic disorders have been identified in cats, many similar to human inborn errors. The high level of similarity among the metabolisms of mammals allows many of these feline diseases to be diagnosed using genetic tests that were originally developed for use in humans, as well as the use of cats in the study of the human diseases.

An interesting example of a mutation that is shared among all felines, including the big cats, is a mutant chemosensor in their taste buds that prevents them from tasting sweetness, which may explain their indifference to fruits, berries, and other sugary foods. In some breeds of cats congenital deafness is very common, with most white cats (but not albinos) being affected, particularly if they also have blue eyes. The genes responsible for this defect are unknown, but the disease is studied in the hope that it may shed light on the causes of hereditary deafness in humans.

Since a large variety of coat patterns exist within the various cat breeds, the cat is an excellent animal to study the coat genetics of hair growth and colouration. Several genes interact to produce cats' hair colour and coat patterns. Different combinations of these genes give different phenotypes. For example, the enzyme tyrosinase is needed to produce the dark pigment melanin and Burmese cats have a mutant form that is only active at low temperatures, resulting in colour appearing only on the cooler ears, tail and paws. A completely inactive gene for tyrosinase is found in albino cats, which therefore lack all pigment. Hair length is determined by the gene for fibroblast growth factor 5, with inactive copies of this gene causing long hair.

The Cat Genome Project, sponsored by the Laboratory of Genomic Diversity at the U.S. National Cancer Institute Frederick Cancer Research and Development Center in Frederick, Maryland, aims to help the development of the cat as an animal model for human hereditary and infectious diseases, as well as contributing to the understanding of the evolution of mammals. This effort led to the publication in 2007 of an initial draft of the genome of an Abyssinian cat called Cinnamon. The existence of a draft genome has led to the discovery of several cat disease genes, and even allowed the development of cat genetic fingerprinting for use in forensics.

Domestic cats are similar in size to the other members of the genus *Felis*, typically weighing between 4 kilograms (8 lb 13 oz) and 5 kilograms (11 lb 0 oz). However, some breeds, such as the Maine Coon, can exceed 11 kilograms (25 lb). Conversely, very small cats (less than 1.8 kilograms (3 lb 15 oz)) have been reported. The world record for the largest cat is 21.297 kilograms (46 lb 15.2 oz). The smallest adult cat ever officially recorded weighed around 1.36 kilograms (3 lb). Cats average about 23-25 centimeters (9-10 in) in height and 46 centimeters (18.1 in) in head/body length (males being larger than females), with tails averaging 30 centimeters (11.8 in) in length.

Cats have 7 cervical vertebrae like almost all mammals, 13 thoracic vertebrae (humans have 12), 7 lumbar vertebrae (humans have 5), 3 sacral vertebrae like most mammals (humans have 5 because of their bipedal posture), and a variable number of caudal vertebrae in the tail (humans retain 3 to 5 caudal vertebrae, fused into an internal coccyx). The extra lumbar and thoracic vertebrae account for the cat's spinal mobility and flexibility. Attached to the spine are 13 ribs, the shoulder, and the pelvis. Unlike human arms, cat forelimbs are attached to the shoulder by free-floating clavicle bones, which allow them to pass their body through any space into which they can fit their heads.

The cat skull is unusual among mammals in having very large eye sockets and a powerful and specialized jaw. Within the jaw, cats have teeth adapted for killing prey and tearing meat. When it overpowers its prey, a cat delivers a lethal neck bite with its two long canine teeth, inserting them between two of the prey's vertebrae and severing its spinal cord, causing irreversible paralysis and death. Compared to other felines, domestic cats have narrowly spaced canine teeth; which is an adaptation to their preferred prey of small rodents, which have small vertebrae. The premolar and first molar together compose the carnassial pair on each side of the mouth, which efficiently shears meat into small pieces, like a pair of scissors. These are vital in feeding, since cats' small molars cannot chew food effectively.

Cats, like dogs, are digitigrades. They walk directly on their toes, with the bones of their feet making up the lower part of the visible leg. Cats are capable of walking very precisely, because like all felines they directly register; that is, they place each hind paw (almost) directly in the print of the corresponding forepaw, minimizing noise and visible tracks. This also provides sure footing for their hind paws when they navigate rough terrain. Unlike most mammals, when cats walk, they use a 'pacing' gait; that is, they move the two legs on one side of the body before the legs on the other side. This trait is shared with camels and giraffes. As a walk speeds up into a trot, a cat's gait will change to be a 'diagonal' gait, similar to other mammals: the diagonally opposite hind and forelegs will move simultaneously.

Like almost all members of the Felidae family, cats have protractable claws. In their normal, relaxed position the claws are sheathed with the skin and fur around the toe pads. This keeps the claws sharp by preventing wear from contact with the ground and allows the silent stalking of prey. The claws on the forefeet are typically sharper than those on the hind feet. Cats can voluntarily extend their claws on one or more paws. They may extend their claws in hunting or self-defense, climbing, 'kneading', or for extra traction on soft surfaces. Most cats have five claws on their front paws, and four on their rear paws. The fifth front claw (the dewclaw) is proximal to the other claws. More proximally, there is a protrusion which appears to be a sixth 'finger'. This special feature of the front paws, on the inside of the wrists, is the carpal pad, also found on the paws of big cats and dogs. It has no function in normal walking, but is thought to be an anti-skidding device used while jumping. Some breeds of cats are prone to polydactylyism, and may have eight or even ten toes. These are particularly common along the North-East coast of North America.

As cats are familiar and easily kept animals, their physiology has been particularly well studied; it generally resembles that of other carnivorous mammals but displays several unusual features probably attributable to cats' descent from desert-dwelling species. For instance, cats are able to tolerate quite high temperatures: humans generally start to feel uncomfortable when their skin temperature passes about 44.5°C (112°F), but cats show no discomfort until their skin reaches around 52°C (126°F), and can tolerate temperatures of up to 56°C (133°F) if they have access to water.

Cats conserve heat by reducing the flow of blood to their skin and lose heat by evaporation through their mouth. They do not sweat, and pant only at very high temperatures. Unusually, a cat's body temperature does not vary throughout the day; this is part of cats' general lack of circadian rhythms and may reflect their tendency to be active both during the day and at night. Cats' feces are usually dry and their urine is also highly concentrated, both of which are adaptations that allow cats to retain as much fluid as possible. Their kidneys are so efficient that cats can survive on a diet consisting only of meat, with no additional water, and can even rehydrate by drinking seawater.

Cats are obligate carnivores: their physiology has evolved to efficiently process meat, and they have difficulty digesting plant matter. In contrast to omnivores such as rats, which only require about 4 per cent protein in their diet, about 20 per cent of a cat's diet must be protein. Cats are unusually dependent on a constant supply of the amino acid arginine, and a diet lacking arginine causes marked weight loss and can be rapidly fatal. Another unusual feature is that the cat also cannot produce the amino acid taurine, with taurine deficiency causing macular degeneration, where the cat's retina slowly degenerates, causing irreversible blindness. Since cats tend to eat all of their prey, they obtain minerals by digesting animal bones, and a diet composed only of meat may cause calcium deficiency.

A cat's digestive tract is also adapted to meat eating, being much shorter than that of omnivores and having low levels of several of the digestive enzymes that are needed to digest carbohydrates. These traits severely limit the cat's ability to digest and use plant-derived nutrients, as well as certain fatty acids. Despite the cat's meat-oriented physiology, several vegetarian or vegan cat foods have been marketed that are supplemented with chemically synthesized taurine and other nutrients, in attempts to produce a complete diet. However, some of these products still fail to provide all the nutrients that cats require, and diets containing no animal products pose the risk of causing severe nutritional deficiencies.

Cats have excellent night vision and can see at only one-sixth the light level required for human vision. This is partly the result of cat eyes having a tapetum lucidum, which reflects any light that passes through the retina back into the eye, thereby increasing the eye's sensitivity to dim light. Another adaptation to dim light is the large pupils of cats' eyes. Unlike some big cats, such as tigers, domestic cats have slit pupils. These slit pupils can focus bright light without chromatic aberration, and are needed since the domestic cat's pupils are much larger, relative to their eyes, than the pupils of the big cats. Indeed, at low light levels a cat's pupils will expand to cover most of the exposed surface of its eyes. However, domestic cats have rather poor colour vision and can only see two colours: blue and green, and are less able to distinguish between red and green, although they can achieve this in some conditions.

Cats have excellent hearing and can detect an extremely broad range of frequencies. They can hear higher-pitched sounds than either dogs or humans, detecting frequencies from 55 Hz up to 79 kHz, a range of 10.5 octaves; while humans can only hear from 31 Hz up to 18 kHz, and dogs hear from 67 Hz to 44 kHz, which are both ranges of about 9 octaves. Cats do not use this ability to hear ultrasound for communication but it is probably important in hunting, since many species of rodents make ultrasonic calls. Cats' hearing is also extremely sensitive and is among the best of any mammal, being most acute in the range of 500 Hz to 32 kHz. This sensitivity is further enhanced by the cat's large movable outer ears (their *pinnae*), which both amplify sounds and help a cat sense the direction from which a noise is coming.

Cats have an acute sense of smell, which is due in part to their well-developed olfactory bulb and also to a large surface of olfactory mucosa, in cats this mucosa is about 5.8 cm^2 in area, which is about twice that of humans and only 1.7-fold less than the average dog. Cats are very sensitive to pheromones such as 3-mercapto-3-methylbutan-1-ol, which they use to communicate through urine spraying and marking with scent glands. Cats also respond strongly to plants such as catnip which contains nepetalactone, as they can detect this substance at less than one part per billion. This response is also produced by other plants, such as Silver Vine and valerian, and may be caused by the smell of these plants mimicking a pheromone and stimulating cats' social or sexual behaviours.

Cats have relatively few taste buds compared to humans. Owing to a mutation in an early cat ancestor, one of two genes necessary to taste sweetness may have been lost by the cat family. Their taste buds instead respond to amino acids, bitter tastes and acids. To aid with navigation and sensation, cats have dozens of movable vibrissae (whiskers) over their body, especially their face. These provide information on the width of gaps and on the location of objects in the dark, both by touching objects directly and by sensing air currents; they also trigger protective blink reflexes to protect the eyes from damage.

In captivity, an average life expectancy for male indoor cats at birth is 12 to 14 years, with females usually living a year or two longer. However, there have been records of cats reaching into their 20s and 30s, with the oldest known cat, Creme Puff, dying at a verified age of 38. Having a cat neutered or spayed confers some health benefits, since castrated males cannot develop testicular cancer, spayed females cannot develop uterine or ovarian cancer, and both have a reduced risk of mammary cancer. The lifespan of feral cats is hard to determine accurately, although one study reported a median age of 4.7 years, with a range between 0 to 10 years.

Diseases

Cats can suffer from a wide range of health problems, including infectious diseases, parasites, injuries and chronic disease. Vaccinations are available for many of these diseases, and domestic cats are regularly given treatments to eliminate parasites such as worms and fleas.

Poisoning

In addition to obvious dangers such as rodenticides, insecticides and weed killers, cats may be poisoned by many chemicals that are usually considered safe. This is because their livers are less effective at some forms of detoxification than those of other animals, including humans and dogs. Some of the most common causes of poisoning in cats are antifreeze and rodent baits. It has also been suggested that cats may be particularly sensitive to environmental pollutants. When a cat has a sudden or prolonged serious illness without any obvious cause, it is therefore possible that it has been exposed to a toxin.

Human medicines should never be given to cats. For example, the painkiller paracetamol (also called acetaminophen, sold as Tylenol and Panadol) is extremely toxic to cats: even very small doses can be fatal and need immediate treatment. Even aspirin, which is sometimes used to treat arthritis in cats, is much more toxic to them than to humans and must be administered cautiously. Similarly, application of minoxidil (Rogaine) to the skin of cats, either accidentally or by well-meaning owners attempting to counter loss of fur, has sometimes been fatal. Essential oils can be toxic to cats and there have been reported cases of serious illnesses caused by tea tree oil, and tea tree oil-based flea treatments and shampoos.

Other common household substances that should be used with caution around cats include mothballs and other naphthalene products. Phenol-based products (Pine-Sol, Dettol (Lysol) or hexachlorophene) are often used for cleaning and disinfecting near cats' feeding areas or litter boxes but these can sometimes be fatal. Ethylene glycol, often used as an automotive antifreeze, is particularly appealing to cats, and as little as a teaspoonful can be fatal. Some human foods are toxic to cats; for example theobromine in chocolate can cause theobromine poisoning, although few cats will eat chocolate. Large amounts of onions or garlic are also poisonous to cats. Many houseplants are also dangerous, such as *Philodendron* species and the leaves of the Easter Lily, which can cause permanent and life-threatening kidney damage.

Free-ranging cats are active both day and night, although they tend to be slightly more active at night. The timing of cats' activity is quite flexible and varied, which means that house cats may be more active in the morning and evening (crepuscular behaviour), as a response to greater human activity at these times. House cats have territories that vary considerably in size, in one study ranging from seven to 28 hectares (69 acres). Although they spend the majority of their time in the vicinity of their home, they can range many hundreds of metres from this central point.

Cats conserve energy by sleeping more than most animals, especially as they grow older. The daily duration of sleep varies, usually 12-16 hours, with 13-14 being the average. Some cats can sleep as much as 20 hours in a 24-hour period. The term *cat nap* refers to the cat's ability to fall asleep (lightly) for a brief period and has entered the English lexicon—someone who nods off for a few minutes is said to be 'taking a cat nap'. During sleep cats experience short periods of rapid eye movement sleep accompanied by muscle twitches, which suggests that they are dreaming.

Sociability

Although wildcats are solitary, the social behaviour of domestic cats is much more variable and ranges from widely dispersed individuals to feral cat colonies that form around a food source, based on groups of co-operating females. Within such groups one cat is usually dominant over the others. Each cat in a colony holds a distinct territory, with sexually active males having the largest territories, which are about ten times larger than those of female cats and may overlap with several females' territories. These territories are marked by urine spraying, by rubbing objects at head height with secretions from facial glands and by defecation. Between these territories are neutral areas where cats watch and greet one another without territorial conflicts. Outside these neutral areas, territory holders usually chase away stranger cats, at first by staring, hissing, and growling, and if that does not work, by short but noisy and violent attacks. Despite some cats cohabiting in colonies, cats do not have a social survival strategy, or a pack mentality and always hunt alone.

Domestic cats use many vocalizations for communication, including purring, trilling, hissing, growling, snarling and several different forms of meowing. In contrast, feral cats are generally silent. Their types of body language, including position of ears and tail, relaxation of whole body, and kneading of paws, are all indicators of mood. The tail and ears are particularly important social signal in cats, with a raised tail acting as a friendly greeting. Tail raising also indicates the cat's position in the group's social hierarchy, with dominant individuals raising their tails less often than subordinate animals. Nose-touching is also a common greeting and may be followed by social grooming, which is solicited by one of the cats raising and tilting its head. However, some pet cats are poorly socialized. In particular older cats may show aggressiveness towards newly arrived kittens, which may include biting and scratching; this type of behaviour is known as Feline Asocial Aggression.

For cats, life in proximity with humans (and other animals kept by humans) amounts to a "symbiotic social adaptation". They may express great affection towards their human companions, especially if they imprint on them at a very young age and are treated with consistent affection. It has been suggested that, ethologically, the human keeper of a cat functions as a sort of surrogate for the cat's mother, and that adult domestic cats live their lives in a kind of extended kittenhood, a form of behavioural neoteny. Conversely, the high-pitched purrs cats make to solicit food may mimic the cries of a hungry human infant, making them particularly hard for humans to ignore.

Grooming

Cats are known for their cleanliness, spending many hours licking their coats. The cat's tongue has backwards-facing spines about 500 micrometres long, which are called papillae. These are quite rigid, as they contain keratin. These spines allow cats to groom themselves by licking their fur, with the rows of papillae acting like a hairbrush. Some cats, particularly longhaired cats, occasionally regurgitate hairballs of fur that have collected in their stomachs from grooming. These clumps of fur are usually sausage-shaped and about two to three centimetres long. Hairballs can be prevented with remedies that ease elimination of the hair through the gut, as well as regular grooming of the coat with a comb or stiff brush.

With domestic cats, males are more likely to fight than females. With feral cats, the most common reason for cat fighting is when two males are competing to mate with a female: here most fights will be won by the heavier male. Another possible reason for fighting in domestic cats is when the cats have difficulties in establishing a territory within a small home. Female cats will also fight over territory or to defend their kittens. Spaying females and neutering males will decrease or eliminate this behaviour in many cases, suggesting that the behaviour is linked to sex hormones.

When fighting, cats make themselves appear more impressive and threatening by raising their fur and arching their backs, thus increasing their apparent size. Often, the ears are pointed down and back to avoid damage to the inner ear and potentially listen for any changes behind them while focussed forward. Attacks usually comprise powerful slaps to the face and body with the forepaws as well as bites, but serious damage is rare; usually the loser runs away with little more than a few scratches to the face, and sometimes the ears. Cats will also throw themselves to the ground in a defensive posture to rake their opponent's belly with their powerful hind legs.

Normally, serious injuries from fighting will be limited to infections of scratches and bites, though these can occasionally kill cats if untreated. In addition, bites are probably the main route of transmission of feline immunodeficiency virus (FIV). Sexually active males will usually be involved in many fights during their lives, and often have decidedly battered faces with obvious scars and cuts to the ears and nose.

Cats feed on small prey, primarily birds and rodents. Feral cats and house cats that are free-fed tend to consume many small meals in a single day, although the frequency and size of meals varies between individuals. Cats use two hunting strategies, either stalking prey actively, or waiting in ambush until an animal comes close enough to be captured. Although it is not certain, the type of strategy used may depend on the prey species in the area, with for example, cats waiting in ambush outside burrows, but tending to actively stalk birds.

Most breeds of cat have a noted fondness for settling in high places, or perching. In the wild, a higher place may serve as a concealed site from which to hunt; domestic cats may strike prey by pouncing from such a perch as a tree branch, as does a leopard. Other possible explanations include that height gives the cat a better observation point, allowing it to survey its territory. During a fall from a high place, a cat can reflexively twist its body and right itself using its acute sense of balance and flexibility. This is known as the cat's 'righting reflex'. It always rights itself in the same way, provided it has the time to do so, during a fall. The height required for this to occur is around 90 cm (3 feet). Cats without a tail also have this ability, since a cat mostly moves its hind legs and relies on conservation of angular momentum to set up for landing, and the tail is in fact little used for this feat. This leads to the proverb 'a cat always lands on its feet'.

One poorly understood element of cat hunting behaviour is the presentation of prey to human owners. Ethologist Paul Leyhausen proposed that cats adopt humans into their social group, and share excess kill with others in the group according to the local pecking order, in which humans are placed at or near the top. However, anthropologist and animal scientist Desmond Morris, in his 1986 book *Catwatching*, suggests that when cats bring home mice or birds, they are teaching their human to hunt, or helping their human as if feeding "an elderly cat, or an inept kitten". However, this proposal is inconsistent with the fact that male cats also bring home prey, despite males having no involvement with raising kittens.

Domestic cats select food based on its temperature, smell and texture, strongly disliking chilled foods and responding most strongly to moist foods rich in amino acids, which are similar to meat. Cats may reject novel flavours (a response termed neophobia) and learn quickly to avoid foods that have tasted unpleasant in the past. They may also avoid sugary foods and milk; since they are lactose intolerant, these sugars are not easily digested and may cause soft stools or diarrhoea. They can also develop odd eating habits.

Some cats like to eat or chew on other things, most commonly wool, but also plastic, paper, string, or even coal. This condition is called pica and can threaten their health, depending on the amount and toxicity of the items eaten.

Since cats cannot fully close their mouths to create suction, they use a lapping method with the tongue to draw liquid upwards into their mouths. Lapping at a rate of four times a second, the cat touches the smooth tip of its tongue to the surface of the water, and quickly retracts it, drawing water upwards.

Domestic cats, especially young kittens, are known for their love of play. This behaviour mimics hunting and is important in helping kittens learn to stalk, capture, and kill prey. Cats will also engage in play fighting, with each other and with humans. This behaviour may be a way for cats to practice the skills needed for real combat, and might also reduce any fear they associate with launching attacks on other animals.

Owing to the close similarity between play and hunting, cats prefer to play with objects that resemble prey, such as small furry toys that move rapidly, but rapidly lose interest (they become habituated) in a toy they have played with before. Cats also tend to play with toys more when they are hungry. String is often used as a toy, but if it is eaten it can become caught at the base of the cat's tongue and then move into the intestines, a medical emergency which can cause serious illness and death. Owing to the risks posed by cats eating string, it is sometimes replaced with a laser pointer's dot, which cats may chase. While concerns have been raised about the safety of these lasers, Professor John Marshall, an ophthalmologist at St Thomas' Hospital, has stated that it would be 'virtually impossible' to blind a cat with a laser pointer.

Female cats are seasonally polyestrous, which means they may have many periods of heat over the course of a year, the season beginning in spring and ending in late autumn. Heat periods occur about every two weeks and last about 4 to 7 days. Multiple males will be attracted to a female in heat. The males will fight over her, and the victor wins the right to mate. At first, the female will reject the male, but eventually the female will allow the male to mate. The female will utter a loud yowl as the male pulls out of her. This is because a male cat's penis has a band of about 120-150 backwards-pointing spines, which are about one millimeter long; upon withdrawal of the penis, the spines rake the walls of the female's vagina, which is a trigger for ovulation. This act also occurs to clear the vagina of other sperm in the context of a 2nd (or more) mating, thus giving the latter males a larger chance of conception.

After mating, the female will wash her vulva thoroughly. If a male attempts to mate with her at this point, the female will attack him. After about 20 to 30 minutes, once the female is finished grooming, the cycle will repeat.

Because ovulation is not always triggered by a single mating, females may not be impregnated by the first male with which they mate. Furthermore, cats are superfecund; that is, a female may mate with more than one male when she is in heat, with the result that different kittens in a litter may have different fathers.

The gestation period for cats is between 64-67 days, with an average length of 66 days. The size of a litter averages three to five kittens, with the first litter usually smaller than subsequent litters. Kittens are weaned at between six and seven weeks, and cats normally reach sexual maturity at 5-10 months (females) and to 5-7 months (males), although this can vary depending on breed. Females can have two to three litters per year, so may produce up to 150 kittens in their breeding span of around ten years.

Cats are ready to go to new homes at about 12 weeks old, or when they are ready to leave their mother. Cats can be surgically sterilized (spayed or castrated) as early as 7 weeks to limit unwanted reproduction. This surgery also prevents undesirable sex-related behaviour, such as aggression, territory marking (spraying urine) in males and yowling (calling) in females. Traditionally, this surgery was performed at around six to nine months of age, but it is increasingly being performed prior to puberty, at about three to six months. In the USA approximately 80 per cent of household cats are neutered.

Cats are a cosmopolitan species and are found across much of the world. They are extremely adaptable and are now present on all continents except Antarctica, and on 118 of the 131 main groups of islands — even on sub-Antarctic islands such as the Kerguelen Islands. Feral cats can live in forests, grasslands, tundra, coastal areas, agricultural land, scrublands, urban areas and wetlands. Their habitats even include small oceanic islands with no human inhabitants. This ability to thrive in almost any terrestrial habitat has led to the cat's designation as one of the world's worst invasive species. Despite this general adaptability, the close relatives of domestic cats, the African Wildcat (*Felis silvestris lybica*) and the Arabian Sand Cat (*Felis margarita*) both inhabit desert environments, and domestic cats still show similar adaptations and behaviours.

Impact on Prey Species

To date, there are few scientific data available to assess the impact of cat predation on prey populations. Cat numbers in the UK are growing annually and their abundance is far above the 'natural' carrying capacity, because their population sizes are independent of their prey's dynamics: *i.e.* cats are 'recreational' hunters. Population densities can be as high as 2000 individuals per km^2 and the current trend is an increase of 0.5 million cats annually.

Even well-fed domestic cats may hunt and kill, mainly catching small mammals, but also birds, amphibians, reptiles, fish and invertebrates. Hunting by domestic cats may be contributing to the decline in the numbers of birds in urban areas, although the importance of this effect remains controversial. In the wild, the introduction of feral cats during human settlement can threaten native species with extinction. In many cases controlling or eliminating the populations of non-native cats can produce a rapid recovery in native animals. However, the ecological role of introduced cats can be more complicated: for example, cats can control the numbers of rats, which also prey on birds' eggs and young, so in some cases eliminating a cat population can actually accelerate the decline of an endangered bird species in the presence of a mesopredator, controlled by cats.

In the Southern Hemisphere, cats are a particular problem in landmasses such as Australasia, where cat species have never been native and there were few equivalent native medium-sized mammalian predators. Native species such as the New Zealand Kakapo and the Australian Bettong, for example, tend to be more ecologically vulnerable and behaviourally 'naive' to predation by feral cats. Feral cats have had a major impact on these native species and have played a leading role in the endangerment and extinction of many animals.

Impact on Birds

The domestic cat is probably a significant predator of birds. Current UK assessments indicate that they may be accountable for an estimated 64.8 million bird deaths each year. Certain species appear more susceptible than others; for example, 30 per cent of house sparrow mortality is linked to the domestic cat. In the recovery of ringed robins and dunnocks, it was also concluded that 31 per cent of deaths were a result of cat predation. The presence of larger carnivores such as coyotes which prey on cats and other small predators reduces the effect of predation by cats and other small predators such as opossums and raccoons on bird numbers and variety. The proposal that cat populations will increase when the numbers of these top predators decline is called the mesopredator release hypothesis.

On islands, birds can contribute as much as 60 per cent of a cat's diet. In nearly all cases, however, the cat cannot be identified as the sole cause for reducing the numbers of island birds, and in some instances eradication of cats has caused a 'mesopredator release' effect; where the suppression of top carnivores creates an abundance of smaller predators that cause a severe decline in their shared prey. Domestic cats are, however, known to be a contributing factor to the decline of many species; a factor that has ultimately led, in some cases, to extinction. The South Island Piopio, Chatham Islands Rail, the Auckland Islands Merganser, and the common diving petrel are a few from a long list, with the most extreme case being the flightless Stephen Island Wren, which was driven to extinction only a few years after its discovery.

Some of the same factors that have promoted adaptive radiation of island avifauna over evolutionary time appear to promote vulnerability to non-native species in modern time. The susceptibility inherent of many island birds is undoubtedly due to evolution in the absence of mainland predators, competitors, diseases and parasites. In addition to lower reproductive rates and extended incubation periods. The loss of flight, or reduced flying ability is also characteristic of many island endemics. These biological aspects have increased vulnerability to extinction in the presence of introduced species, such as the domestic cat. Equally, behavioural traits exhibited by island species, such as 'predatory naivety' and ground-nesting, have also contributed to their susceptibility.

Domesticated Cats

Cats are a common companion animal in Europe and North America, and their worldwide population exceeds 500 million. In 1998 there were around 43 million cats in Western Europe, 33 million in Eastern Europe, seven million in Japan and three million in Australia. A 2007 report stated that about 37 million US households owned cats, with an average of 2.2 cats per household giving a total population of around 82 million. This is slightly more than the 72 million pet dogs in that country. Although cat ownership has commonly been associated with women, a 2007 Gallup poll reported that men and women were equally likely to own a cat. The ratio of pedigree/purebred cats to random-bred cats varies from country to country. However, generally speaking, purebreds are less than 10 per cent of the total population.

According to the Humane Society of the United States, as well as being kept as pets, cats are also used in the international fur trade. Cat fur is used in coats, gloves, hats, shoes, blankets and stuffed toys. About 24 cats are needed to make a cat fur coat. This use has now been outlawed in several countries, including the United States, Australia and the European Union. However, some cat furs are still made into blankets in Switzerland as folk remedies that are believed to help rheumatism.

It has long been common for cats to be eaten in some parts of China and in some other Asian countries. According to the *Chengdu Business Daily*, people in southern China's Guangdong province ate 10,000 cats a day. Animal People estimates that 4 million cats are killed and consumed in Asia every year.

The concept of a cat breed appeared in Britain during the late 19th century. The current list of cat breeds is quite large: with the Cat Fanciers' Association recognizing 41 breeds, of which 16 are 'natural breeds' that probably emerged before humans began breeding pedigree cats, while the others were developed over the latter half of the 20th century. The owners and breeders of show cats compete to see whose animal bears the closest resemblance to the 'ideal' definition and standard of the breed. Because of common crossbreeding in populated areas, many cats are simply identified as belonging to the homogeneous breeds of domestic longhair and domestic shorthair, depending on their type of fur. In the United Kingdom and Australasia, non-purebred cats are referred in slang as moggies (derived from 'Maggie', short for Margaret, reputed to have been a common name for cows and calves in 18th century England and latter applied to housecats during the Victorian era). In the United States, a non-purebred cat is sometimes referred to in slang as a barn or alley cat, even if it is not a stray.

Cats come in a variety of colours and patterns. These are physical properties and should not be confused with a breed of cat. Furthermore, cats may show the colour and/or pattern particular to a certain breed without actually being of that breed. For example, cats may have seal point colouration, but not be Siamese.

Some original cat breeds that have a distinct phenotype that is the main type occurring naturally as the dominant domesticated cat type in their region of origin are sometimes considered as subspecies and also have received names as such in nomenclature, although this is not supported by feline biologists. Some of these cat breeds are:

- *F. catus anura* — the Manx — The Manx is a stocky, solid cat with a dense double coat (long or short), a compact body, very short back, hind legs that are visibly longer than the front legs, big bones, a wide chest, and greater depth of flank (sides of the cat nearest the rear) than other cats. A female Manx would not weigh more than 10 pounds and a male does not weigh over 12 pounds. Specific to this breed is the way their ears appear as a 'cradle' when looked at from behind. A Manx cat is mainly recognized by its appearance as it does not have a tail. Although some of them may have a small tail, most Manx cats are tailless. Because of the genetic deformation of these cats they are susceptible of developing what is called Manx Syndrome, a condition that could be fatal for a kitten. Although the gene normally affects only the tail, there is the risk of causing damage to the spine such as fused vertebrae.

- *F. catus siamensis* — the Siamese — Siamese cats are amongst the firstly recognized Oriental cats, a type of cat with a long body but an elegant posture. The length is the main characteristic based on which these cats are distinguished. Their body, legs and tail are all long and still Siamese cats are known for their grace. Also, they are famous because of their blue almond eyes and they are also called 'people cats' because of the affection they show to their owners.
- *F. catus cartusenensis* — the Chartreux — The Chartreux is a natural French breed, which is easily recognized by its size, grayish colour and double coat. These cats are also famous because of the paradox coming from the combination between a massively build body and smiling expression and sweet voice.
- *F. catus angorensis* — the Turkish Angora.

This pattern varies between the tuxedo cat which is mostly black with a white chest, and possibly markings on the face and paws/legs, all the way to the *Van* pattern (so named after the Lake Van area in Turkey, which gave rise to the Turkish Van breed), where the only coloured parts of the cat are the tail (usually including the base of the tail proper), and the top of the head (often including the ears). There are several other terms for amounts of white between these two extremes, such as *Harlequin* or *jellicle cat*. Bicolour cats can have as their primary (non-white) colour black, red, any dilution thereof, and tortoiseshell (see below for definition).

Tabby

Striped, with a variety of patterns. The classic blotched tabby (or marbled) pattern is the most common and consists of butterflies and bullseyes. The mackerel or striped tabby is a series of vertical stripes down the cat's side (resembling the fish). This pattern broken into spots is referred to as a spotted tabby. Finally, the tabby markings may look like a series of ticks on the fur, thus the ticked tabby, which is almost exclusively associated with the Abyssinian breed of cats. The worldwide evolution of the cat means that certain types of tabby are associated with certain countries; for instance, blotched tabbies are quite rare outside NW Europe, where they are the most common type.

Tortoiseshell and Calico

This cat is also known as a calimanco cat or clouded tiger cat, and by the abbreviation 'tortie'. In the cat fancy, a tortoiseshell cat is patched over with red (or its dilute form, cream) and black (or its dilute blue) mottled throughout the coat. Additionally, the cat may have white spots in its fur, which make it a 'tortoiseshell and white' cat; if there is a significant amount of white in the fur and the red and black colours form a patchwork rather than a mottled aspect, in North America the cat will be called a calico. All calicos are tortoiseshell (as they carry both black and red), but not all tortoiseshells are calicos (which requires a significant amount of white in the fur and patching rather than mottling of the colours). The calico is also sometimes called a tricolour cat. The Japanese refer to this pattern as *mi-ke* (meaning 'triple fur'), while the Dutch call these cats *lapjeskat* (meaning 'patches cat'). A true tricolour must consist of three colours: a reddish colour, dark or light; white; and one other colour, typically a brown, black, or blue. Both tortoiseshell and calico cats are typically female because the coat pattern is the result of differential X chromosome inactivation in females (which, as with all normal female mammals, have two X chromosomes). Conversely, cats where the overall colour is ginger (orange) are commonly male (roughly in a 3:1 ratio). In a litter sired by a ginger tom, the females will be tortoiseshell or ginger. Male tortoiseshells can occur as a result of chromosomal abnormalities (often linked to sterility) or by a phenomenon known as mosaicism, where two early stage embryos are merged into a single kitten.

Colourpoint

The colourpoint pattern is most commonly associated with Siamese cats, but may also appear in any domesticated cat. A colourpointed cat has dark colours on the face, ears, feet, and tail, with a lighter version of the same colour on the rest of the body, and possibly some white. The exact name of the colourpoint pattern depends on the actual colour, so there are seal points (dark brown), chocolate points (warm lighter brown), blue points (dark gray), lilac or frost points (silvery gray-pink), red or flame points (orange), and tortie (tortoiseshell mottling) points, among others. This pattern is the result of a temperature sensitive mutation in one of the enzymes in the metabolic pathway from tyrosine to pigment, such as melanin; thus, little or no pigment is produced except in the extremities or points where the skin is slightly cooler. For this reason, colourpointed cats tend to darken with age as bodily temperature drops; also, the fur over a significant injury may sometimes darken or lighten as a result of temperature change.

The tyrosine pathway also produces neurotransmitters, thus mutations in the early parts of that pathway may affect not only pigment, but also neurological development. This results in a higher frequency of cross-eyes among colourpointed cats, as well as the high frequency of cross-eyes in white tigers.

White Cat

True albinism (a mutation of the tyrosinase gene) is quite rare in cats. Much more common is the appearance of white coat colour that is caused by a lack of melanocytes in the skin. A higher frequency of deafness in white cats is due to a reduction in the population and survival of melanoblast stem cells, which in addition to creating pigment producing cells, develop into a variety of neurological cell types. White cats with one or two blue eyes have a particularly high likelihood of being deaf.

Smoke Cats

The bottom eighth of each hair is white or creamy-white, with the rest of the hair being a solid colour. Genetically this colour is a non-agouti cat with the dominant inhibitor gene; a non-agouti version of the silver tabby. Smoke cats will look solid coloured until they move, when the white undercoat becomes apparent. It is mostly found in pedigreed cats (especially longhair breeds) but also present in some domestic longhaired cats.

Body Types

Cats can also come in several body types, ranging between two extremes:

1. *Oriental:* Not a specific breed, but any cat with an elongated slender build, almond-shaped eyes, long nose, large ears (the Siamese and Oriental Shorthair breeds are examples of this).
2. *Foreign:* Less slender than the oriental type, but nevertheless a cat with a slight build and generally athletic look. Typical example breeds would be the Abyssinian cat and the Turkish Angora. Some people consider the foreign and oriental body types as being the same, however.

Semi-Foreign

More or less the middle range of body conformation types, this type of cat is less slender without being stocky. Example breeds would be the Devon Rex and the Egyptian Mau.

Semi-Cobby

These cats look more rounded without looking too stocky. Example breeds would be the American Shorthair and British Shorthair.

Cobby

Any cat with a short, muscular, compact build, roundish eyes, short nose, and small ears. Persian cats and Exotic cats are two prime examples of such a body type.

Effects on Human Health

Because of their small size, domesticated house cats pose little physical danger to adult humans. However, in the USA cats inflict about 400,000 bites per year, with 90 per cent of these bites coming from provoked animals; this number represents about one in ten of all animal bites. Many cat bites will become infected, sometimes with serious consequences such as cat-scratch disease, or, more rarely, rabies. Cats may also pose a danger to pregnant women and immunosuppressed individuals, since their feces can transmit toxoplasmosis. A large percentage of cats are infected with this parasite, with infection rates ranging from around 40 to 60 per cent in both domestic and stray cats worldwide.

Allergic reactions to cat dander and/or cat saliva are common. Some humans who are allergic to cats—typically manifested by hay fever, asthma, or a skin rash—quickly acclimate themselves to a particular animal and live comfortably in the same house with it, while retaining an allergy to cats in general. Whether the risk of developing allergic diseases such as asthma is increased or decreased by cat ownership is uncertain. Some owners cope with this problem by taking allergy medicine, along with bathing their cats frequently, since weekly bathing will reduce the amount of dander shed by a cat. There have also been attempts to breed hypoallergenic cats, which would be less likely to provoke an allergic reaction.

As well as posing health risks, interactions with cats may improve health and reduce physical responses to stress: for example the presence of cats may moderate increased blood pressure. Cat ownership may also improve psychological health by providing emotional support and dispelling feelings of depression, anxiety and loneliness. Their ability to provide companionship and friendship are common reasons given for owning a cat.

From another point of view, cats are thought to be able to improve the general mood of their owners by alleviating negative attitudes. According to a Swiss study carried out in 2003, cats may change the overall psychological state of their owner as their company's effect appears to be comparable to that of a human partner. The researchers concluded that, while cats were not shown to promote positive moods, they do alleviate negative ones.

Several studies have shown that cats develop affection towards their owners. However, the effect of these pets on human health is closely related to the time and effort the cat owner is able to invest in it, in terms of bonding, playing and buying accessories for their pet.

Indoor Scratching

A natural behaviour in cats is to periodically hook their front claws into suitable surfaces and pull backwards. This marks their territory and exercises their legs, in addition to cleaning and sharpening their claws. Indoor cats benefit from being provided with a scratching post so that they are less likely to use carpet or furniture which they can easily ruin. Commercial scratching posts typically are covered in carpeting or upholstery, but some authorities advice against this practice, as not making it clear to the cat which surfaces are permissible and which are not; they suggest using a plain wooden surface, or reversing the carpeting on the posts so that the rougher texture of the carpet backing is a more attractive alternative to the cat than the floor covering. Scratching posts made of sisal rope or corrugated cardboard are also common.

Although scratching can serve cats to keep their claws from growing excessively long, their nails can be trimmed if necessary. Another response to indoor scratching is onychectomy, commonly known as declawing. This is a surgical procedure to remove the claw and first bone of each digit of a cat's paws. Declawing is most commonly only performed on the front feet. A related procedure is tendonectomy, which involves cutting a tendon needed for cats to extend their claws. Declawing is a major surgical procedure and can produce pain, infections and permanent lameness.

Since this surgery is almost always performed for the benefit of owners, it is controversial and remains uncommon outside of North America. In many countries, declawing is prohibited by animal welfare laws and it is ethically controversial within the veterinary community. While both the Humane Society of the United States and the American Society for the Prevention of Cruelty to Animals strongly discourage or condemn the procedure, the American Veterinary Medical Association supports the procedure under certain guidelines and finds "no scientific evidence that declawing leads to behavioural abnormalities when the behaviour of declawed cats is compared with that of cats in control groups." They further argue that many cats would be given up and euthanized were declawing not performed.

Waste

Cats bury their urine and feces. Indoor cats are usually provided with a box containing litter, typically bentonite, but sometimes other absorbent material such as shredded paper or wood chips, or sometimes sand or similar material. It should be cleaned daily and changed often, depending on the number of cats in a household and the type of litter; if it is not kept clean, a cat may be fastidious enough to find other locations in the house for urination or defecation. This may also happen for other reasons; for instance, if a cat becomes constipated and defecation is uncomfortable, it may associate the discomfort with the litter box and avoid it in favour of another location.

Daily attention to the litter box also serves as a monitor of the cat's health. Bentonite or clumping litter is a variation which absorbs urine into clumps which can be sifted out along with feces, and thus stays cleaner longer with regular sifting, but has sometimes been reported to cause health problems in some cats. Those with toxoplasmosis-infected cats living in habitat areas of sea otters may wish to dispose of droppings in the trash, rather than flushing them down the toilet. Some cats can be trained to use the human toilet, eliminating the litter box and its attendant expense, unpleasant odour, and the need to use landfill space for disposal. Training may involve four to six weeks of incremental moves, such as moving and elevating the litter box until it is near the toilet, as well as employing an adapter such as a bowl or small box to suspend the litter above the toilet bowl. When training is complete, the cat uses the toilet by squatting on the toilet seat over the bowl.

Feral Cats

Feral cats are wild cats that are unfamiliar with humans and roam freely in urban or rural areas. The numbers of feral cats are not known, but estimates of the US feral population range from 25 to 60 million. Feral cats may live alone, but most are found in large groups called feral colonies, which occupy a specific territory and are usually associated with a source of food. Famous feral cat colonies are found in Rome around the Colosseum and Forum Romanum, with cats at some of these sites being fed and vetted by volunteers.

Public attitudes towards feral cats vary widely: ranging from seeing them as free-ranging pets, to regarding them as vermin. One common approach to reducing the feral cat population is termed *trap-neuter-return*, where the cats are trapped, neutered, immunized against rabies and the feline leukemia virus, and then released. Before releasing them back into their feral colonies, the attending veterinarian often nips the tip off one ear to mark the feral as neutered and inoculated, since these cats may be trapped again. Volunteers continue to feed and give care to these cats throughout their lives, and not only is their lifespan greatly increased, but behaviour and nuisance problems caused by competition for food are also greatly reduced.

History and Mythology

Traditionally, historians tended to think that ancient Egypt was the site of cat domestication, owing to the clear depictions of house cats in Egyptian paintings about 3,600 years old. However, in 2004, a Neolithic grave was excavated in Shillourokambos, Cyprus, that contained the skeletons, laid close to one another, of both a human and a cat. The grave is estimated to be 9,500 years old, pushing back the earliest known feline-human association significantly. The cat specimen is large and closely resembles the African wildcat (*Felis silvestris lybica*), rather than present-day domestic cats. This discovery, combined with genetic studies, suggest that cats were probably domesticated in the Near East, in the Fertile Crescent around the time of the development of agriculture and then they were brought to Cyprus and Egypt.

In ancient Egypt cats were sacred animals, with Bast often depicted in cat form, sometimes taking on the warlike aspect of a lioness. The Romans are often credited with introducing the domestic cat from Egypt to Europe; in Roman Aquitaine, a 1st or 2nd century epitaph of a young girl holding a cat is one of two earliest depictions of the Roman domesticated cat. However, it is possible that cats were already kept in Europe prior to the Roman Empire, as they may have already been present in Britain in the late Iron Age. Domestic cats were spread throughout much of the rest of the world during the Age of Discovery, as they were carried on sailing ships to control shipboard rodents and as good-luck charms.

Several ancient religions believed that cats are exalted souls, companions or guides for humans, that they are all-knowing but are mute so they cannot influence decisions made by humans. In Japan, the Maneki Neko is a cat that is a symbol of good fortune. Although there are no sacred species in Islam, some writers have stated that Muhammad had a favourite cat, Muezza. He is reported to have loved cats so much that "he would do without his cloak rather than disturb one that was sleeping on it".

Freyja—the goddess of love, beauty, and fertility in Norse mythology—is depicted as riding a chariot drawn by cats.

Many cultures have negative superstitions about cats. An example would be the belief that a black cat 'crossing your path' leads to bad luck, or that cats are witches' familiars used to augment a witch's powers and skills. This led to the widespread extermination of cats in Europe in mediaeval times. The Black Plague was spread by fleas carried by infected rats, and the killing of cats ostensibly caused an increase in the rat population. The killing of cats in Mediaeval Ypres is commemorated in the innocuous present-day Kattenstoet (cat parade).

According to a myth in many cultures, cats have multiple lives. In many countries, they are believed to have nine lives, but in some Spanish-speaking regions they are said to have seven lives, while in Turkish and Arabic traditions the number of lives is six. The myth is attributed to the natural suppleness and swiftness cats exhibit to escape life-threatening situations. Also lending credence to this myth is that falling cats often land on their feet because of an inbuilt automatic twisting reaction and are able to twist their bodies around to land feet first, though they can still be injured or killed by a high fall.

16 Domestic Duck

Domesticated ducks are ducks that are raised for meat, eggs and down. Many ducks are also kept for show, as pets or for their ornamental value. Almost all of the varieties of domesticated ducks are descended from the Mallard (*Anas platyrhynchos*), apart from the Muscovy Duck (*Cairina moschata*).

Ducks have been farmed for thousands of years, possibly starting in Southeast Asia. They are not as popular as the chicken, because chickens have much more white lean meat and are easier to keep confined, making the total price much lower for chicken meat, whereas duck is comparatively expensive and, while popular in the haute cuisine, appears less frequently in mass market food industry and restaurants in the lower price range.

Ducks are farmed for their meat, eggs, and down. A minority of ducks are also kept for foie gras production. In Vietnam, their blood is used in a food called ti?t canh. Their eggs are blue-green to white depending on the breed.

Ducks can be kept free range, in cages, in barns, or in batteries. To be healthy, ducks should be allowed access to water, though battery ducks are often denied this. They should be fed a grain and insect diet. It is a popular misconception that ducks should be fed bread; bread has limited nutritional value and can be deadly when fed to developing ducklings. Ducks should be monitored for avian influenza, as they are especially prone to infection with the dangerous H5N1 strain.

The females of many breeds of domestic ducks are unreliable at sitting their eggs and raising their young. Notable exceptions include the Rouen

Duck and especially the Muscovy Duck. It has been a custom on farms for centuries to put duck eggs under a broody hen for hatching; nowadays incubators are often used. However, young ducklings rely on their mother for a supply of preen oil to make them waterproof, and a chicken hen does not make as much preen oil as a duck hen; and an incubator makes none. Once the duckling sprouts its own feathers it will produce preen oil from the sebaceous gland near the base of its tail.

As Pets and Ornamentals

Domesticated ducks can be kept as pets. They can be kept in a garden or backyard, and with special accessories, have also been known to be kept in the house. They will often eat insects and slugs. A pond or deep water dish is recommended. Without access to plentiful water, ducks will not thrive. If ducks are given access to a pond they will dabble in the mud, dredging out and eating wildlife and frogspawn, and swallow adult frogs and toads up to the size of the British common frog *Rana temporaria*, as they have been bred to be much bigger than wild ducks with a 'hull length' (base of neck to base of tail) of up to a foot or more; the wild mallard's 'hull length' is about 6 inches (150 mm). A coop should be provided for shelter from predators such as foxes, hawks, coyotes, and racoons, as many breeds of domestic ducks are unable to fly.

Ducks are also kept for their ornamental value. Breeds have been developed with crests and tufts or striking plumage. Exhibition shows are held in which ducks, along with other breeds of poultry, are exhibited in competition. These shows can be 'open' (meaning any exhibitor who pays the required entry fee can enter), or 'closed' (accessible only to members of a given group). The most common of these is a 4-H poultry show.

Duck is the common name for a number of species in the Anatidae family of birds. The ducks are divided between several subfamilies in the Anatidae family; they do not represent a monophyletic group but a form taxon, since swans and geese are not considered ducks. Ducks are mostly aquatic birds, mostly smaller than the swans and geese, and may be found in both fresh water and sea water.

Ducks are sometimes confused with several types of unrelated water birds with similar forms, such as loons or divers, grebes, gallinules, and coots.

The word *duck* comes from Old English **duce* 'diver', a derivative of the verb **ducan* "to duck, bend down low as if to get under something, or dive", because of the way many species in the dabbling duck group feed by upending; compare with Dutch *duiken* and German *tauchen* 'to dive'.

This word replaced Old English *ened/ænid* 'duck', possibly to avoid confusion with other Old English words, like *ende* 'end' with similar forms. Other Germanic languages still have similar words for 'duck', for example, Dutch *eend* 'duck' and German *Ente* 'duck'. The word *ened/ænid* was inherited from Proto-Indo-European; compare: Latin *anas* 'duck', Lithuanian *ántis* 'duck', Ancient Greek *nessa/netta* (??ssa, ??tta) 'duck', and Sanskrit *atí* 'water bird', among others.

Some people use 'duck' specifically for adult females and 'drake' for adult males, for the species described here; others use 'hen' and 'drake', respectively.

A duckling is a young duck in downy plumage or baby duck; but in the food trade young adult ducks ready for roasting are sometimes labelled 'duckling'.

The overall body plan of ducks is elongated and broad, and the ducks are also relatively long-necked, albeit not as long-necked as the geese and swans. The body shape of diving ducks varies somewhat from this in being more rounded. The bill is usually broad and contains serrated lamellae which are particularly well defined in the filter-feeding species. In the case of some fishing species the bill is long and strongly serrated. The scaled legs are strong and well developed, and generally set far back on the body, more so in the highly aquatic species. The wings are very strong and are generally short and pointed, and the flight of ducks requires fast continuous strokes, requiring in turn strong wing muscles. Three species of steamer duck are almost flightless, however. Many species of duck are temporarily flightless while moulting; they seek out protected habitat with good food supplies during this period. This moult typically precedes migration.

The drakes of northern species often have extravagant plumage, but that is moulted in summer to give a more female-like appearance, the 'eclipse' plumage. Southern resident species typically show less sexual dimorphism, although there are exceptions like the Paradise Shelduck of New Zealand which is both strikingly sexually dimorphic and where the female's plumage is brighter than that of the male. The plumage of juvenile birds generally resembles that of the female.

Ducks exploit a variety of food sources such as grasses, aquatic plants, fish, insects, small amphibians, worms, and small molluscs.

Diving ducks and sea ducks forage deep underwater. To be able to submerge more easily, the diving ducks are heavier than dabbling ducks, and therefore have more difficulty taking off to fly.

Dabbling ducks feed on the surface of water or on land, or as deep as they can reach by up-ending without completely submerging. Along the edge of the beak there is a comb-like structure called a pecten. This strains the water squirting from the side of the beak and traps any food. The pecten is also used to preen feathers.

A few specialized species such as the mergansers are adapted to catch and swallow large fish.

The others have the characteristic wide flat beak designed for dredging-type jobs such as pulling up waterweed, pulling worms and small molluscs out of mud, searching for insect larvae, and bulk jobs such as dredging out, holding, turning headfirst, and swallowing a squirming frog. To avoid injury when digging into sediment it has no cere. but the nostrils come out through hard horn.

Breeding

The ducks are generally monogamous, although these bonds generally last a single year only. Larger species and the more sedentary species (like fast river specialists) tend to have pair-bonds that last numerous years. Most duck species breed once a year, choosing to do so in favourable conditions (spring/summer or wet seasons). Ducks also tend to make a nest before breeding.

Communication

Despite widespread misconceptions, only the females of most dabbling ducks 'quack'. For example, the scaup — which are diving ducks — make a noise like 'scaup' (hence their name), and even among the dabbling ducks, the males never quack. In general, ducks make a wide range of calls, ranging from whistles cooing, yodels and grunts. Calls may be loud displaying calls or quieter contact calls.

A common urban legend claims that duck quacks do not echo; however, this has been shown to be false. This myth was first debunked by the Acoustics Research Centre at the University of Salford in 2003 as part of the British Association's Festival of Science. It was also debunked in one of the earlier episodes of the popular Discovery Channel television show *MythBusters*.

Distribution and Habitat

The ducks have a cosmopolitan distribution occurring across most of the world except for Antarctica. A number of species manage to live on sub-Antarctic islands like South Georgia and the Auckland Islands. Numerous ducks have managed to establish themselves on oceanic islands such as Hawaii, New Zealand and Kerguelen, although many of these species and populations are threatened or have become extinct.

Some duck species, mainly those breeding in the temperate and Arctic Northern Hemisphere, are migratory; those in the tropics, however, are generally not. Some ducks, particularly in Australia where rainfall is patchy and erratic, are nomadic, seeking out the temporary lakes and pools that form after localised heavy rain.

Ducks have become an accepted presence in populated areas. Migration patterns have changed such that many species remain in an area during the winter months. In spring and early summer ducks sometimes influence human activity through their nesting; sometimes a duck pair nests well away from water, needing a long trek to water for the hatchlings: this sometimes causes an urgent wildlife rescue operation (e.g. by the RSPCA) if the duck nested somewhere unsuitable like in a small enclosed courtyard.

Predators

Worldwide, ducks have many predators. Ducklings are particularly vulnerable, since their inability to fly makes them easy prey not only for predatory birds but also large fish like pike, crocodilians, and other aquatic hunters, including fish-eating birds such as herons. Ducks' nests are raided by land-based predators, and brooding females may be caught unaware on the nest by mammals such as foxes, or large birds, such as hawks or eagles.

Adult ducks are fast fliers, but may be caught on the water by large aquatic predators including big fish such as the North American muskie and the European pike. In flight, ducks are safe from all but a few predators such as humans and the Peregrine Falcon, which regularly uses its speed and strength to catch ducks.

Ducks have many economic uses, being farmed for their meat, eggs, feathers, (particularly their down). They are also kept and bred by aviculturists and often displayed in zoos. All domestic ducks are descended from the wild Mallard *Anas platyrhynchos*, except the Muscovy Duck. Many domestic breeds have become much larger than their wild ancestor, with a 'hull length' (from base of neck to base of tail) of 30 cm (12 inches) or more and routinely able to swallow an adult British Common Frog *Rana temporaria* whole; the wild mallard's 'hull length' is about 6 inches.

FAO reports that China is the top duck market in 2004 followed by Vietnam and other South East Asian countries.

In many areas, wild ducks of various species (including ducks farmed and released into the wild) are hunted for food or sport, by shooting, or formerly by decoys. Because an idle floating duck or a duck squatting on land cannot react to fly or move quickly, 'a sitting duck' has come to mean 'an easy target'.

Wild ducks of many species and domesticated breeds are widely consumed around the world.

References

'Breeds of Livestock'. Department of Animal Science—Oklahoma State University.

Alderson, L. and Dowling, R. (1995). *Rare Breeds.* London: Bulfinch Press. p. 144.

CIP-UPWARD (2003). *Conservation and Sustainable Use of Agricultural Biodiversity: A Sourcebook.* CIP-UPWARD, in Partnership with GTZ GmbH, IDRC of Canada, IPGRI and SEARICE.

DAD-IS: *Information System for the Global Strategy for the Management of Farm Animal Genetic Resources* (AnGR).

FAO (2001). *Agricultural Biological Diversity.* The First Report on the State of the World's AnGR for Food and Agriculture: Paper Submitted by FAO for the 7th SBSSTA Meeting, 12-16 November 2001, Montreal, Canada.

Geerlings, E., Mathias, E. and Köhler-Rollefson, I. (2002). *Securing Tomorrow's Food. Promoting the Sustainable Use of Farm Animal Genetic Resources.* Information for Action. League for Pastoral Peoples, Ober-Ramstadt, Germany. PDF Gura, S. and League for Pastoralist Peoples. (2003). *Losing Livestock, Losing Livelihoods.* GRAIN.

Intermediate Technology (1996). *Dynamic Diversity: Livestock Keepers Safeguarding Domestic Animal Diversity Through Their Animal Husbandry.* Intermediate Technology Development Group, Myson House, Railway Terrace, Rugby, CV21 3HT, UK.

Köhler-Rollefson, I. (2001). Intellectual Property Rights Regime Necessary for Traditional Livestock Raisers. *Indigenous Knowledge and Development Monitor*, March 2001.

Köhler-Rollefson, I. (2003). Managing Animal Genetic Resources at the Community Level. Ch.50 in *Conservation and Sustainable Use of Agricultural Biodiversity: A Sourcebook*. CIP-UPWARD, in Partnership with GTZ GmbH, IDRC of Canada, IPGRI and SEARICE.

Mason, I.L. (1988). *World Dictionary of Livestock Breeds*. Wallingford: CAB International. p. 348.

Rare Breeds Survival Trust (UK) (January 2008). 'Sheep'. *Rare Breeds Watchlist*. Archived from the Original on June 22, 2008.

"Sheep Grazing Reduces Pesticide Use in Alfalfa". *ucanr.org*. University of California Agriculture and Natural Resources.

Schoenian, Susan. 'Sheep Basics'. *Sheep101.info*. Retrieved 2007-11-27.

Thomas, Heather Smith. 'True Horse Sense'. *Thoroughbred Times*. Thoroughbred Times Company. Retrieved 2008-07-08.

Miller, Robert M. and Rick Lamb (2005). *Revolution in Horsemanship and What It Means to Mankind*. Guilford, Connecticut: Lyons Press.

Anthony, David W. (1996). "Bridling Horse Power: The Domestication of the Horse". *Horses Through Time* (First ed.). Boulder, CO: Roberts Rinehart Publishers.

S.G. Pierzynowski; R. Zabielski (1999). *Biology of the Pancreas in Growing Animals*. Volume 28 of Developments in Animal and Veterinary Sciences. Elsevier Health Sciences.

"The Efficacy of the Model-rival Method When Compared to Operant Conditioning for Training Domestic Dogs to Perform a Retrieval-selection Task." *AABS*. 2003.

Feichtenberger, Klaus, Jill Clarke, Elyse Eisenberg, and Otmar Penker (Writers and Directors). (2008). *Prince of the Alps*. [Television Production]. ORF/Nature. Event Occurs at Shortly After Birth. Retrieved 2009-05-05. "The Mother Eats the Placenta to Prevent Predators from Getting the scent".

Devendra, C., and M. Burns. 1970. Goat Production in the Tropics. Commonwealth Bur. Anim. Breeding and Genetics,Tech. Commun. No. 19.

Greta Stamberg and Derek Wilson (1997-09-02). 'Behaviour: Sounds'. *Llamapaedia*.

Greta Stamberg and Derek Wilson (2007-04-12). 'Induced Ovulation'. *Llamapaedia*.

Beula Williams (2007-04-17). 'Llama Fibre'. *International Llama Association*.

Index